A Book of Emblems

To all aspiring *artisti emblematici*

A Book of Emblems

The Emblematum Liber *in Latin and English*

Andrea Alciati

translated and edited by
John F. Moffitt

McFarland & Company, Inc., Publishers
Jefferson, North Carolina, and London

LIBRARY OF CONGRESS CATALOGUING-IN-PUBLICATION DATA

Alciati, Andrea, 1492–1550
[Emblematum liber. English & Latin]
A book of emblems : the Emblematum liber
in Latin and English / Andrea Alciati ;
translated and edited by John F. Moffitt
p. cm.
Includes bibliographical references and index.

ISBN 0-7864-1807-9 (softcover : 50# alkaline paper)

1. Emblems— Early works to 1800. 2. Emblem books.
I. Moffitt, John F. (John Francis), 1940– II. Title.
PN6349.A413 2004 871'.04 — dc22 2004004457

British Library cataloguing data are available

On the cover: Emblema III, Numquam Procrastinandum
(Emblem 3, Never Procrastinate)

Manufactured in the United States of America

McFarland & Company, Inc., Publishers
Box 611, Jefferson, North Carolina 28640
www.mcfarlandpub.com

Contents

Preface

My purpose here is to make available to all English-speaking persons interested in the arts an accessible translation of a key text in post-medieval European culture. For centuries, the *Emblematum liber* by Andrea Alciati was considered an essential part of the library of anyone who participated in humanistic learning and creativity. Since its initial publication in 1531, scholars had depended upon this often-reprinted picture book to interpret the meaning of contemporary art and literature. Likewise, writers and artists turned to Alciati's *Book of Emblems* in order to invest their creative work with an understood moral significance.

Alciati's illustrated text was shared by all the well-educated. For the culture of Humanism, which flourished during the Renaissance and Baroque periods, it was the common leaven, just as the Bible had provided the intellectual structure of the Middle Ages, or the Qu'ran furnishes the basic key to understanding Islamic culture. Without Alciati's *Emblematum liber* one lacks an essential key to the once easily read meanings attached to many of the greatest artworks produced from the sixteenth century through the eighteenth century. With this new English translation I hope to offer the student of the liberal arts a necessary tool to understand that culture.

Presented here are the complete Latin texts, along with the illustrations, belonging to each of the 211 emblems making up the Alciatian canon. Below each text I have placed a literal but readable English translation; bracketed words and phrases represent once-understood references now likely to be missed by the modern reader. Also recovered here, and offered as an appendix, is the "suppressed" emblem, which appeared in the first edition (as number 80) but was subsequently removed because of its "offensive" subject matter. For this emblem I have added, and translated, the erudite seventeenth-century commentary on the emblem composed by Johann Thuilius.

For those unfamiliar with emblematics, Thuilius's commentary is a useful supplement, especially as it provides the contemporary reader with a literary sampling explaining the way Renaissance and Baroque era artists and writers had actually come to understand the whole range of humanistic subtleties potentially incorporated into one, apparently simple, image. Besides Thuilius, the learned commentators on Alciati's emblems included the likes of Claude Mignault, Francisco Sánchez ("el Brocense"), Diego López, and others. Artists who incorporated Alciatian motifs into their works would have also read these often lengthy commentaries on the somewhat enigmatic illustrations. The Thuilius extract is representative of this extensive interpretive tradition.

A number of years ago, I began to use Alciati to interpret a series of important artworks whose primary meanings had previously escaped scholars. Since there was then no accessible edition in English, and certainly none in Latin at a price I could afford, I turned to a bilingual paperback edition in Spanish and Latin, published in Madrid in 1975. This Castilian translation had been prepared by Bernadino Daza Pinciano and was first published in Lyons by Guillaume Rovillé in 1549. It provided only paraphrases (rather than a literal translation), and Daza arbitrarily chose to reassemble the original order of Alciati's emblems. Flawed as it may have been, however, with that essential interpretive tool in hand — Alciati's original texts and a contemporary Romance language version enabling me to sort out the tricky, somewhat tangled Latin syntax — I was then able to begin to immerse myself in the study of emblematics. Subsequently, I began to publish what became some three-dozen studies of various artworks.

Rather like the better known work of a police detective, the interpretive procedure is easy to explain. Initially, one simply looks for a general visual relation between one of Alciati's emblems and a given artwork. Then one reads Alciati's text to see whether his meaning logically applies to the particular picture or sculpture. If so, the shared, emblem-to-artwork, meaning should additionally prove flattering to the person who is known to have commissioned the masterpiece. In order, however, to extract the full connotation likely intended by any artist who had later appropriated a given Alciatian motif, the modern interpreter still must consult one of the standard commentaries listed in the select bibliography (until recently, the only one not published in Latin was Diego López's).

Now that the basic procedure has been explained, some specific examples may be cited. Alciati's emblem no. 15 explains why it is still the custom to place sculptures of lions in front of government buildings, and particularly in places where lions have never roamed in the wild (and even in the rustic town where I live). His emblem no. 25 reveals the underlying political message belonging to innumerable royal equestrian portraits commissioned during the Baroque era. Knowledge of the *Emblematum liber* has also enabled scholars to ascertain the underlying meanings informing such famous artworks as (among many, many others) Bernini's *Aeneas and Anchises* (emblem no. 194), and his *Triton Fountain* (emblem no. 132); Brueghel's *Fall of Icarus* (emblem no. 103); Caravaggio's *Boy Bitten by a Lizard* (emblem no. 49), and his *Narcissus* (emblem no. 69); Goya's "Strange Devotion" (*Desastres de la Guerra*, 66, emblems nos. 6, 7), and his *Disparate Matrimonial* and *Capricho* 75 (emblem no. 197); Holbein's *The Ambassadors* (emblem no. 10); Rembrandt (attrib.), *Man with a Golden Helmet* (emblem no. 132), Rembrandt's *Rape of Ganymede* (emblem no. 4), and his *Terminus* (emblem no 157); Rubens's *Self-Portrait with Isabella Brant* (emblem no. 190), his *Democritus and Heraclitus* (emblem no. 151), his *Three Graces* (emblem no. 162), and his *Rape of Ganymede* (emblem no. 4); Velázquez's *Water Carrier of Seville* (emblem no. 101), his *Los Borrachos* (emblems nos. 23–25), and his *Surrender at Breda* (emblems nos. 39, 167). And so it goes, and among many other notable artists.

The illustrations in this edition are derived from the Bernadino Daza Pinciano text published in 1549. Rather than following Daza's rearrangement, however, this book restores the essential organic order of the original; see the introduction for more on this subject.

At the end of this book I have included a select bibliography, which cites the studies explaining the Alciatian basis of some of these examples. By immersion in these published investigations, one may then become a participating interpreter of the crucial emblematic tradition. But first one must have in hand the basic source: Alciati's conjoined pictures and explanatory texts.

The daunting task facing the translator here may be briefly described. In English, the exact placement of words within a sentence is crucial in revealing their function or clear-cut meaning. To the contrary, in Latin the declensions attached to the end of each word define the function of each declarative component, allowing for greater mobility of their placement within the given sentence than is the case with English. In fact, word order can be arbitrarily assigned, according to the whim of the author. In the case of Alciati, one can imagine the compositional technique as something like this: Label a number of poker chips individually as "verb," "noun," "adjective," "adverb," and so forth. Next, place the chips in a paper sack, and then give that a vigorous shake. Cast the chips upon a table, then align them horizontally more or less as they have fallen. This procedure yields a given sentence — or so it may have for Alciati; many, many casts later, the *Emblematum liber* was deemed complete.

One example, typically bereft of articles and pronouns, will suffice to illustrate this point (and, comparing the Latin texts appended here, the reader will find any number of similar verbal conundrums). Retaining the original word-order and punctuation belonging to the opening sentence of Emblem 66, one is confronted with the following jumble of words: "While wolf famished chews deer-seeking food before and hunger prey devours fawn, sees if by chance something else or perhaps glance diverts, presently forgotten which has in mouth food, searches uncertain (such is forgetfulness) prey." To complicate things, some words (e.g., *prae* + *que*) are understood to be repeated, and with repetitions these are given different meanings in their new applications.

As you see, making sense of all this can often be rather a complicated business. After reviewing many previous translations of Alciati's usually brief, but very compressed, texts — in Spanish, French, German, Italian and English (and mostly as these are gathered together in the invaluable edition compiled by Peter M. Daly and Virginia W. Callahan) — one often finds many minor variations attached to the meaning of any given passage. Hence, with the help of a Latin-English dictionary, the reader is further encouraged to compare the two texts given here, in Latin and English, for each emblem. In this way, you yourself become an active interpreter of the primordial text—and that is just what a Renaissance humanist would have done. *Vale*!

John F. Moffitt
Las Cruces, NM
April 2004

Introduction

Alciati's *Emblematum liber* is a key monument of Renaissance culture. As we know, this age had a unique sense of history: it looked *back* into time. The previous period then became the "Middle Ages," *media aetas*. In spite of a recently imposed sense of chronological distance, the Middle Ages handed down to the Renaissance a rich legacy of moralized allegory and a tradition of "typological" (or prefiguring) exegesis of history (whereby Samson "prefigures" Christ, and so forth). A characteristic example of symbol-propelled medieval thought strictly applying to natural phenomena is found in the bestiaries, where innumerable animals and birds (usually pictured) were "allegorized," that is, more or less arbitrarily assigned symbolic meanings applicable to the human condition. But the practice of composing moralizing maxims goes back at least to the sixth century BCE, when "Aesop" (likely an invented name) assembled a collection of 358 folk-wisdom tales, the "Fables," told to highlight human follies and foibles; according to his simple two-part formula, he would first relate an anecdote about an unfortunate animal encounter, then he would add a succinct moral injunction for the human reader.

The broader context later impelling all this interpretive ingenuity became that of a "meaningful universe," the one created by God in order to reveal himself and his divine plan to mankind; hence, everything that exists necessarily points to a meaning lying beyond any given *res*, the thing itself. Since each natural *res* contains potential meaning, it simultaneously becomes a *res significans*. As such, it next points to its *sensus spiritualis, sive mysticus* (spiritual meaning), with this deduction then directing the individual's conduct in this world and enhancing his hope for salvation in the next. Typically, this interpretive undertaking was addressed to the "Book of Nature" (*Liber naturae*), and Alan of Lille summed up the twelfth-century position in a rhyme: *Omnis mundi creatura / Quasi liber et pictura / Nobis est et speculum* ("Every creature [and object] in the world is like a book [providing a] picture and mirror of ourselves"). Around 1450, Thomas à Kempis succinctly explained the still ongoing procedure in his *Imitatio Christi* ("Imitation of Christ"): *Si rectum cor tuum esset, tunc omnis creatura speculum vitae et liber santae doctrinae esset* ("If your heart is upright, then every creature [and object] is like the mirror of life, and it serves you as a book of holy doctrine"). The new and self-conscious age labeled itself, however, a "rebirth," that is, of the first great age, classical antiquity. Nonetheless, the medieval way of thinking in "anagogical" (upward-leading) terms of symbolic analogies and correspondences remained in force.

Alciati inherited this pre–Renaissance tradition, including its aristocratic heraldry, or coats-of-arms, combining recondite pictorial motifs with a laconic inscription in Latin. The rules for the Renaissance reappropriation of medieval blazons, with the two-part devices now called *imprese, dévises* or *empresas*, were laid down by Paolo Giovio in his *Dialogo dell'imprese militari et amorose* (1555). As opposed to an emblem, the *impresa* has only two components, a title and a graphic image; unlike an emblem, the *impresa* contains no explanatory text. Giovio sets forth the conditions of its construction:

> In order that the invention, or *impresa*, may have a pleasing grace, it is obligatory that it conforms to five conditions. First, there must be established a just proportion between the soul [the inscribed motto] and the body [the graphic image]. Second, its meaning must not be so obscure that it is necessary to call upon the Sibyl in order to interpret it; however, neither should its meaning be so transparent that any common person might understand it. Third, above all it must have a handsome appearance, with this appearing delightful and most attractive, it being accompanied by stars, suns, moons, flames, waters, trees, mechanical instruments, fantastic animals and birds. The fourth condition is that it is not suitable that any human figure should appear therein. The fifth condition is that the motto, which is its soul, should be stated in a different language from that of the author of the device, so that its sentiments should be somewhat more concealed.

Another source for Alciati's emblems was considerably older. In their desire to recuperate antiquity, Renaissance scholars often found themselves with a problem of language; the historical texts and monuments sometimes appeared to them in an unintelligible form. The hieroglyphs (literally, "secret writings") of ancient Egypt proved to be particularly inscrutable. Their enigmatic, symbolic and pictorial language was in itself considered to represent a sign of the *priscorum theologia* ("theology of the ancients"), a hidden form of lost but profound wisdom, likely itself of divine origin and thus prefiguring Christian *sapientia*. The key date is 1419, when the illustrated Greek manuscript of Horopollo's *Hieroglyphica* arrived in Florence. It took a century before it was translated into Latin, then published (in 1517). In that work the learned translator, Filippo Fasanini, described hieroglyphics as "short sayings ... which can, in combination with painted or sculpted figures, wrap in shrouds the secrets of the mind."

Andrea Alciati had been a student of Fasanini in Bologna, and his pictorial treatise followed shortly after, in 1531. The link with the ancient Egyptian precedent had been made explicit by Alciati slightly earlier in his *De verborum signficatione* ("On the significations of words," 1530): "Words indicate; things are indicated. But things can also indicate, for example, in the 'Hieroglyphics of

Horapollo' [*hieroglyphica apud Horum*]. Working from their arguments, we have also written a book in verse with the title *Emblemata*."

It was Alciati who propagated the word *emblema* throughout sixteenth-century Europe. As he must have known, the Greek word εμβλεμα stands for, in the first place, any "inserted part," and such *emblemas* can range from the insole inserted within a shoe to a cultivated branch grafted on to a wild tree. In Latin, however, *emblema* was always a technical term for works of art of the inlaid sort, particularly mosaics and even the ornamental reliefs covering precious metal objects. Much later, Francesco Colonna used *emblematura* to signify "mosaic work" in his *Hypnerotomachia* (1499), a fantastic "dream-novel" acknowledged to have been a great influence on later emblematic creativity. Taking that "inlaid" application a bit further, the Roman rhetoricians had used *emblema* in a figurative sense; Lucilius, Quintilian and Cicero, for instance, used it in an ironical way to characterize a speech which is composed of ingeniously interwoven, or grafted, points. As described in 1517 by Ludovicus Coelius Rhodiginus, "everything cultivated [*urbana*], when grafted on to what is uncultivated [*sylvestre*], is called an *emblema*." Later, the term "emblema" was frequently taken by Alciati's contemporaries to represent the modern equivalent of the ancient hieroglyphs, for these also combined an enigmatic (or "uncultivated") image with a mostly inscrutable (but clearly "cultivated" and urbane) text. As was explained in French by Gilles Corrozet in 1540, an "*emblème*" is that which "*on peut nommer lettre hiéroglyphique*" (one could call hieroglyphic writing).

In their canonic form, emblems are, in short, symbolic combinations of pictures and words. The internal harmony of an emblem is established by its three essential components; hence, it is known as an *emblema triplex*, so distinguishing it from the two-part *impresa*. The first component of an emblem is the *inscriptio*, or terse motto, which provides the title, typically cast in the form of a proverb, providing a clearly defined declaration of purpose through Aesop-like "conventional wisdom." The second element is the *pictura*, or symbolic illustration of the central motif, an anecdote often drawn from classical mythology. Absent in an *impresa*, the essential third feature of an *emblema* is the *subscriptio*, or declaration appended below ("sub") the picture, and this is most often presented as an epigram. The meaningful symbiotic relationship between the mute and the speaking halves ("*muta Poesis et Pictura loquens*") in an emblem is connotative rather than denotative.

In its characteristic application, the subscribed written declaration commences with an anecdote, usually the subject of the *pictura*, from which (in the venerable manner of Aesop) there is derived a moral message, with a concluding admonition being addressed to the reader. The broad moral conclusion declared by the title of the emblem is exemplified by the particular case-history recreated in the picture, and a timeless truth is meant to be distilled from the particular, time-bound and localized, action illustrated in the *pictura*. The emblematic "method" is to evoke meaning by assigning "likeness," but that implied similitude is rarely seen from the outset or necessarily inherent in the initial linkage. Instead, as initially prodded by *inscriptio* and then further impelled by the *subscriptio*, perception was assumed to be gradual. This process conforms to another major Renaissance theme, that of *discordia concors*, or bringing "concord," or resolution, to an initial sense of "discord."

Like Giovio, Alciati and the emblematists following him regarded the picture as the "body" of the emblem, and the written parts were referred to as its "soul," so expressing the Renaissance belief that external human form reflects inner character. In actual practice, the text extracts and discovers couched in the picture-puzzle a deeper meaning than the one initially apparent to the innocent (or uninformed) eye. Naturally, the usually cryptic *pictura* was what that eye first perceived in the emblem, what had initially invited the mind to interpret it, and one's initial perception was to be later confirmed (more or less) by what was written in the interpretive *subscriptio*. The ostensible function of the discursive *subscriptio* is to resolve the enigma produced by the conjoined *inscriptio* and *pictura*. Nonetheless, since the compressed *subscriptio* is typically ambiguous (as you shall soon see), the viewer-reader was further encouraged to individually exercise his or her intellect, which is always a flattering invitation. Emblematic interpretation required controlled *associative* thinking, that is, conceptualization. Since, however, a single emblematic motif usually allows of a variety of interpretations, the potential meanings would expand according to the individual's reader's store of accumulated cultural knowledge.

The larger strategies (*el conceptualismo*) belonging to that kind of historical mentality were perhaps best explained by Baltasar Gracián in his 1642 treatise on *Agudeza y arte de ingenio* ("Wit and the Art of Ingenuity"), where many illustrations of applied literary "wit" had been drawn from Alciati's emblems. In his *L'art des emblèmes* (1662), the Jesuit author Claude-François Menestrier dealt with the more focused issue of the approved function of an emblem:

> Images are what constitute the matter of emblems, for emblems are instructions which must enter through the eyes in order to pass through them toward the soul. These images are obtained from all perceivable objects, and from these we can represent spiritual things by using human figures. Hence, Nature, the Arts, Fables, the [Ovidian] Metamorphoses, Proverbs, Apologetics, Moral Sentences, Axioms drawn from the Sciences, examples taken from History and the fictions of the Poets are all material proper to emblems; for all these [subjects] provide images which can instruct us.... Images applicable to an emblem are natural figures, symbolic figures and poetic figures. Natural figures are the images of things with which we are familiar, such as an eagle, a lion, a rock, a river. Symbolic figures are the symbols or hieroglyphs denoting certain things, such as the Caduceus of Mercury, the Horns of Plenty, etc. Poetic figures are images belonging to virtues, vices, passions and other moral, civic and spiritual things which do not submit to the senses; for they only represent a moral state or a spiritual state, such as virtue, the angels, the soul, life, honor glory, etc.

Emmanuele Tesauro proposed another definition in his *Il Cannocchiale Aristotelico* ("The Aristotelian Telescope," 1670), and he did so by citing specific examples drawn from Alciati's *Emblematum liber*:

> Among these [emblematic] figures, some are historical, for instance, the example

> of the inhabitants of Finland [sic. Scythia], who, according to Cornelius Tacitus, are so impoverished that fortune can do them no harm, and they may be employed to allude to the security belonging to those who carry all their goods with them, as is shown in Alciati's Emblem 37. Other emblematic figures are drawn from fable, such as that one showing Phaeton, with this example reprimanding the reckless, as is shown in Emblem 56. Others are taken from nature, such as the example of the piety of the offspring of the stork, who feed their mother when she grows old; Emblem 30 encourages us to express gratitude to our benefactors. Others are by nature artificial, such as is the sepulcher of Archilochus, which becomes a symbol standing for the slanderer in Emblem 51. Yet others are chimerical, such as is the remora; coiled around a shaft, it becomes a symbol of pondered haste in Emblem 20.

Consequently, any attempt at clarification and analysis of the emblem must take into account both the central illustrative element, the *res picta* (the pictured object), and its discursive commentary, the *res significans* (the thing signified). As Sebastián Covarrubias explained in his *Tesoro de la Lengua Castellana* (1611): "Metaphorically, one calls an 'emblem' those verses which are written beneath a picture or print, and with which there is given meaning to some [larger] concept, this being either military, moralizing, amorous or the like, and the verses help to declare the [somewhat concealed] purpose of the emblem and the [latent] intention of its author." In the larger sense, emblem-books served as unsurpassable visual aids to the *ars memorativa* ("art of memory"). The major Renaissance statement of mnemotechnics is the *Exercitia Spiritualia*, or "Spiritual Exercises," of St. Ignatius of Loyola; composed in 1533, it is a near-exact contemporary to the first edition of the *Emblematum liber*. For "The First Exercise" Ignatius recommends what may be called an Alciatian technique, namely, one produces a concrete "mental image" and "contemplation is [focused] on a visible object," and "the image will consist of seeing with the mind's eye the physical place with the object that we wish to contemplate." The ultimate purpose is, of course, moral, for instance, to "weigh my sins, considering the loathsomeness and the malice that every mortal sin committed has in itself."

In an even broader context, the emblem itself finally provided a concrete realization of the perennial Renaissance goal of *Ut pictura poësis*—"As in poetry, so too in painting." And so was the painter linked spiritually to the poet, and the common connection was *l'acutezza*, "wit," meaning a shared intellectual acuity. Accordingly, in their search for prestige, it was only natural that the Renaissance artists would introduce into their "witty" pictorial art the prestigious "poetic" devices of the contemporary emblematist; and by flattering the viewer as a knowing accomplice, they made him, too, an erudite interpreter of the typically veiled, potential moral meanings attached to the emblematic messages. Whether cast as a poem or a painting, the "emblematic" artwork is one that has been consciously structured upon the symbiotic organization of abstract, interpretive statements deriving from an implicitly pictorial exemplification.

For us today, psychologically reshaped by a post-modernist era manipulated by the electronic mass-media, who bedazzle us with the ephemeral fashions deriving from a crassly commercial pop-culture, emblem-books provide unique insights into a historical relic, the humanist mentality of the Renaissance. To the contrary of our mostly passive mental condition, theirs was a *mentalité* which delighted in strenuously active demonstrations of individual feats of mental ingenuity. The emblematic authors and their many readers belonged to an age driven to search for and extract the deep significance perhaps embedded in the inter-relationships imposed upon superficially disparate parts. The act (or art) of unveiling, and then defining as similes, those previously obscured linkages also then defined intelligence, *l'acutezza*, a literally "sharp" wit. Besides affording repositories of often striking visual motifs and their immediately attendant meanings, the emblem-books lent service as portable "treasuries" (*thesauri*) full of standard classical tags (*topoi*) and mutually shared proverbial wisdom.

Providing us today with important cross-references to specific motifs in sixteenth- and seventeenth-century literature and art, the emblem-books also explain the habitual formulation of poetic ideas through concrete images. Viewed as a once-standard mode of thought (a "period *mentalité*"), the emblem-books indicate to us in detail what educated people once knew about history and mythology, the physical world and, especially, the slipperiness and fallibility of human nature. Most importantly, they show us today just how the participants in humanist culture zestfully set about to interpret, then morally apply to contemporary life, that now mostly forgotten, traditional knowledge.

The commercial success of the new, as much entertaining as educational, genre initiated by Alciati is unquestionable, and it was comparable in scale (if scarcely in quality) to the post-modernist, pop-culture "blockbuster." More than 150 editions of the *Emblematum liber*, including translations into the vernacular tongues, were issued by European printing presses. Making emblems quickly became a popular intellectual game among the *cognoscenti*. By the end of the eighteenth century, there were more than 1,300 emblematic authors, and it has been estimated that they had collectively published at least 5,300 different titles. Although many of these publications were frivolous, the humanists had insisted from the outset that the prevailing taste for such intellectual subtleties should be turned to didactic ends. As they stipulated, emblems must consistently be given an encoded *content*, either broadly moral or more narrowly religious.

Alciati's commentators, along with the dozens of new emblematists following in his path, saw the condensed, pictorial-verbal hybrid as the ideal vehicle by which to inculcate virtue, wisdom and good customs. According to a standard motto, the task of the humanists was *docere cum delectatione* ("to instruct through delight"), and the emblem-books were the perfect means by which to realize this didactic goal. Coinciding with the Renaissance interest in the Platonic "universalia" (deep truths lying beyond material reality), the new genre inaugurated by Alciati quickly became a picture-driven alternative to traditional philosophical and theological discourse. Not only did it serve as an elegant stylistic model for Latin literary expression; because it additionally offered a focused medium by which the diverse topics of classical history, mythology, antiquarianism, linguistics and epigraphy could be presented and systematically analyzed, Alciati's *Emblematum liber* was also eagerly taken up by both schoolmasters and university professors. A similar role is played by William Shakespeare and John Milton in the postmodernist classroom (and it is now often forgotten that both these authors had themselves employed emblem-books for their writings).

What we do know about the life of the instigator of the emblematic genre may be quickly recounted. On May 8, 1492, Andrea Alciati was born in Alzate, near Milan, whence his cognomen. His family moved to Milan in 1504, and, between 1507 and 1514, he went to Pavia and Bologna to study law. In 1516, at age twenty-four, the University of Ferrara granted him a doctorate (*laurea*) in civil and canon law, and he then practiced jurisprudence in Pavia and Bologna. Soon renowned for his intellectual acumen, in 1518 he was invited to teach in France, where he took up his first academic post in the papal city of Avignon. Equally fluent in Latin and Greek, he regularly corresponded with notable European humanists, the likes of Desiderius Erasmus in Rotterdam and Konrad Peutinger in Augsburg. In 1521, he was made a Palatine count by Pope Leo X. Although the prestige he enjoyed in France was enormous, he was driven to return to his homeland in 1522. Unfortunately, for the next four years northern Italy was to become the battle ground between Charles V and François I for dominion over Milan, so Alciati reluctantly left Italy in 1527 to take up academic posts in Avignon and, later, in Bourges. In 1533, he was recalled to Milan by Duke Francesco Sforza II. Back in Italy, besides teaching at Pavia, Bologna and Ferrara, Alciati worked tirelessly to reestablish political harmony, and Pope Paul II appointed him an apostolic first notary. At the age of fifty-seven, covered with honors, he died in Pavia on January 12, 1550. His posthumously published (1582) writings on the interpretation of laws filled two volumes.

Throughout his busy career, during his rare moments of leisure Alciati tirelessly applied himself to his erudite hobby, the composition of emblematic declarations. As an applied humanist, he knew intimately the surviving principal literary monuments of Greco-Roman culture. However, for his innovative emblematic endeavor the most important literary source was a collection of Greek epigrams which had been edited by the Byzantine scholar Maximus Planudes (ca. 1255–1305) and published in 1484 as the *Anthologia graeca*. This connection is easily documented; as early as November 1522, Alciati wrote a letter to a friend in which he announced, "I have composed a little book of epigrams [*libellum composui epigrammaton*], which is entitled the *Emblemata*." Alciati was also one of the three translators of a new edition of the Planudean collection, then called *Selecta epigrammata Graeca Latine versa* (Basel, 1529), and it turns out that a quarter of Alciati's epigrammatical emblems (perhaps 50 out of 212) were translations or paraphrases directly taken from the *The Greek Anthology* (itself now readily available as a Penguin paperback).

The primary meaning of *epigrama* is "inscription," as on a tombstone. Most of these inscriptions came to be written in the elegiac couplet, a verse-form which was initially developed around 500 BCE. Almost all Greek epigrams were "occasional," meaning composed for or upon specific occasions, either public or private. Typically, and this is a crucial point, an epigram describes something—but only that it may serve to signify something else. In Alciati's application, an epigram—now called the *emblema*—verbally pictures a specific situation in such a way as to give it additional meaning, and what is described specifically serves to introduce an abstract idea with broader applications; thereby, it may additionally acquire a pleasing moral sense. In Planudes' *Greek Anthology*, the encoded poems (up to 4,000) were grouped by subject matter and type, and Alciati later hewed to this venerable format for his 212 illustrated texts.

Besides *The Greek Anthology*, the other decisive, strictly literary influence on Alciati's emblematic endeavor was contemporary, namely, the series of moralized interpretations of proverbs composed by his friend Erasmus and published under the collective title of *Adagia* (and successively published in 1500, 1508, 1515, 1518, and 1533); by the final edition, 4,251 traditional sayings had been subjected to Erasmus's erudite scrutiny. Erasmus defined a proverb in a way that parallels Alciati's understanding of an epigram, that is, as meaning something other than what is actually said. Specifically, Erasmus called a proverb a "dark" declaration which is useful for the conduct of life; it is, moreover, an "enigma," "a saying in which a manifest truth is wrapped in obscurity": *proverbiam est sermo rem manifestam obscuritate tegens.* In fact, besides hewing to learned "obscurity," many of Alciati's specific turns of phrase are those of Erasmus.

A clear precedent for the physical format of the *Emblematum libellus* is found in Sebastian Brant's *Das Narrenschiff* ("The Ship of Fools"). Brant's work was perhaps the most famous book of its time, and it appeared between 1494 and 1548 in German, Latin, French, English, Flemish and Dutch editions. Erasmus was himself one of its many avid readers, and his moralizing *Adagia* share many themes with Brant's *Ship of Fools*. Like Alciati's forthcoming emblem-book, *Das Narrenschiff* provided a series of moralizing tales illustrated with prints. Like Alciati, Brant criticized human foibles, and the major topics of his opprobrium were vicious or criminal offenses, insolence, sedition, sloth, presumptuousness, perversities, and so forth. Like Alciati, Brant quoted from a host of Greek and Roman authors. Like Alciati, Brant began with a "motto" (for instance, no. 28, "Von Wider-Gott-Reden"—"Of Speaking Against God"); next was inserted a woodcut, and this was followed by a discursive poem concluding with a moral injunction. However, unlike Brant's explicitly narrative and populist text, Alciati's elitist and learned, poetic expositions are typically dense and elliptic. Moreover, and to the contrary of Brant's explicit woodcut illustrations, Alciati's *picturae* are often fantastic, if not outright ambiguous. In short, whereas Brant's pictures usually only allow one interpretation, Alciati's *picturae* permit many; indeed, they are taken as the interpretive point of departure. Nonetheless, most likely it was the unquestionable commercial success of *Das Narrenschiff* which directly accounts for the decision reached in 1531 by Heinrich Steyner, Alciati's first publisher, to add illustrations to the author's manuscript.

The first version of Alciati's emblem-book appeared in Augsburg in 1531 with a title, naming the author as a

Milanese jurist and dedicating the work to the Augsburger jurist Peutinger: *Viri Clarissimi D. Alciati Iurisconsultiss. Mediol. ad. C. Chonradam Peutingerum Augustanum, Iurisconssultiss. Emblematum liber.* Alciati had prepared his initial manuscript with only 104 emblems—and no illustrations. He presented his poetic anthology to the imperial legal counselor Peutinger, who in turn (and apparently without Alciati's permission) gave it to the Augsberger printer, Heinrich Steyner. And it was Steyner, rather than Alciati, who made the crucial decision that each emblem should be illustrated, and Steyner then commissioned the engravings from an artist named Jörg Breu. The success of the *Emblematum liber* was immediate, and Steyner reissued the picture book in 1532, 1533 and 1534. Nonetheless, the first edition to be actually published with Alciati's express approval was the one issued in Paris by Christian Wechel in 1534, to which were added nine more emblems; this edition bore the streamlined title *Andreae Aliciati Emblematum Libellus.* Other publishers, including Guillaume Rovillé and Mathieu Bonhomme in Lyons, Jean de Tournes and Jérome Marnef in Paris, and also Christopher Plantin publishing in Antwerp and Leiden, quickly issued their own editions following the Wechel model. In 1546, the famous Venetian publisher Aldus Manutius surprised the world by issuing a second volume of Alciati's emblems, then adding 86 new examples to the canon.

The *Emblematum libellus* was additionally translated into French in 1536, and into German in 1542; a Spanish version, with 210 emblems, appeared in 1549, and it finally was translated into Italian in 1551. Oddly, given the well-documented Netherlandish taste for emblematic art, neither a Dutch nor a Flemish translation of Alciati was ever published, nor was there ever to be a complete English translation (but a number of the emblems, 86, were paraphrased in Geoffrey Whitney's *A Choice of Emblemes*, 1586). Given the commercial triumph of his emblem-book throughout Europe, Alciati was continually encouraged to make corrections and expansions, and eventually his popular pictorial anthology included some 212 emblems (all of which are now gathered together here). And so was created a post-medieval ideographic language, one primarily based on images as tersely explained by adjacent texts. The complementary exegetical tradition of deciphering the inherent obscurity of Alciati's epigrammatic declarations was inaugurated in 1573 with Plantin's publication of Claude Mignault's notes and extensive commentaries (560 pages) on all of Alciati's 211 emblems. But the monster commentary, occupying a doubled-columned quarto of 1,004 pages discussing *in extenso* all 212 emblems, was that one published in 1621 by Johann Thuilius (of which the Appendix quotes an extract, explaining the one emblem which had been previously "suppressed" from the canon of 211 entries). But none of this would have been made possible without the advent of a distinctively post-medieval technological phenomenon: the invention of the printing press.

The larger architectural plan of the *Emblematum liber* needs to be clarified. Alciati's literary model was the *Greek Anthology* (naturally unillustrated), where the epigrammatic poems had been grouped according to their designated subject matter and type. Alciati did not, however, at first employ this logical format; the initial editions of his emblem-book were a rather a disorganized jumble, with the entries placed without any regard to a proper succession of the diverse subjects. The definitive order was finally determined only in 1549 by Bartholomé Aneau, who placed the 201 emblems—Alciati then having added eleven new ones—"according to topical commonplaces, and by certain subject classifications" (*in locos communes, et tamquam in certas classes*), with these being arranged commencing "from the supreme God, and ending with trees" (*à Deo optimo maximo ad arbores*). Alciati himself approved of this curriculum-like compositional layout. Now entitled *Emblemata D. A. Alciati* (etc.), the first edition with the full complement of 211 emblems (Alciati having provided yet another batch, this time ten new items) was published posthumously in 1550 by Rovillé, Aneau's employer. According to the didactic scheme worked out in the final editions, the arrangement can be understood as embracing six informal divisions, including five major themes.

Complying here with the now-canonical format, first there comes an introductory grouping, a sort of dedication, including a reference to the Milan-Alciati connection: emblems 1–3. This is followed by the first major thematic grouping, which concerns *God and Religion*: emblems 4–8. The third, much larger, grouping then deals with the *Virtues*, including Faithfulness, 9–13; Prudence, 14–26; Justice, 27–32; Fortitude, 33–37; Concord, 38–42; Hope, 43–46; and Chastity, 47. As seems only fitting, next come the *Vices*, including Perfidy, 48–54; Ignorance, 55–66; Pride, 67–71; Lust, 72–79; Sloth, 80–83; Avarice, 84–89; and Gluttony, 90–96. The fifth grouping may be called the *Human Macrocosm*, and this sequentially examines the transcendental issues of Nature, 97–100; Astrology, 101–104; Love, 105–117; Fate, 118–130; Honor, 131–142; and the Ruler and the Republic, 143–150. The sixth, and final, grouping of elements may likewise be labeled the *Human Microcosm*, and here we deal with such obviously important topics as Life and Death, 151–158; Friendship and Enmity, 159–170; Revenge, 171–175; Peace, 176–178; Knowledge and Ignorance, 179–189; Marriage, 190–197; and, finally, Trees (as a mirror of human nature), 198–211. Last (that is, in the present edition), there is included the formerly "suppressed" emblem: "Against Those Sinning Against Nature" (formerly no. 80, and so belonging to the *Vices*, specifically "Lust").

A Book of Emblems

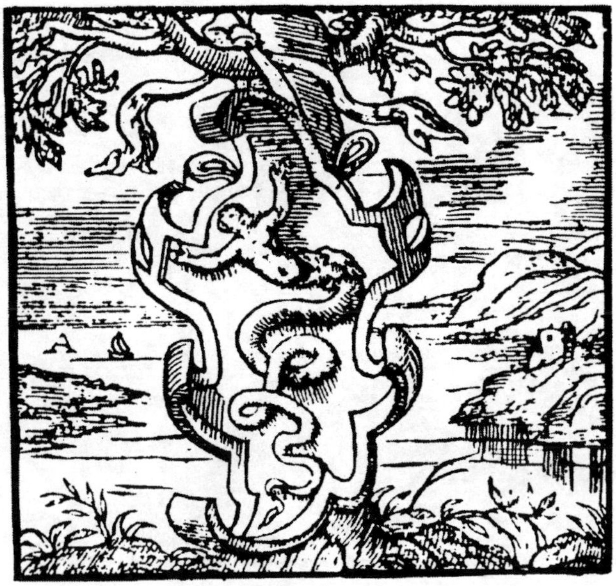

Emblema I

SUPER INSIGNI DUCATUS MEDIOLANI

Ad Illustrissimum Maximilianum, Ducem Mediolanensem

Exiliens infans sinuosi e faucibus anguis,
Est gentilitiis nobile stemma tuis.
Talia Pellaeum gessisse nomismata regem
Vidimus, hisque suum concelebrasse genus:
Dum se Ammone satam, matrem anguis imagine lusam,
Divini et sobolem seminis esse docet.
Ore exit. Tradunt sic quosdam enitier angues.
An quia sic Pallas de capite orta Iovis?

Emblem 1

THE COAT OF ARMS OF THE DUCHY OF MILAN

To the most illustrious Maximilian, Duke of Milan

A child escaping from the jaws of a sinuous serpent represents the pedigree of your noble [Visconti] family. We saw such things on the coinage of the king of Pella [Alexander the Great], and with these he celebrated his lineage: he showed himself to be the son of Ammon [Jupiter] and born from divine seed, for his mother had been seduced by [Jupiter appearing in] the guise of a serpent. The infant exits by the mouth. So also, so they say, do some serpents give birth. Or is this perhaps to mean that Pallas [Athena] was born from the head of Jupiter?

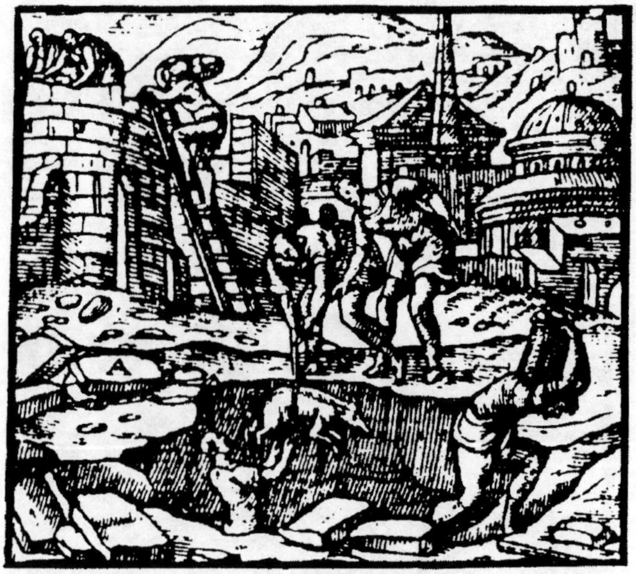

Emblema II

MEDIOLANUM

Biturigis vervex, Aeduis dat sucula signum:
His populis patriae debita origo meae est,
Quam Mediolanum sacram dixere puellae
Terram: nam vetus hoc Gallica lingua sonat.
Culta Minerva fuit, nunc est ubi numine Tecla
Mutato, Matris virginis ante domum.
Iam niger huic signum sus est, animalque biforme,
Acribus hinc setis lanitio inde levi.

Emblem 2

MILAN

The lamb symbolizes the people of Bourges, and the little pig those from Autun; to these peoples is owed the origin of my homeland, and the maidens called this sacred land "Mediolanum," for that is how Milan was pronounced in the ancient Gallic tongue. Then Minerva was worshipped; now, the divine will having been changed, it is [Santa] Tecla who is placed in front of the house of the Virgin Mother. Now the city's symbol is a black pig, an animal of double aspect [lamb and boar], having both rough bristles and, at the same time, soft wool [so making Milan *media lana*, "half-wool"].

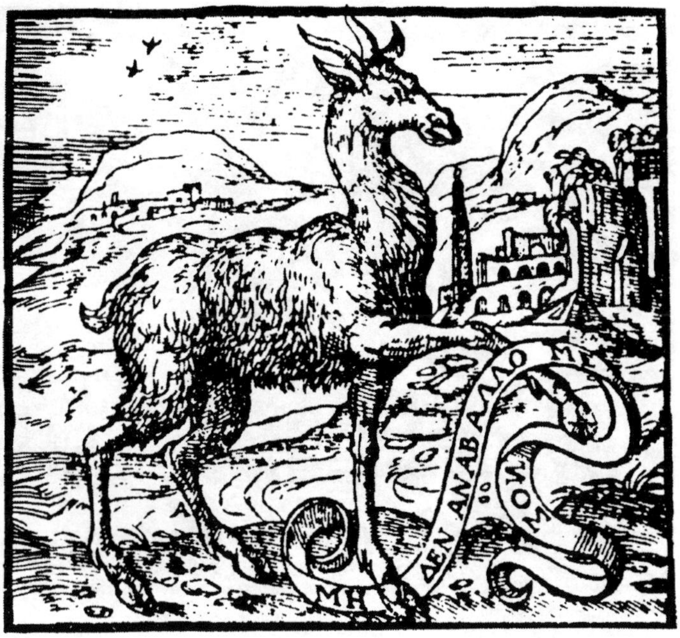

Emblema III

NUMQUAM PROCRASTINANDUM

Alciatae Gentis insignia sustinet Alce,
Unguibus et *midén* fert *anballómenos*
Constat Alexandrum sit respondisse roganti,
Qui tot obivisset tempore gesta brevi?
Nunquam, inquit, differe volens, quod et indicat Alce:
Fortior haec, dubites, ocior anne fiet.

Emblem 3

NEVER PROCRASTINATE

An elk [*alce*] holds the coat of arms of the Alciati family; this states [in Greek] "nothing should be postponed." It is well known how Alexander [the Great] had responded to a person who had asked him how he was able to accomplish so much in such a brief span of time. He said, "By never wanting to postpone anything [*miden anaballomenos*]," and that thought is indicated by the elk: you might be uncertain as to whether it is stronger or swifter.

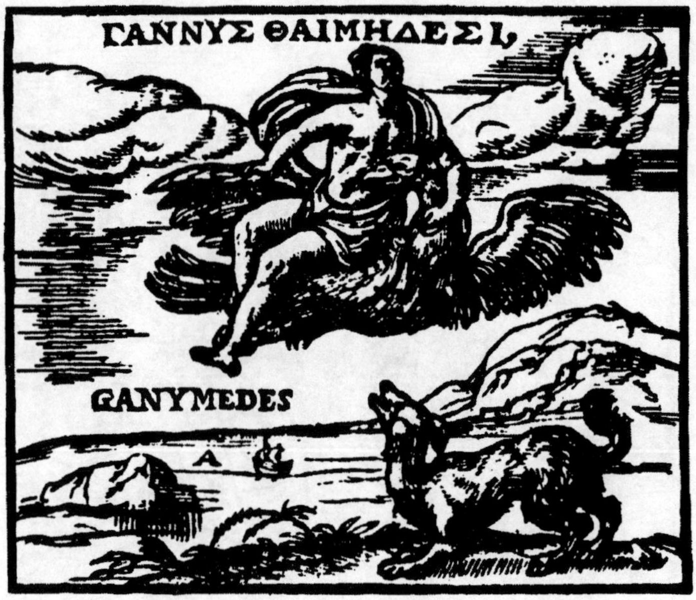

Emblema IV

IN DEO LAETANDUM

Aspice ut egregius puerum Iovis alite pictor
Fecerit Iliacum summa per astra vehi.
Quisne Iovem tactum puerili credat amore?
Dic, haec Maeonius finxerit unde senex?
Consilium, mens atque Dei cui gaudia praestant,
Creditur is summo raptus adesse Iovi.

Emblem 4

ABOUT TAKING JOY IN GOD

(a dialogue)

"See here how an outstanding painter showed the son of Illium [Ganymede] carried away to the distant stars by Jupiter's bird." "Who would have believed that Jupiter would be affected by love for a small boy? Tell me, whence did the old Meonian [Homer] contrive such an idea?" "It is believed that he who takes joy in God's judgment and mind is taken away [in rapture] to be with Jupiter on high."

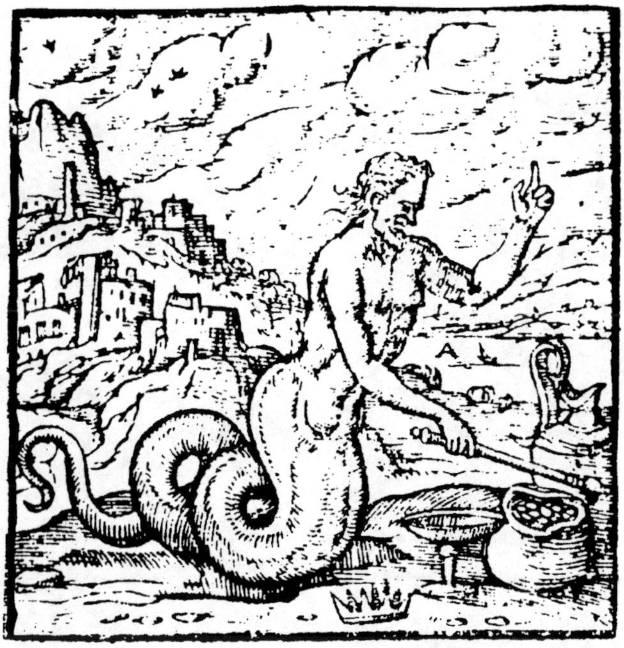

Emblema V

SAPIENTIA HUMANA, STULTITIA EST APUD DEUM

Quid dicam? Quonam hoc compellem nomine monstrum
Biforme, quod non est homo, nec est draco?
Sed sine vir pedibus, summis sine partibus anguis.
Vir anguipes dici, et homiceps anguis potest.
Anguem pedit homo, hominem eructavit et anguis:
Nec finis hominis est, initium nec est ferae.
Sic olim Cecrops doctis regnavit Athenis:
Sic et gigantes terra mater protulit.
Haec vafrum species, sed religione carentem,
Terrena tantum quique curet, indicat.

Emblem 5

HUMAN KNOWLEDGE IS BUT FOOLISHNESS TO GOD

What can I say? What name shall I give to this double-form monster, it being neither a man nor a snake? It is instead a man without feet and a serpent in the rest. It could be called a man with serpent feet and a serpent with a human head. The man farted the serpent and the serpent belched out the man: it has no human ending and no beastly beginning. Such was Cecrops, who formerly ruled over learned Athens, and thus the giants were given birth by Mother Earth. This image refers to one who is crafty but lacking religion; hence, he who only attends to worldly things.

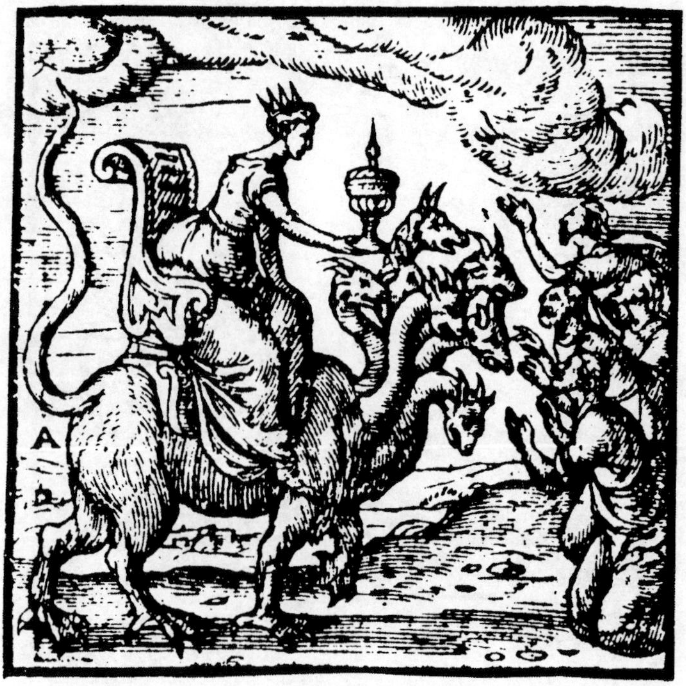

Emblema VI

FICTA RELIGIO

Regali residens meretrix pulcherrima sella,
Purpureo insignem gestat honore peplum.
Omnibus et latices pleno e cratere propinat:
At circum cubitans ebria turba iacet.
Sic Babylona notant: quae gentes illice forma,
Et ficta stolidas religione capit.

Emblem 6

FALSE RELIGION

A most beautiful whore resides upon a royal chair and wears the purple peplum of honor. She hands out wine to all, pouring it from a full vessel, and all around her the mob falls down drunk. This is how Babylon is pictured, she who traps stupid peoples with her seductive beauty and a false religion.

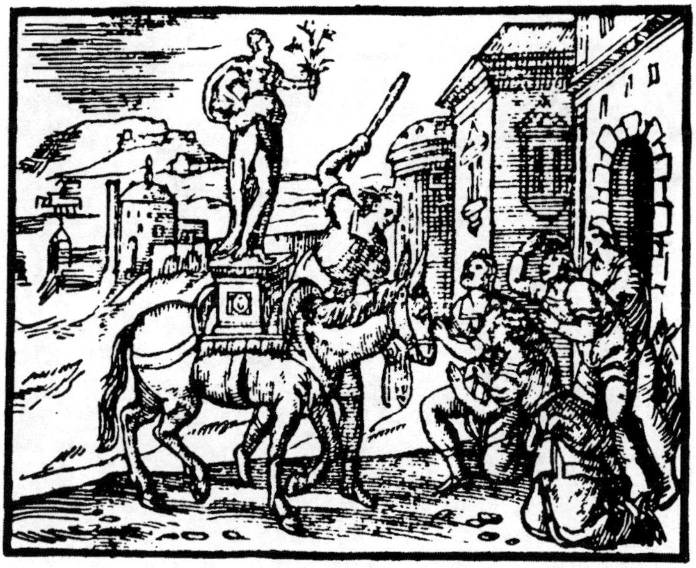

Emblema VII

NON TIBI, SED RELIGIONI

Isidis effigiem tardus gestabat asellus,
Pando verenda dorso habens mysteria.
Obvius erga Deam quisquis reverenter adorat,
Piasque genibus concipit flexis preces.
Ast asinus tantum praestari credit honorem
Sibi, et intumescit, admodum superbiens:
Donec eum flagris compescens, dixit agaso,
Non es Deus tu, aselle, sed Deum vehis.

Emblem 7

NOT FOR YOU, BUT FOR RELIGION

A dim-witted ass was carrying an image of [the goddess] Isis, so bearing upon its bent back the venerated mysteries. Every passerby along its route worshipped the Goddess with reverence, falling to their knees to offer her their pious prayers. The ass, however, assumed that the honors were only being given to himself, and he swelled up with pride. This stopped when the donkey driver, correcting him with some whiplashes, told him: "You are not God, you half-baked ass, but only the bearer of God."

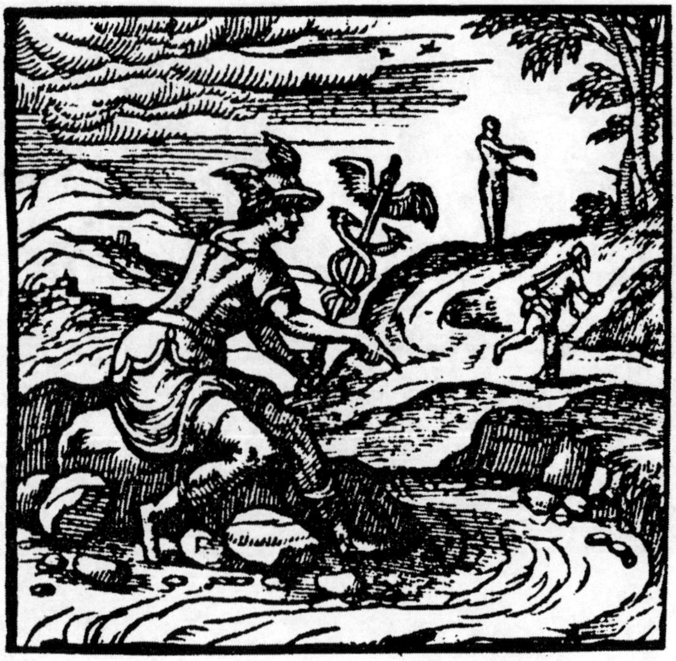

Emblema VIII

QUA DII VOCANT, EUNDUM

In trivio mons est lapidum: supereminet illi
Trunca Dei effigies, pectore facta tenus.
Mercurii est igitur tumulus, suspende viator
Serta Deo, rectum qui tibi monstret iter.
Omnes in trivio sumus, atque hoc tramite vitae
Fallimur, ostendat ni Deus ipse viam.

Emblem 8

WHERE THE GODS TELL US TO, WE MUST GO

In the crossroads there is a pile of stones, on the top of which there rises a truncated image of God, fashioned from the waist up. This is the tomb of Mercury; dedicate to the god, oh traveler, a garland, so that he will show you the correct path to take. We are all in a crossroads, and in this path of life we will turn to error if God himself does not show us the path.

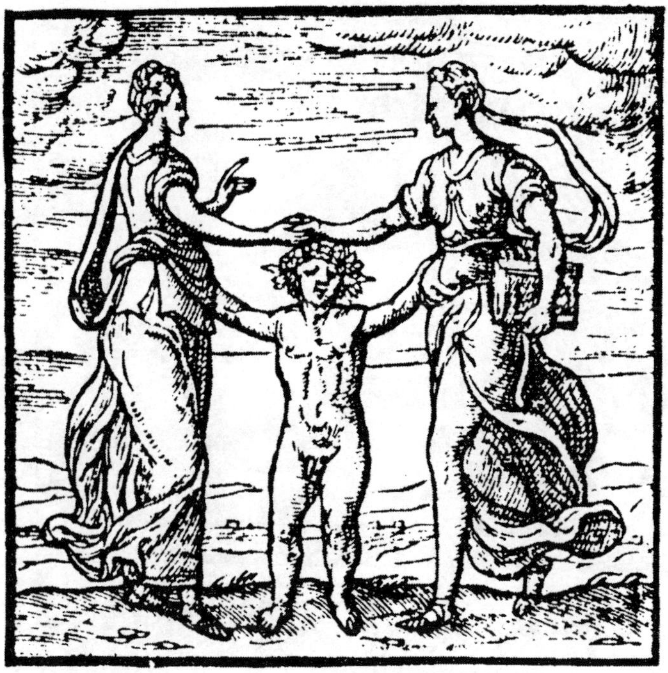

Emblema IX

FIDEI SYMBOLUM

Stet depictus Honos tyrio velatus amictu,
Eiusque iungat nuda dextram Veritas.
Sitque Amor in medio castus, cui tempora circum
Rosa it, Diones pulchrior Cupidine.
Constituunt haec signa Fidem, Reverentia Honoris
Quam fovet, alit Amor, parturitque Veritas.

Emblem 9

THE SYMBOL OF FIDELITY

Honor is to be pictured clothed in a purple mantle. Holding her right hand is the Naked Truth, and between them is chaste Love; with roses encircling his temples, he is more beautiful than the Cupid of Dione [Venus's mother]. These figures constitute the symbols of Fidelity, which is warmed by reverence of Honor, feeding Love and birthing Truth.

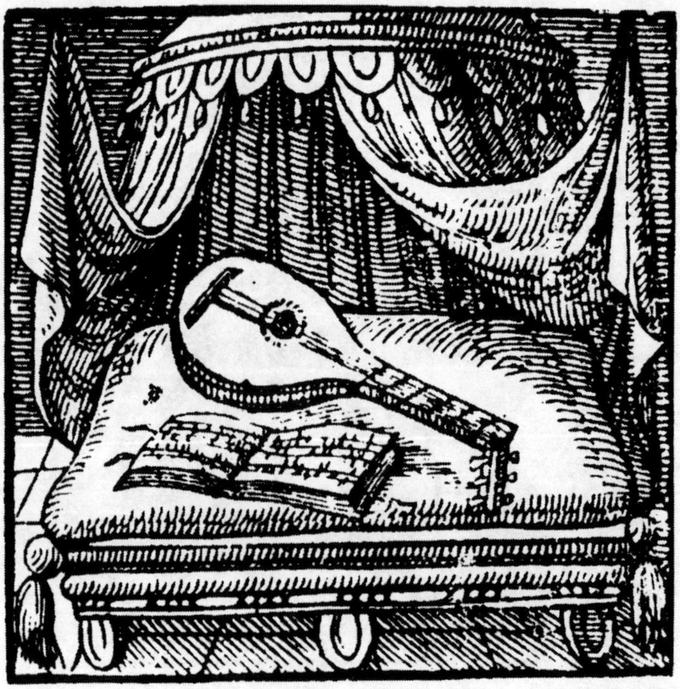

Emblema X
FOEDERA

Ad Maximilianum, Mediolanensem Ducem

Hanc citharam, a lembi quae forma halieutica fertur,
Vendicat et propriam Musa Latina sibi,
Accipe Dux: placeat nostrum hoc tibi tempore munus,
Quo nova cum sociis foedera inire paras.
Difficile est, nisi docto homini, tot tendere chordas;
Unaque si fuerit non bene tenta fides,
Ruptave (quod facile est) perit omnis gratia conchae,
Illeque praecellens cantus, ineptus erit.
Sic Itali coeunt proceres in foedera: concors
Nil est quod timeas, si tibi constet amor.
At si aliquis desciscat (uti plerumque vidamos)
In nihilum illa omnis solvitur harmonia.

Emblem 10

ALLIANCES

To Maximilian, Duke of Milan

Take, oh Duke, this lute, which, due to its boat-like shape, is called *halieutica* [oceanic], and which the Latin Muse flaunts as her own. It is hoped you will enjoy our present, for in this moment you are preparing to enter upon new alliances with your allies. It is difficult, except by the man who is well informed, to tune so many strings [*chorda*]; if only one string [*fides*, also "word of honor"] is not well stretched, or should it break — which can easily happen — then all the grace of the seashell-like instrument is destroyed and the superb song turns out ineffectual. Hence, the nobles of Italy are forming federations: there is nothing to fear if there is concord and they still love you. But if one breaks from the rest, such as we see so often, then all that harmony dissolves into nothingness.

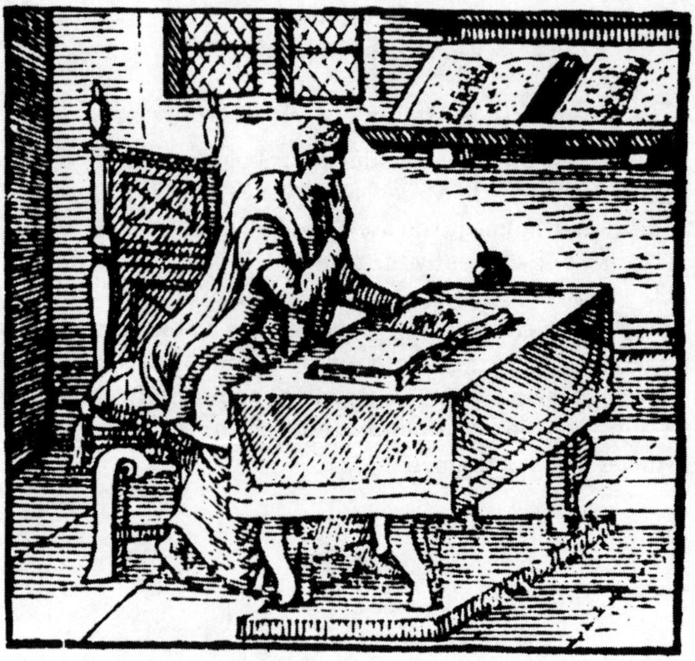

Emblema XI

SILENTIUM

Cum tacet, haud quicquam differt sapientibus amens:
Stultitiae est index linguaque voxque suae.
Ergo premat labias, digitoque silentia signet:
Et sese Pharium vertat in Harpocratem.

Emblem 11

SILENCE

As long as he remains silent, in no way can the fool be distinguished from the wise men. His tongue and his voice are the signs of his stupidity. Therefore, have him press his lips together, and with his finger he shall make the sign of silence: so doing, he turns into an Egyptian Harpocrates [or god of silence].

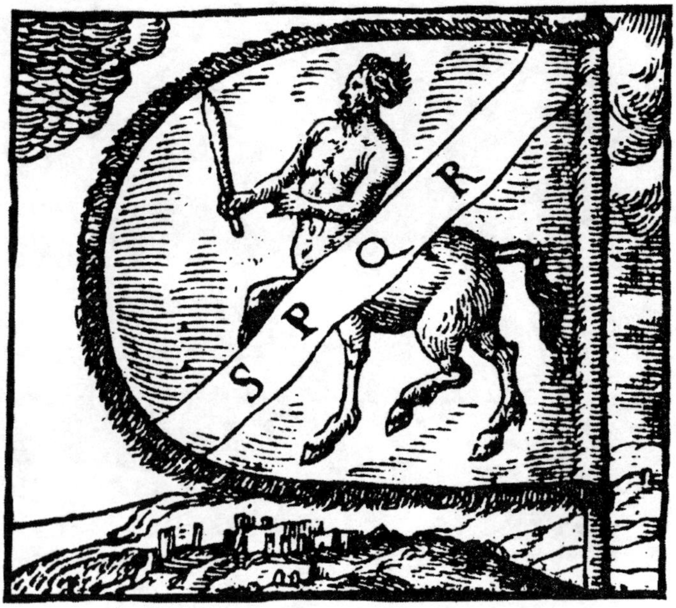

Emblema XII

NON VULGANDA CONSILIA

Limine quod caeco, obscura et caligine monstrum
Gnosiacis clausit Daedalus in latebris,
Depictum Romana phalanx in proelia gestat,
Semiviroque nitent signa superba bove:
Nosque monent, debere Ducum secreta latere
Consilia. Auctori cognita techna nocet.

Emblema 12

SECRETS ARE NOT TO BE DIVULGED

The Roman phalanx carries into battle a painted scene of the monster which Dedalus had imprisoned within the labyrinth of Cnossos with its hidden entrance and shadowy darkness, and signs of arrogance shine forth from the half-human bull [the Minotaur]. These advise us that the secret deliberations of the leaders must remain secret; detected, a cunning trick harms its author.

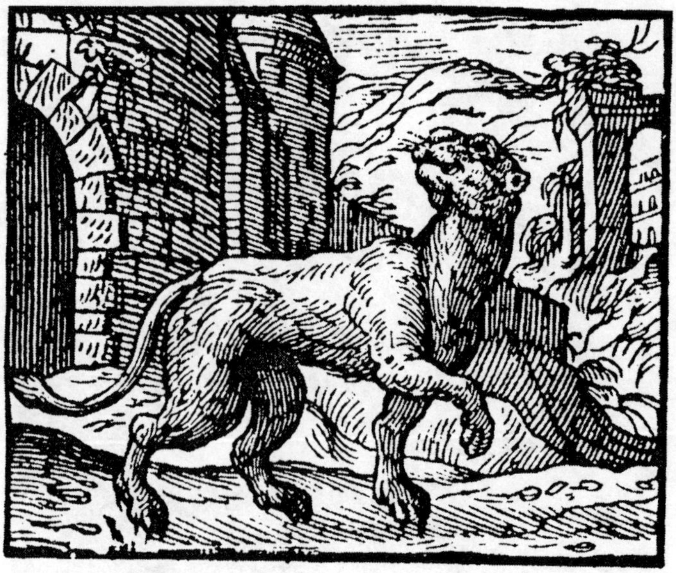

Emblema XIII

NEC QUAESTIONI QUIDEM CEDENDUM

Cecropia effictam quam cernis in arce Leaenam,
Harmodii an nescis hospes? Amica fuit.
Sic animum placuit monstrare viraginis acrem
More fera, nomen quia tale tulit.
Quod fidibus contorta, suo non prodidit ullum
Indicio, elinguem reddidit Iphicrates.

Emblem 13

ONE MUST NEVER YIELD UNDER QUESTIONING

Leaena, whom you see pictured [as a lioness] upon the [Athenian] fortress of Ceropes, was a friend of Harmodius; did you not know this, oh stranger? It pleased the artist to show the fierce spirit of the heroine in the form of a beast, or perhaps he painted her this way because of her name [Leaena, or "lioness"]. Although tied to the rack, she betrayed no one with her testimony; hence, Iphicrates [the painter] showed her without a tongue.

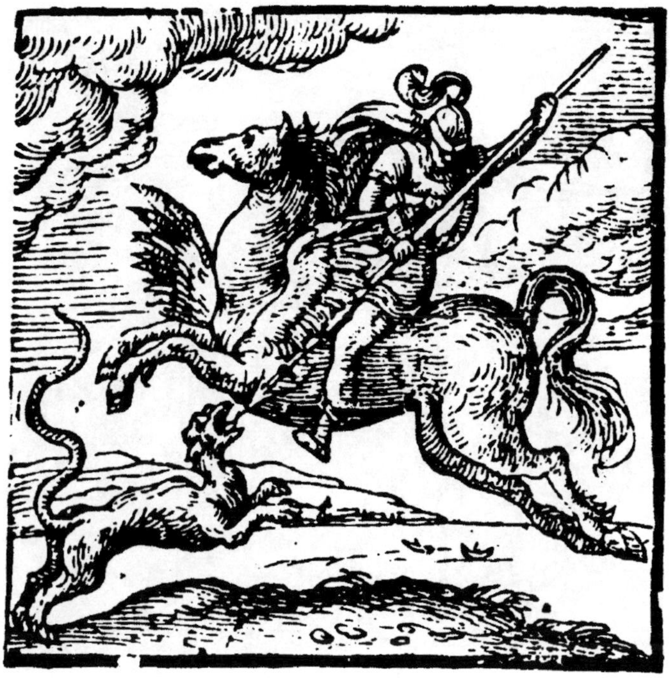

Emblema XIV

CONSILIO ET VIRTUTE CHIMAERAM SUPERARI, HOC EST, FORTIORES ET DECEPTORES

Bellerophon ut fortis eques superare Chimaeram
Et Lycii potuit sternere monstra soli:
Sic tu Pegaseis vectus petis aethera pennis,
Consilioque animi monstra superba domas.

Emblem 14

BY COUNSEL AND VIRTUE, THE CHIMERA SHALL BE OVERCOME, MEANING THE STRONGER AND THE DECEIVERS

Just as the mighty knight Bellerophon was able to conquer the Chimera and to slay the Lycian monsters, so can you, too, rise up to heaven, carried aloft on the wings of Pegasus. As well counseled by the intellect, you can tame all the haughty monsters.

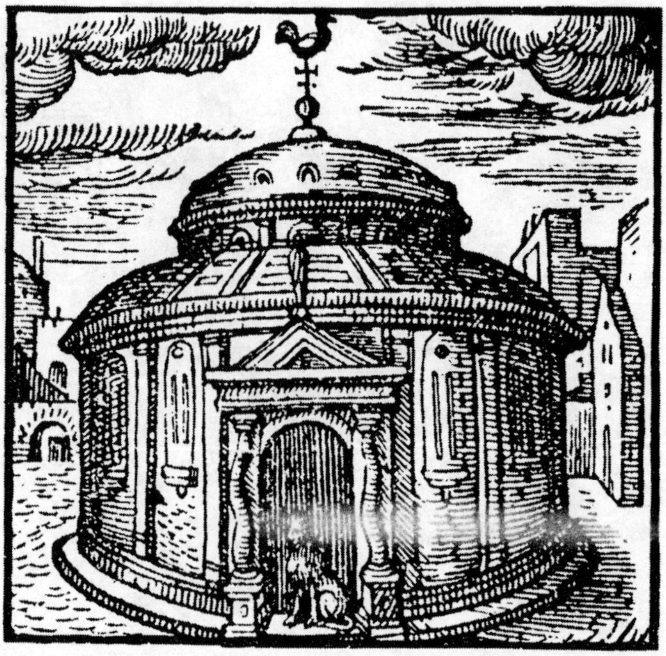

Emblema XV

VIGILANTIA ET CUSTODIA

Instantis quod signa canens det gallus Eoi,
Et revocet famulas ad nova pensa manus:
Turribus in sacris effingitur aerea pelvis,
Ad superos mentem quod revocet vigilem.
Est leo: sed custos oculis quia dormit apertis,
Templorum idcirco ponitur ante fores.

Emblem 15

VIGILANCE AND PROTECTION

The rooster is the herald of the approaching dawn and, crowing, he calls the toiling hands to new tasks. Because it summons the vigilent mind again to heavenly things, a bronze bell is shown on the towers of sacred places. Because he sleeps with his eyes open, as a guardian there will also be placed a lion before the gates of the temples.

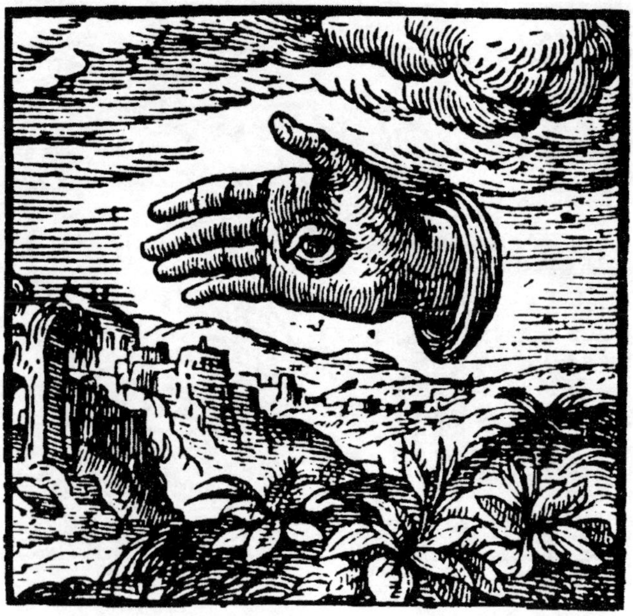

Emblema XVI

SOBRIE VIVENDUM ET NON TEMERE CREDENDUM

(Nephe, kai memnes hapistein harthra tauta phrenon)

Ne credas, ne (Epicharmus ait) non sobrius esto:
Hi nervi humanae membraque mentis erunt.
Ecce oculata manus credens id quod videt: ecce
Puleium antiquae sobrietatis holus:
Quo turbam ostenso sedaverit Heraclitus,
Mulxerit et tumida seditione gravem.

Emblem 16

LIVE SOBERLY AND DO NOT ACCEPT BELIEFS HEEDLESSLY

(repeated in Greek)

States Epicharmus: "Never be credulous nor cease to be sober." These are the sinews and members of the human mind. Behold the hand with an eye upon it; it only believes what it sees. Here is shown the mint, the herb symbolizing ancient sobriety. Brandishing this plant, Heraclitus pacified and soothed the maddened mob bursting into frenzied revolt.

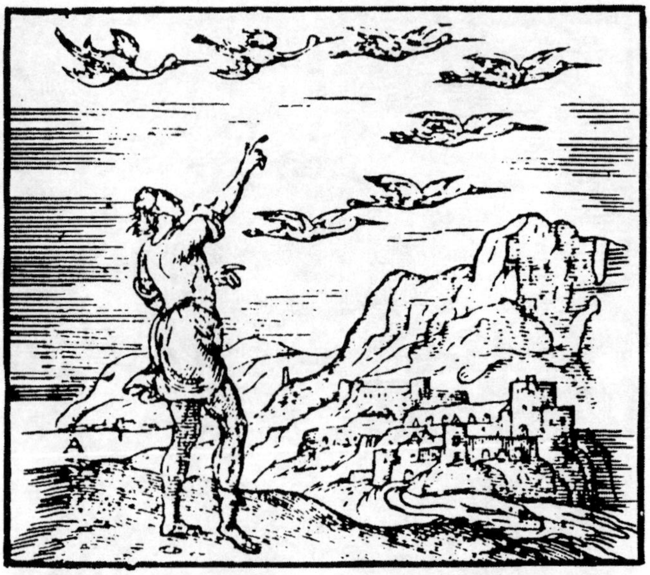

Emblema XVII

QUID EXCESSI? QUID ADMISI? QUID OMISI?

(pe parebio; ti d'erexa; ti moi deon ouk hetlephe?)

Italicae Samius sectae celeberrimus auctor
Ipse suum clausit carmine dogma brevi:
Quo praetergressus? Quid agis? Quid omittis agendum?
Hanc rationem urgens reddere quemque sibi.
Quod didicisse Gruum volitantum ex agmine fertur,
Arreptum gestant quae pedibus lapidem:
Ne cessent, neu transversas mala flamina raptent.
Qua ratione, hominum vita regenda fuit.

Emblem 17

WHERE HAVE I ERRED? WHAT HAVE I DONE? WHAT HAVE I OMITTED?

(repeated in Greek)

The celebrated author from Samos, founder of the Italic sect [Pythagoras], himself compressed his teachings into a brief epigram: "Where did you err? What did you do? What have you failed to accomplish?" He urged every one to render this account individually. It is said that he taught this [maxim] referring to a flock of cranes; when they are flying, they all carry a stone in their claws so that they won't tarry or be blown from their course by contrary gusts of wind. A man's life should be governed by the same rule.

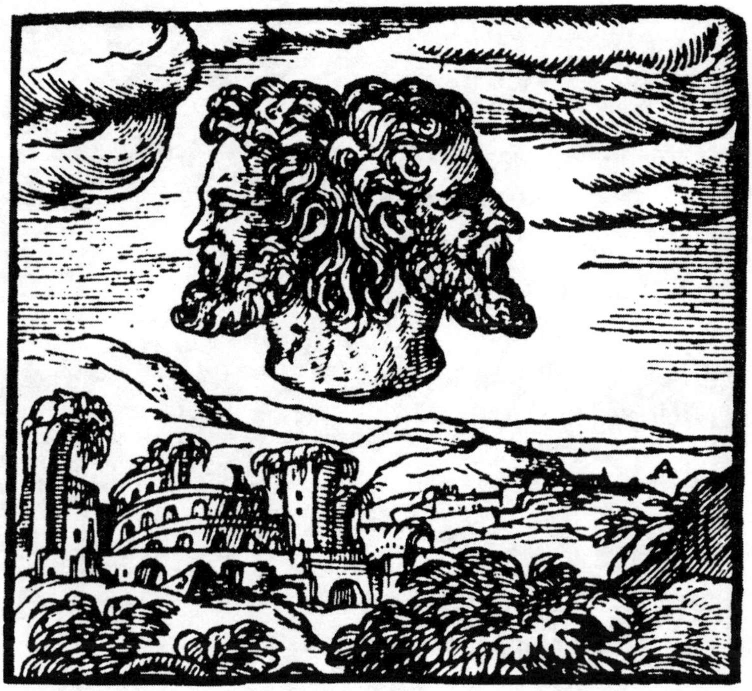

Emblema XVIII

PRUDENTES

Iane bifrons, qui iam transacta futuraque calles,
Cuique retro sannas, sicut et ante, vides:
Te tot cur oculis, cur fingunt vultibus? An quod
Circumspectum hominem forma fuisse docet?

Emblem 18

PRUDENT PEOPLE

Two-faced Janus, how well you know both past and the future transactions, and you see the mocking grimaces behind and in front of you. Why do they portray you with so many eyes and faces? Is it not, perhaps, because this image symbolizes the man who is watchful on every side?

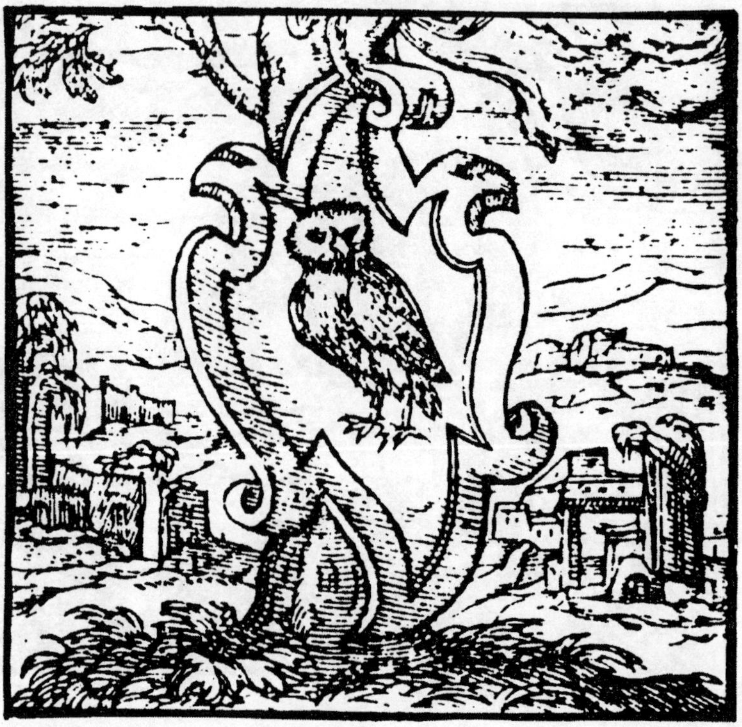

Emblema XIX

PRUDENS MAGIS QUAM LOQUAX

Noctua Cecropiis insignia praestat Athenis,
Inter aves sani noctua consilii.
Armiferae merito obsequiis sacrata Minervae,
Garrula quo cornix cesserat ante loco.

Emblem 19

MORE PRUDENT THAN LOQUACIOUS

The barn-owl is the attribute of Athens founded by Cecrops, for this one belongs among the birds of good counsel. Due to its merits, it was consecrated to serve armed Minerva, so displacing the chattering crow.

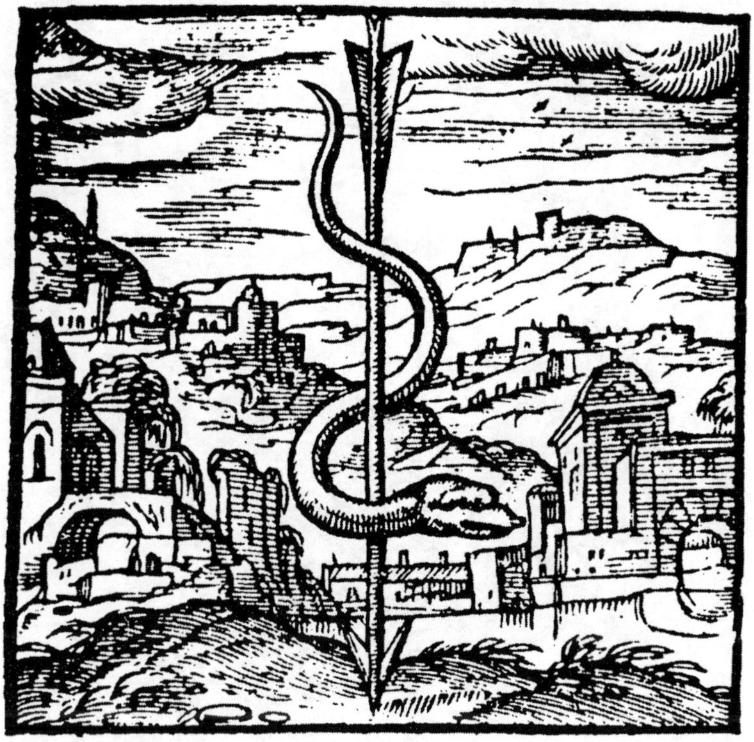

Emblema XX

MATURANDUM

Maturare iutent propere, et cunctarier omnes;
Ne nimium praeceps, neu mora longa nimis.
Hoc tibi declaret connexum echeneide telum:
Haec tarda est, volitant spicula missa manu.

Emblem 20

MATURING

They all advise us to ripen with speed and [yet] to take our time, acting neither precipituously nor without a long delay. This is announced to you by the remora coiled around a shaft: while the fish is slow, the arrows fly from the hand which throws them.

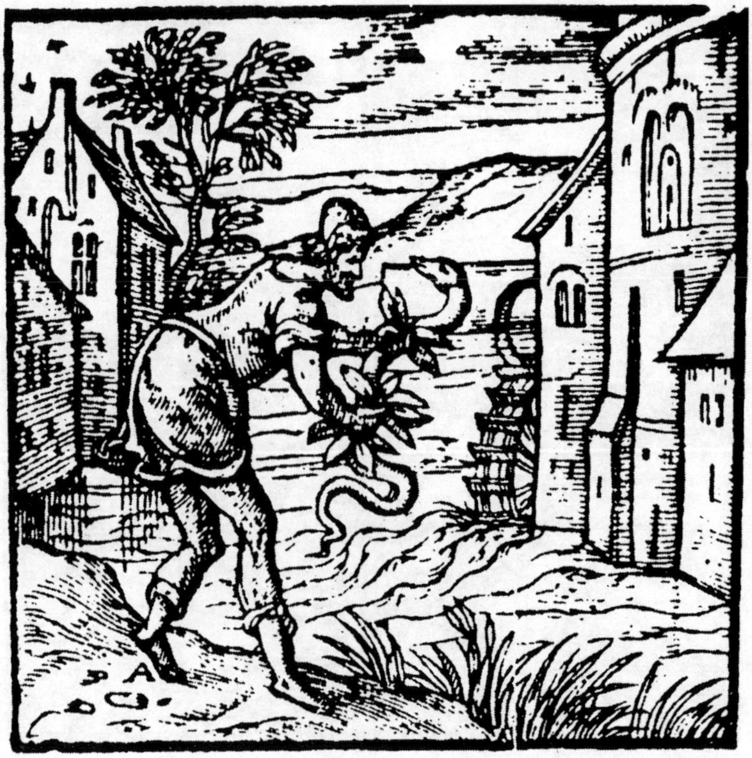

Emblema XXI

IN DEPREHENSUM

Iamdudum quacunque fugis, te persequor: at nunc
Cassibus in nostris denique captus ades.
Amplius haud poteris vires eludere nostras:
Ficulno anguillam strinximus in folio.

Emblem 21

ABOUT THE CAPTIVE

For a long time I have pursued you to where ever you chose to flee, but now, finally, you have been trapped in our nets. You will no longer slip away from our power: we have tied the eel in a fig leaf.

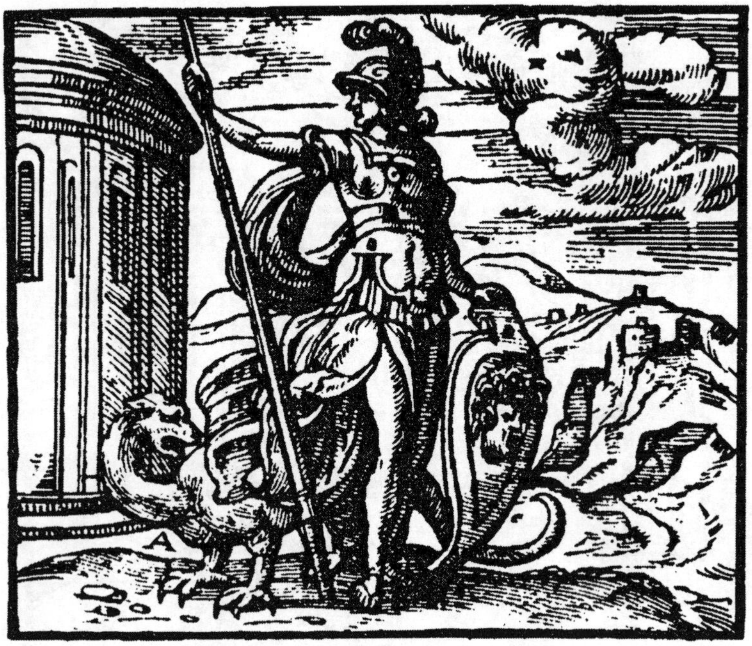

Emblema XXII

CUSTODIENDAS VIRGINES

Vera haec effigies innuptae est Palladis: eius
Hic Draco, qui dominae constitit ante pedes.
Cur Divae comes hoc animal? Custodia rerum
Huic data: sic lucos, sacraque templa colit.
Innuptas opus est cura asservare puellas
Pervigili: Laqueos undique tendit amor.

Emblem 22

VIRGINS MUST BE GUARDED

This is the true image of the virgin Pallas [Athena], and she is the mistress of the dragon seen at her feet. Why is this animal the companion of the goddess? The protection of things was entrusted to it; it guards the sacred forests and temples. It is necessary to warily guard unwed maidens, for love lays its lures everywhere.

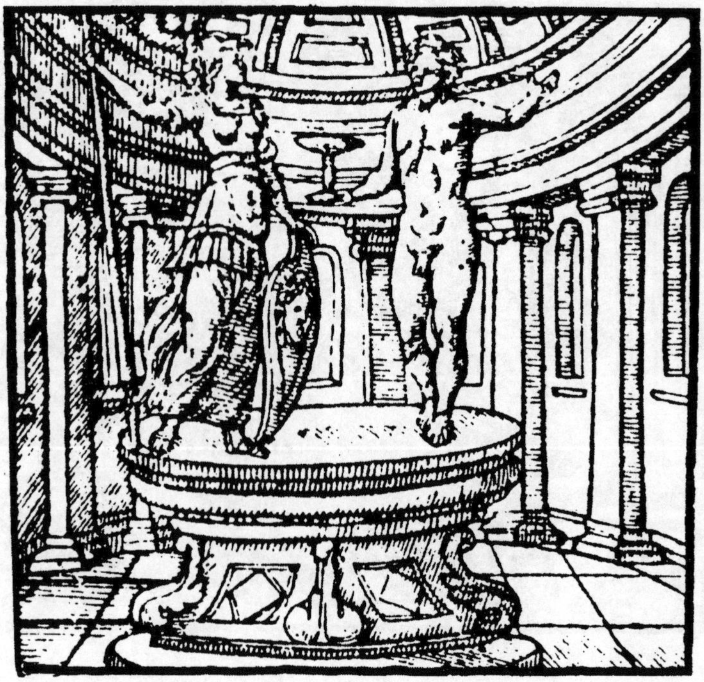

Emblema XXIII

VINO PRUDENTIAM AUGERI

Haec Bacchus pater et Pallas communiter ambo
Templa tenent, soboles utraque vera Iovis.
Haec caput, ille femur solvit: huic usus olivi
Debitus, invenit primus at illle merum.
Junguntur merito: quod si qui abstemius odit
Vina, Deae nullum sentiet auxilium.

Emblem 23

AUGMENT PRUDENCE WITH WINE

Father Bacchus and Athena share together this temple; both are the true offspring of Jupiter. She sprang from the head of Jupiter; he arose from his thigh. To her [Minerva] is due the use of the olive, but he [Dionysus] first discovered fortified wine. Rightly are they linked; for if an abstemious man hates wine [and Bacchus], he will experience no aid whatsoever from the Goddess [of the Arts and Sciences].

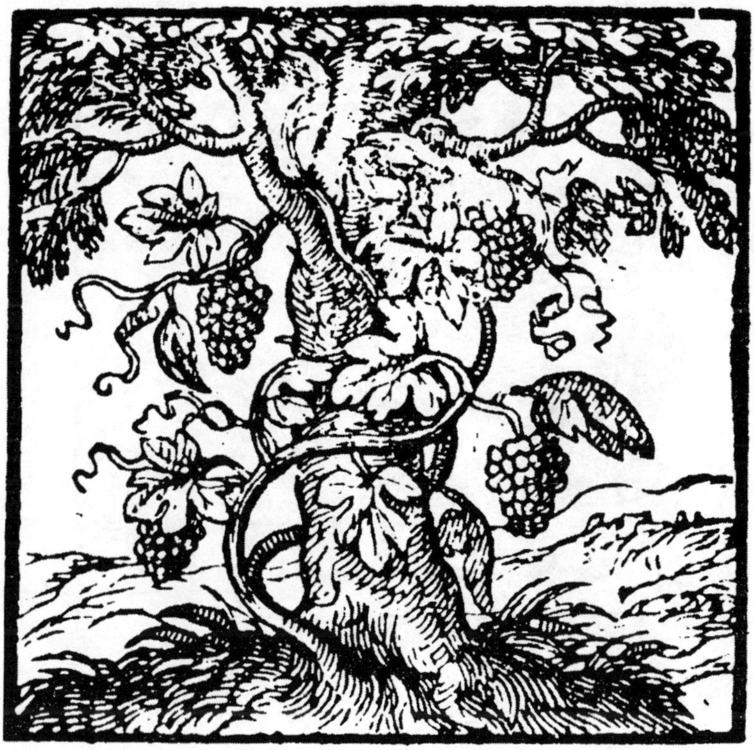

Emblema XXIV

PRUDENTES VINO ABSTINENT

Quid me vexatis rami? Sum Palladis arbor.
Auferte hinc botros, virgo fugit Bromium.

Emblem 24

THE PRUDENT ABSTAIN FROM WINE

Why do you vex me so, oh branches? I am the tree of Pallas [Athena]. Remove from here your clusters of grapes: the virgin [Athena] flees from Bromius [Bacchus].

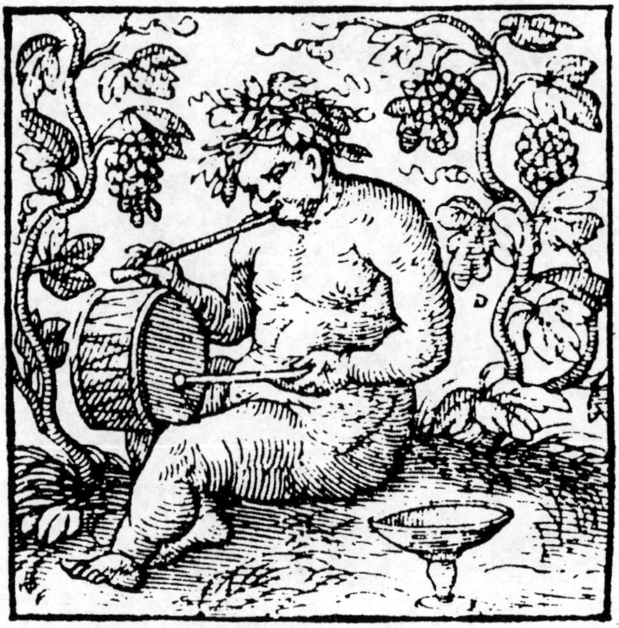

Emblema XXV
IN STATUAM BACCHI

Dialogismus

Bacche pater, quis te mortali lumine novit,
Et docta effinxit quis tua membra manu?
Praxiteles, qui me rapientem Gnossida vidit,
Atque illo pinxit tempore, qualis eram.
Cur iuvenis teneraque etiam lanugine vernat
Barba, queas Pylium cum superare senem?
Muneribus quandoque meis si parcere disces,
Iunior et forti pectore semper eris.
Tympana non manibus, capiti non cornua desunt:
Quos nisi dementeis talia signa decent?
Hoc doceo, nostro quod abusus munere sumit
Cornua, et insanus mollia sistra quatit.
Quid vult ille color membris pene igneus? Omen
Absit, an humanis ureris ipse focis?
Cum Semeles de ventre parens me fulmine traxit
Ignivomo, infectum pulvere mersit aquas.
Hinc sapit hic, liquidis qui nos bene diluit undis:
Qui non, ardenti torret ab igne iecur.
Sed nunc me doceas, qui vis miscerier? Et qua
Te sanus tutum prendere lege queat?

Quadrantem addat aquae, calicem sumpsisse falerni
Qui cupit, hoc sumi pocula more iuvat.
Stes intra heminas: nam qui procedere tendit
Ultra, alacer, sed mox ebrius, inde furit.
Res dura haec nimium, sunt pendula guttura, dulce
Tu fluis. Heu facile commoda cadunt!

Emblem 25

CONCERNING THE IMAGE OF BACCHUS

(a dialogue)

"Father Bacchus, whose mortal eyes saw you, and who modeled your limbs with such a skilled hand?" "It was [the sculptor] Praxiteles, who saw me while I was abducting the girl [Ariadne] from Cnossos, and he portrayed me in that moment and just as I was then." "Why does he have you sprout a youthful and downy beard, since you must be superior in age to the ancient of Pylos [Nestor]?" "Once you learn to abstemious of my gifts [wine], then you too will always be as young as I am — and with a heart as strong as mine is." "You are not lacking tambourines in your hands nor horns on your hands: to whom are suitable such attributes, if not the demented?" "This is what I teach: the abuse of my gifts acquires horns; then, maddened, he rattles effeminate sistrums." "What does that fire-like color of your limbs mean? Is it perhaps a sign that you were yourself burnt at a human hearth?" "When my father [Jupiter] ripped me from the belly of Semele with his fiery lightening-bolt, since I was spotted with ashes, he dipped me in the water. Hence, you understand what happens to he who dilutes me [wine] well in waves of liquid: he doesn't burn his liver with ardent fire." "Now, however, teach me in what proportion you have to be mixed, and by what rule may you be drunk without damage." "He who wishes to drink a goblet of Falernian wine is advised to add to it a quarter part of water; it is pleasing for the cup to be so drained. Stick to the *herminas* [measuring 27 cl], since whoever exceeds this limit, rather than just lively, will get drunk immediately, and later he goes mad." "This edict is much too stringent. My throat is open wide — and you flow so sweetly. Oh my: nothing pleasant comes without trouble!"

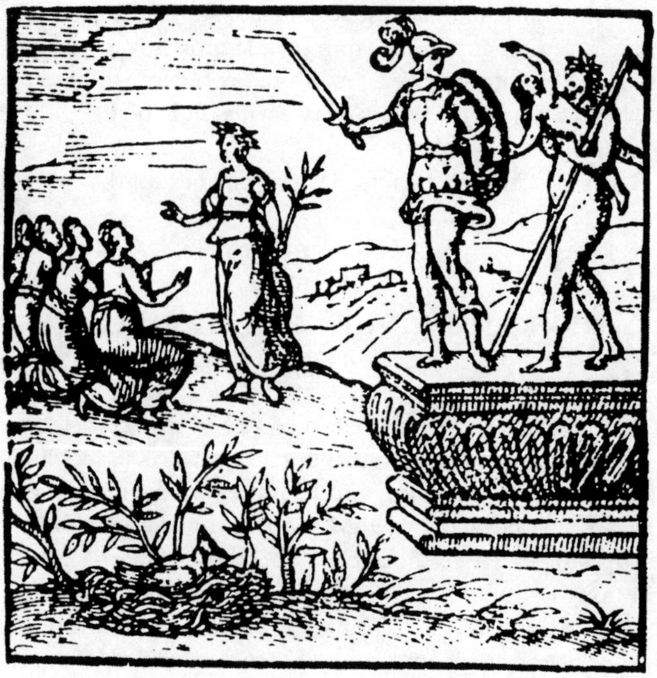

Emblema XXVI
GRAMEN

Gramineam Fabio patres tribuere corollam,
Fregerat ut Poenos Hannibalemque mora.
Occulit inflexo nidum sibi gramine alauda,
Vulgo aiunt, pullos sic fovet illa suos.
Saturno Martique sacrum, quo Glaucus adeso
Polybides, factus creditur esse Deus.
His merito arguitur nodis tutela salusque:
Herbaque tot vires haec digitalis habet.

Emblem 26
GRAMA GRASS

Since he had defeated Hannibal and the Punic troops with his delaying tactics, the senators gave Fabius a garland of grama grass. According to folk wisdom, the lark hides its nest with folded grama to shelter its chicks. This grass was sacred to Saturn and Mars and, after eating it, it is believed that Glaucus, the son of Polybius, became a god. Its buds qualify the herb to be a proper symbol of protection and health: such are the virtues of this plant of the foxglove family.

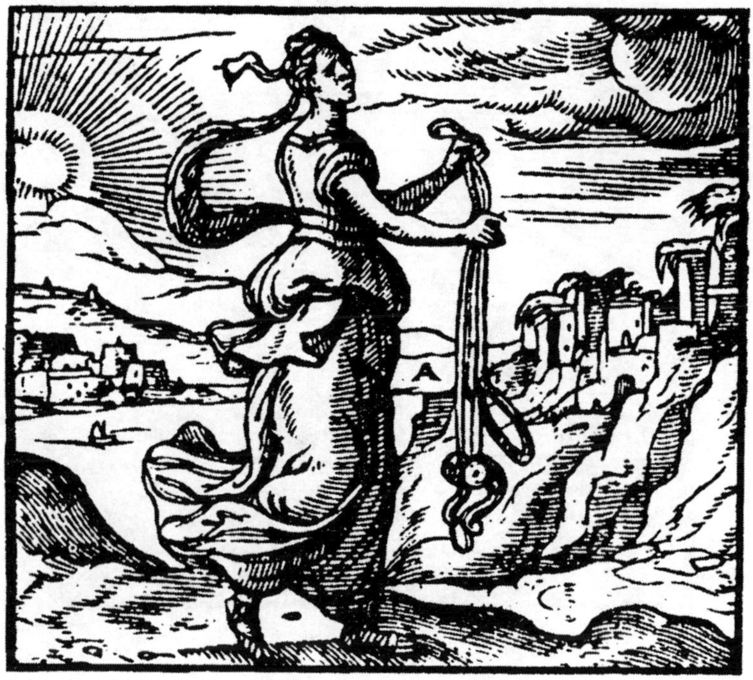

Emblema XXVII

NEC VERBO, NEC FACTO QUEMQUAM LAEDENDUM

Assequitur, Nemesisque virum vestigia servat,
Continet et cubitum duraque frena manu.
Ne male quid facias, neve improba verba loquaris:
Et iubet in cunctis rebus adesse modum.

Emblem 27

NEVER WOUND ANYBODY, NEITHER BY WORD OR BY DEED

Nemesis follows and observes the footprints of men, and she holds in her hand the measure and the hard bit. This is so that you will do no evil nor say any improper words, and she orders that limits should be observed in all things.

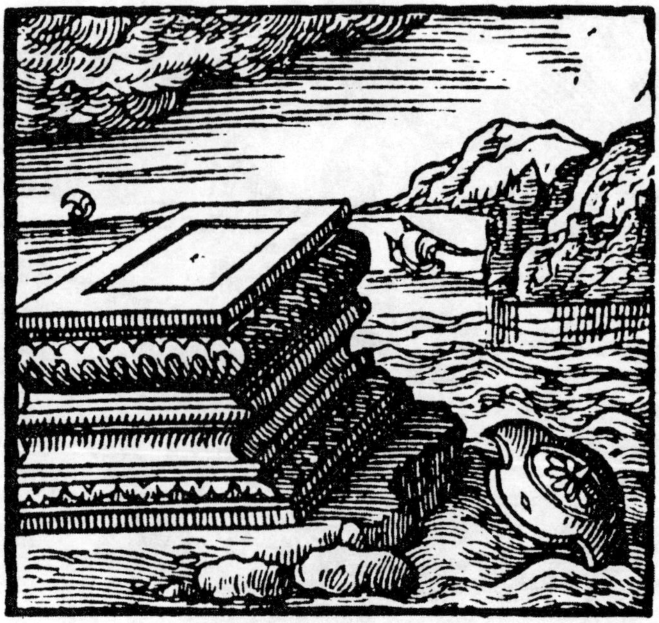

Emblema XXVIII

TANDEM, TANDEM IUSTITIA OBTINET

Aeacidae Hectoreo perfusum sanguine scutum,
Quod Graecorum Ithaco contio iniqua dedit,
Iustior arripuit Neptunus in aequora iactum
Naufragio, ut dominum posset adire suum:
Littoreo Aiacis tumulo namque intulit unda,
Quae boat, et tali voce sepulchra ferit:
Vicisti, Telamoniade, tu dignior armis
Affectus. Fas est cedere iustitiae.

Emblem 28

SOONER OR LATER, JUSTICE PREVAILS

Covered with the blood of Hector, the shield of Achilles, which the unjust assembly of the Greeks had granted to the Ithacan [Ulysses], was tossed into the waters after a shipwreck; Neptune, more just, pulled it out so that he could be sent to its rightful owner. The waves, in fact, carried it toward the tomb of Ajax on the coast and, beating against his sepulcher, it resounded with these words: "You conquered, oh son of Telamon; you are more worthy to possess these weapons. It is right for emotion to yield to justice."

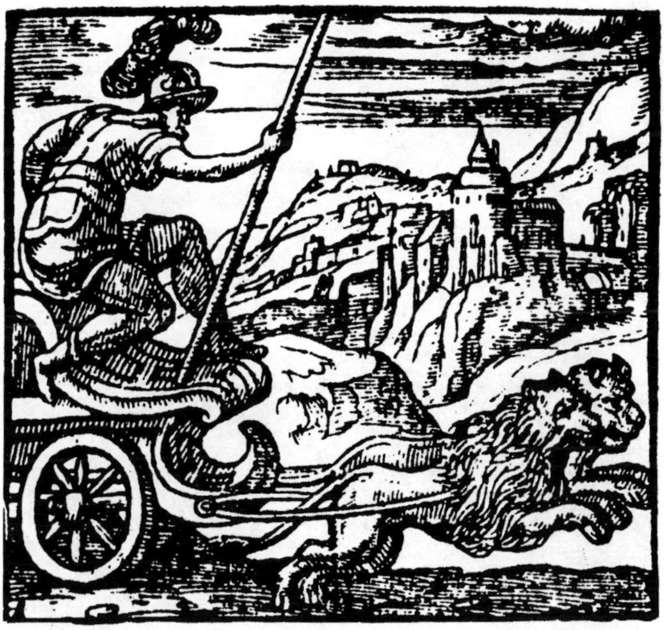

Emblema XXIX

ETIAM FEROCISSIMOS DOMARI

Romanum postquam eloquium, Cicerone perempto,
Perdiderat patriae pestis acerba suae:
Inscendit currus victor, iunxitque leones,
Compulit et durum colla subire iugum:
Magnanimos cessisse suis Antonius armis,
Ambage hac cupiens significare duces.

Emblem 29

EVEN THE FIERCEST ARE TAMED

A bitter plague in his own homeland destroyed Roman eloquence after Cicero's death; then [Mark] Antony mounted as a victor upon his chariot and harnessed lions to it, forcing them to suffer the harsh yoke upon their necks. By means of this enigma Antony wished to show that the great-hearted leaders [Brutus and Cassius] had yielded to his arms [at Philippi].

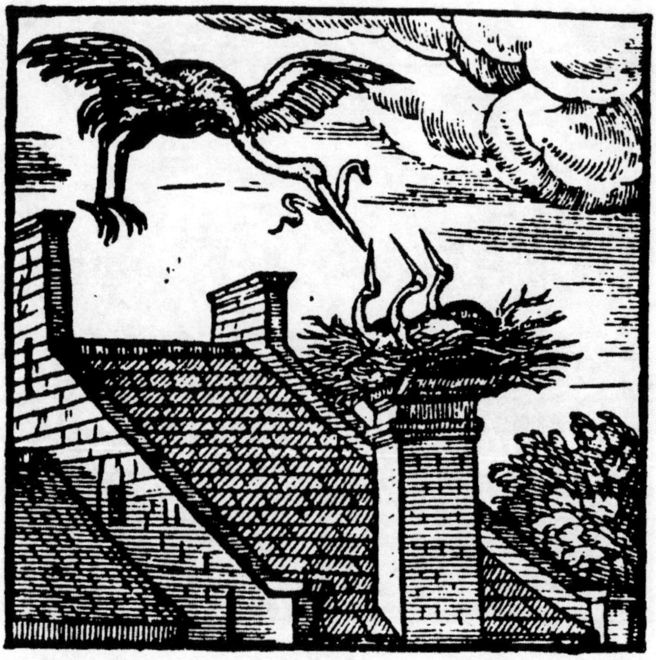

Emblema XXX

GRATIAM REFERENDAM

Aerio insignis pietate Ciconia nido,
Investes pullos pignora grata fovet.
Taliaque exspectat sibi munera mutua reddi,
Auxilio hoc quoties mater egebit anus.
Nec pia spem soboles fallit, sed fessa parentum
Corpora fert humeris, praestat et ore cibos.

Emblem 30

FAVORS MUST BE RETURNED

The stork, famous for its piety, nourishes its unclothed chicks in its airy nest with thankful pledges. The mother stork hopes that such gifts will be reciprocated when, now old, she has need of the same succor. The pious offspring do not betray this hope; instead, they carry upon their backs the exhausted bodies of their parents and give them food from their mouths.

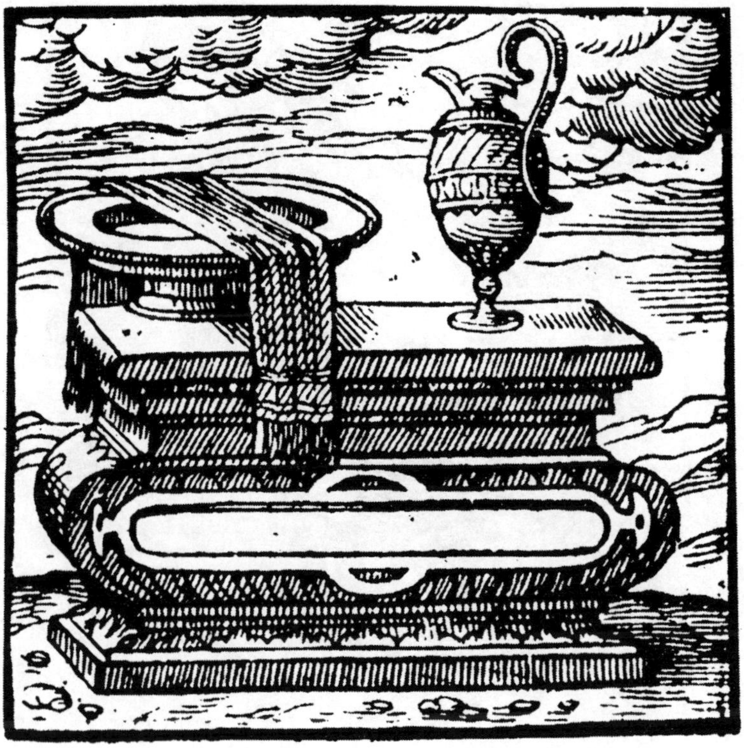

Emblema XXXI

ABSTINENTIA

Marmoreae in tumulis una stat parte columnae
Urceus, ex alia cernere malluvium est.
Ius haec forma monet dictum sine sordibus esse,
Defunctum puras atque habuisse manus.

Emblem 31

ABSTINENCE

Upon one side of the marble-columned tomb there stands a water-pitcher, and on the other side a wash basin is seen. This image indicates laws administered without filth [bribery], and that the deceased [judge] kept his hands clean.

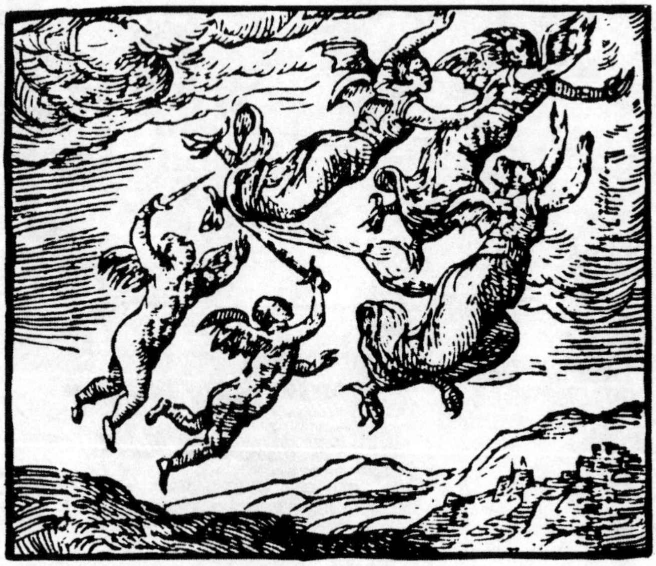

Emblema XXXII

BONIS A DIVITIBUS NIHIL TIMENDUM

Iunctus contiguo Marius mihi pariete, nec non
Subbardus, nostri nomina nota fori,
Aedificant bene nummati, sataguntque vel ultro
Obstruere heu, nostris undique luminibus.
Me miserum! Geminae quem tamquam Phinea raptant
Harpyae, ut propriis sedibus eiiciant,
Integritas nostra, atque animus quaesitor honesti,
His nisi sint Zetes, his nisi sint Calais.

Emblem 32

GOOD PEOPLE SHOULDN'T HAVE TO FEAR THE RICH

The wall of Marius is joined to mine, and so is that of Subbardus; their names are well known in our criminal courts. Since they are filthy rich, they build higher and bigger, and they busy themselves— oh my!— in taking away everywhere our daylight. Oh woe is me! Just like they did to Phineus, these twin harpies would plunder me. They would even throw me out of my own house, were it not for my integrity and determination, it seeking only honesty, and for them [my resolution] becomes a Zetes and a Calais [who chased the Harpies out of the kingdom of Phineus].

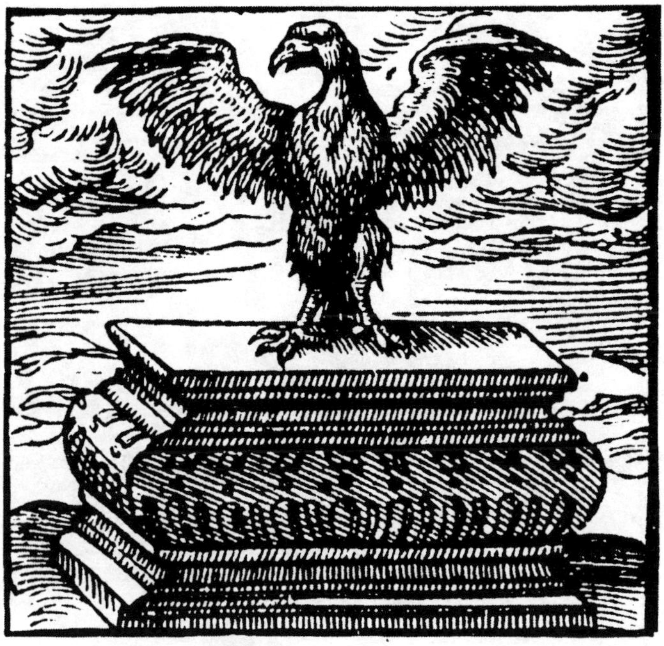

Emblema XXXIII

SIGNA FORTIUM

Dialogismus

Quae te causa monet, volucris Saturnia, magni
Ut tumulo insideas ardua Aristomenis?
Hoc moneo, quantum inter aves ego robore praesto,
Tantum semideos inter Aristomenes.
Insideant timidae timidorum bustae columbae;
Nos aquilae intrepidis signa benigna damus.

Emblem 33

ATTRIBUTES OF THE MIGHTY

(a dialogue)

"Which cause has impelled you, oh bird of Saturn, to alight upon the tomb of the great Aristomenes?" "I attest that as I excel among birds in strength, so does Aristomenes excel among the semi-gods. Let timid doves perch upon the tombs of the timid, but we, the eagles, provide signs favorable to the intrepid."

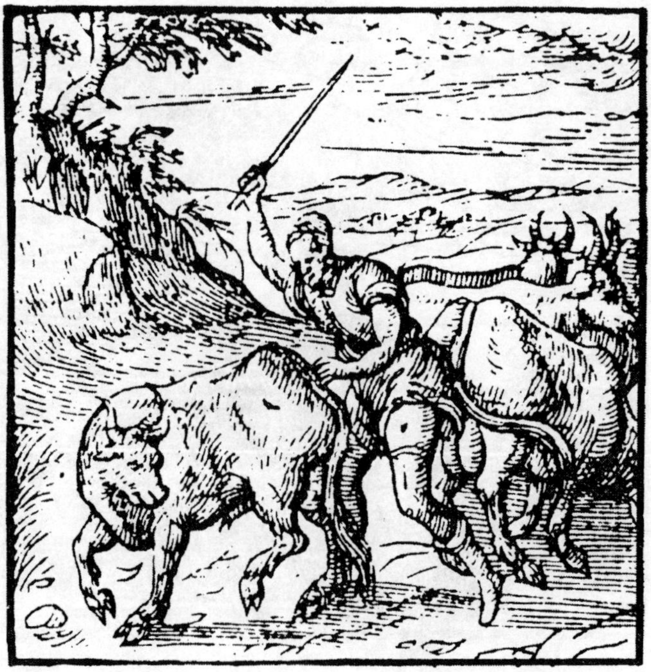

Emblema XXXIV

SUSTINE ET ABSTINE

Anecho kai hapecho

Et toleranda homini tristis fortuna ferendo est,
Et nimium felix saepe timenda fuit.
Sustine (Epictetus dicebat) et abstine. Oportet
Multa pati, illicitis absque tenere manus.
Sic ducis imperium victus fert poplite taurus
In dextro: sic se continet a gravidis.

Emblem 34

SUFFER AND ABSTAIN

(repeated in Greek)

In the same way that a man must endure joyless fortune, so too is happy fortune often to be feared. As Epictetus stated, "Suffer and abstain." One must suffer many things and it is fitting that one's hand be kept away from what is unlawful. Similarly, the bull, with his right leg tethered, must suffer the commands of its master. In this manner, he is constrained from [coupling with] the pregnant cows.

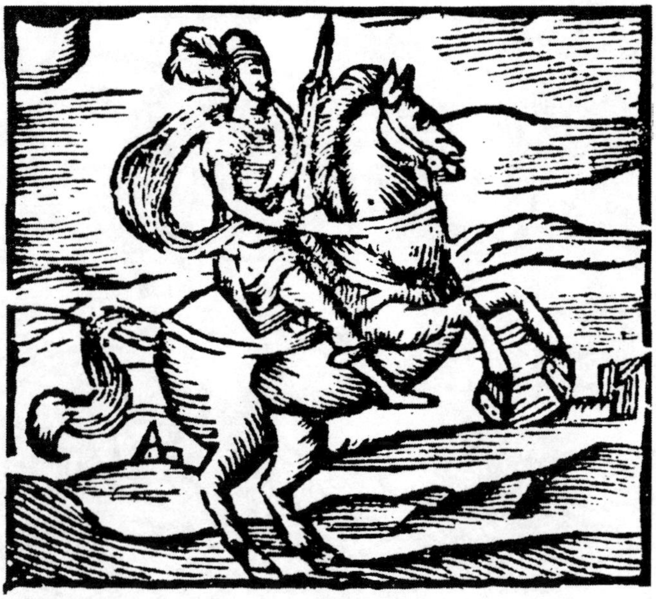

Emblema XXXV

IN ADULARI NESCIENTEM

Scire cupis dominos toties cur Thessalis ora
Mutet, et ut varios quaerat habere duces?
Nescit adulari, cuiquamve obtrudere palpum,
Regia quem morem Principis omnis habet.
Sed veluti ingenuus sonipes, dorso excutit omnem,
Qui moderari ipsum nesciat Hippocomom.
Nec saevire tamen domino fas: ultio sola est,
Dura ferum ut iubeat ferre lupata magis.

Emblem 35

HE WHO IS IGNORANT OF FLATTERY

Would you like to know why the land of Thessaly constantly changes its masters, and why it tries to have so many different leaders? It does not know [like the untamed horse] how to flatter or fawn upon anybody, which is a custom to be observed by the prince in every royal court. To the contrary [of flatterers] is the purebred horse, who throws from his back every rider who does not really know how to govern him properly. It is not, however, allowed that the ruler may vent his anger: the only vengeance allowed to him is to order that the beast suffer the application of a harsher bridle.

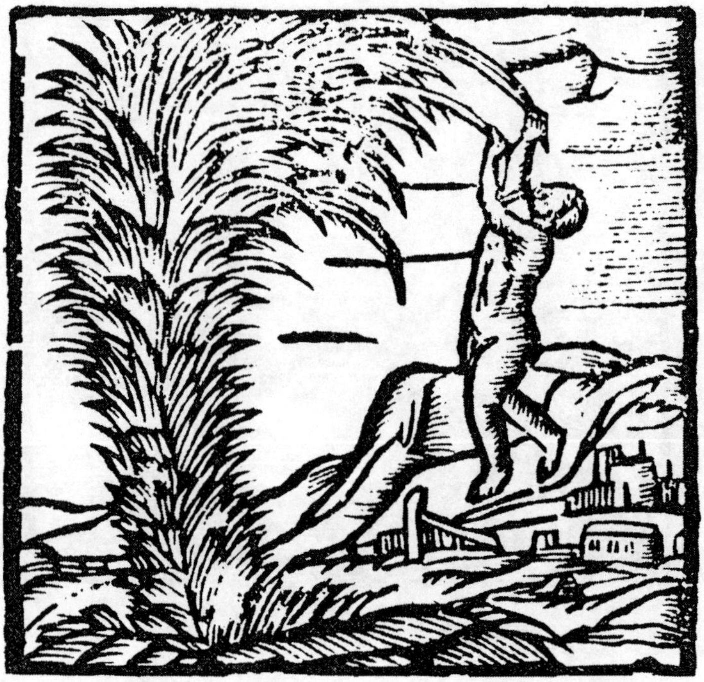

Emblema XXXVI

OBDURANDUM ADVERSUS URGENTIA

Nititur in pondus palma, et consurgit in arcum,
Quod magis, et premitur, hoc mage tollit onus:
Fert, et odoratas, bellaria dulcia glandes,
Queis mensas inter primus habetur honos.
I, puer, et reptans ramis has collige: mentis
Qui constantis erit, praemia digna feret.

Emblem 36

STEADFAST UNDER PRESSURE

Straining under the weight, the palm-tree exerts itself and rises up in an arch, and the more it is burdened, the more it lifts the load. It bears perfumed berries, sweet tidbits [dates], which are enjoyed in banquets as the prime honor. Go, oh boy, and climbing up the branches, gather these: the mind which remains steadfast [in its goal] goes away with worthy prizes.

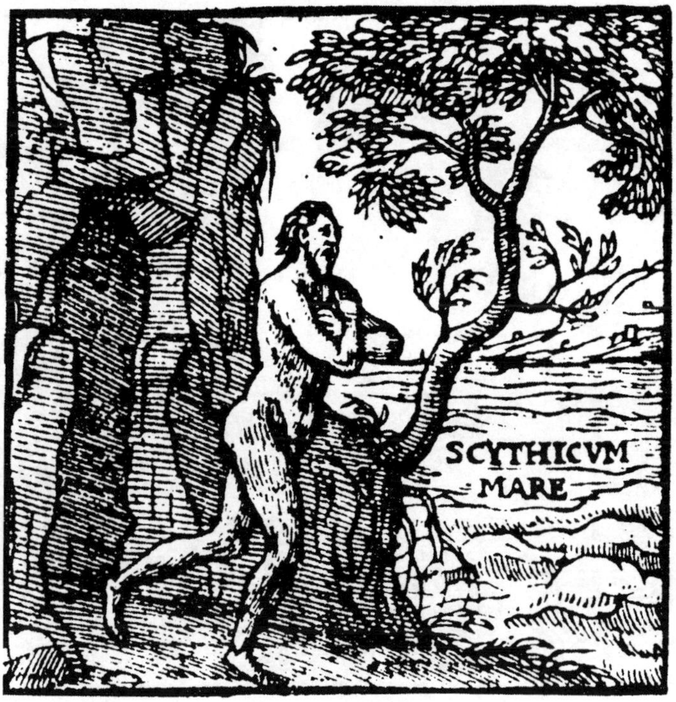

Emblema XXXVII

OMNIA MEA MECUM PORTO

Hunnus inops, Scythicique miserrimus accola Ponti,
Ustus perpetuo livida membra gelu:
Qui Cereris non novit opes, nec dona Lyaei,
Et pretiosa tamen stragula semper habet.
Nam myrrhinae illum perstringunt undique pelles:
Lumina sola patent, caetera opertus agit.
Sic furem haud metuit, sic ventos temnit et imbres;
Tutus apudque viros, tutus apudque Deos.

Emblem 37

I CARRY WITH ME ALL I OWN

The indigent Hun, an impoverished inhabitant of the Scythian Sea, burns his livid limbs in perpetual frost. But he who knows neither the gifts of Ceres [wheat] nor the legacy of Bacchus [wine] always has a precious bedspread, and he [the Hun] envelopes all his parts in the skins of ermines: only his eyes are seen and all the rest is hidden. Hence, fearing no thief and disdaining winds and rain storms, he is safe among men and secure with the gods.

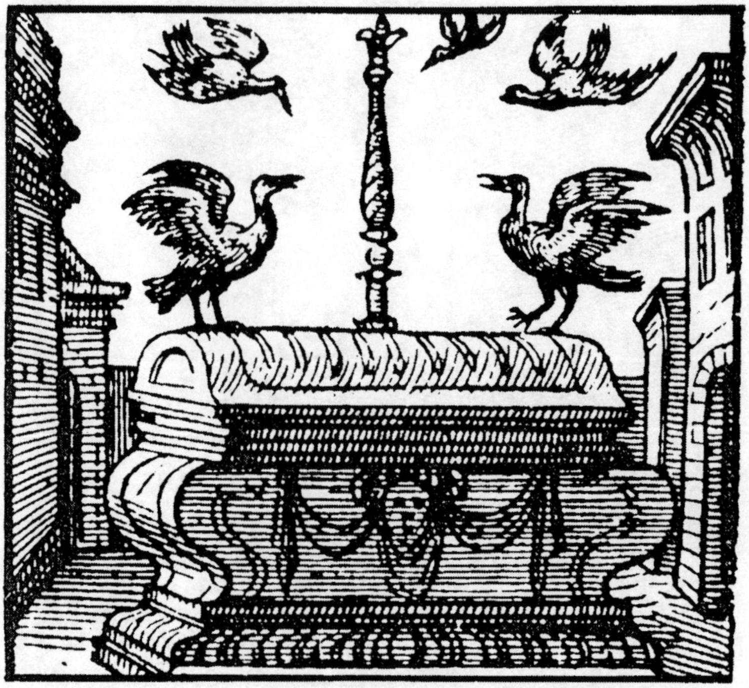

Emblema XXXVIII

CONCORDIAE SYMBOLUM

Cornicum mira inter se concordia vitae est,
Mutua statque illis intermerata fides.
Hinc volucres haec sceptra gerunt, quod scilicet omnes
Consensu populi stantque caduntque duces:
Quem si de medio tollas, discordia praeceps
Advolat, et secum regia fata trahit.

Emblem 38

THE SYMBOL OF CONCORD

To be admired is the concord enjoyed among hooded-crows during their lifetime, and there exists among them a mutual and pure fidelity. Hence, such birds may carry these scepters; this means that all rulers rise and fall by the consensus of the people. If you take this consensus away, then discord rapidly rushes in and flies away, carrying away with it the destiny of royalty.

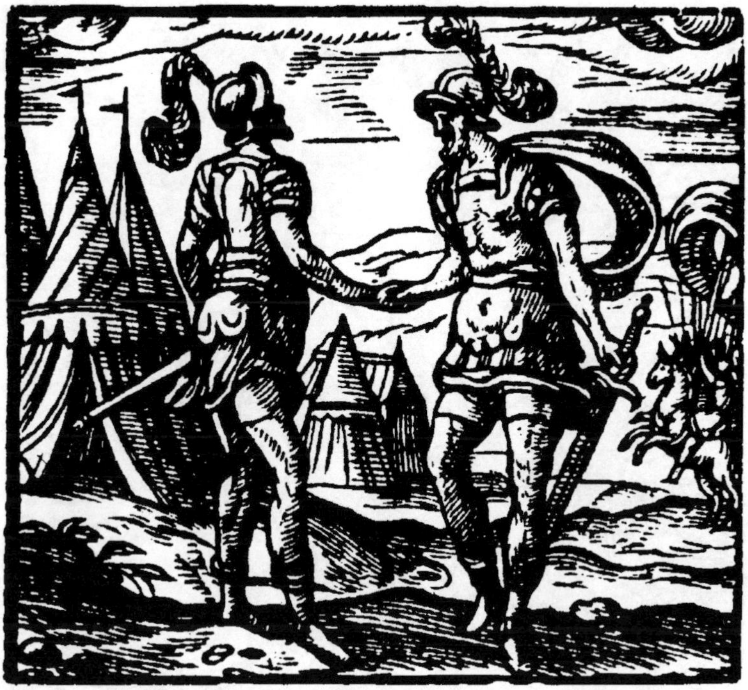

Emblema XXXIX
CONCORDIA

In bellum civile duces cum Roma pararet,
Viribus et caderet Martia terra suis:
Mos fuit in partes turmis coeuntibus easdem
Coniunctas dextras mutua dona dare.
Foederis haec species: id habet concordia signum,
Ut quos iungit amor, iungat et ipsa manus.

Emblem 39
CONCORD

When Rome was preparing its leaders for civil wars, and the land of Mars was being destroyed by its own forces, it became the custom for the troops coming together in the same regions to make an alliance by extending the right hand, so mutually regaling one another. This is the sign of alliance. Concord takes this [handshake] for its symbol; hence, those who may become united by affection also are to be joined by the hand.

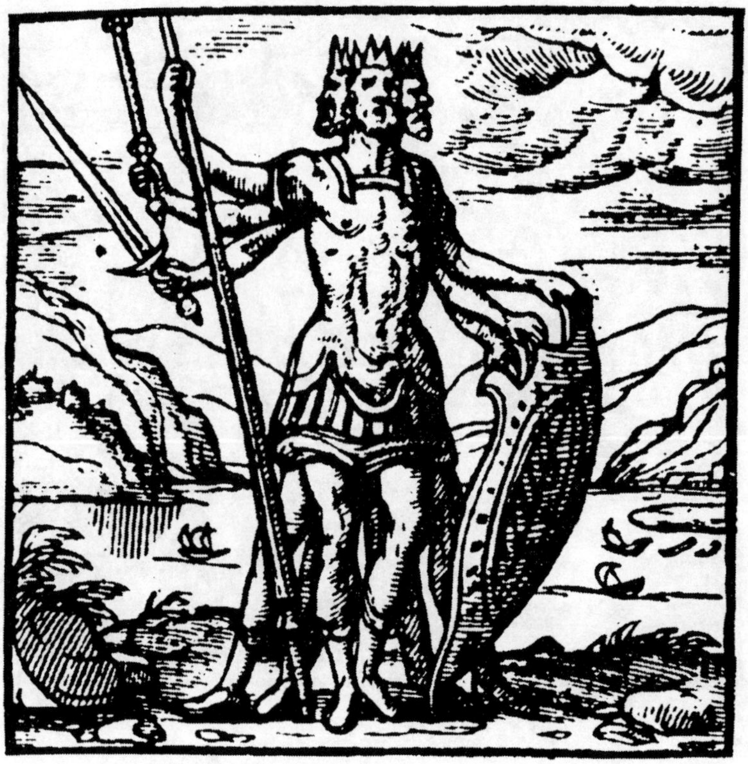

Emblema XL

CONCORDIA INSUPERABILIS

Tergeminos inter fuerat concordia fratres,
Tanta simul pietas mutua, et unus amor:
Invicti humanis ut viribus ampla tenerent
Regna, uno dicti nomine Geryonis.

Emblem 40

INVINCIBLE CONCORD

Among these triplet brothers, there was concord and, similarly, much mutual devotion and a single love. Never conquered by human forces, they gained an immense kingdom under a single name, that of Geryon.

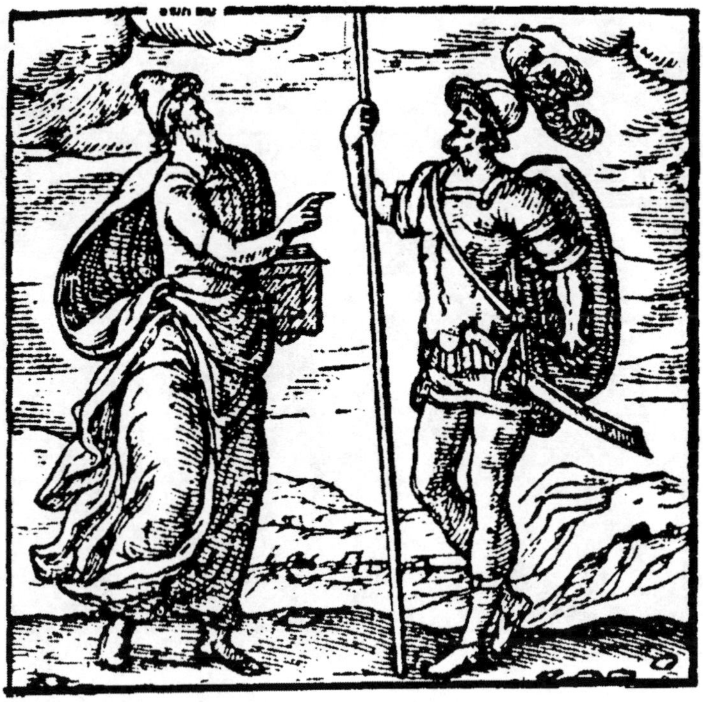

Emblema XLI

UNUM NIHIL, DUOS PLURIMUM POSSE

Laerte genitum, genitum quoque Tydeos una,
Hac cera expressit Zenalis apta manus.
Viribus hic praestat, hic pollet acumine mentis,
Nec tamen alterius non eget alter ope.
Cum duo coniuncti veniunt, victoria certa est,
Solum mens hominem, dextrave destituit.

Emblem 41

ONE CAN DO NOTHING, BUT TWO CAN DO MUCH

The sons of Laertes and Tydeus [Ulysses and Diomedes] were portrayed upon this panel with encaustic [paint] by the able hand of Zenalus. One [Ulysses] is outstanding for his might, and the other [Diomedes] is esteemed for the sharpness of his mind. Nonetheless, they have mutual need of one another. Once they are joined together, victory is certain. Just the mind, or only the hand, leave a man incomplete.

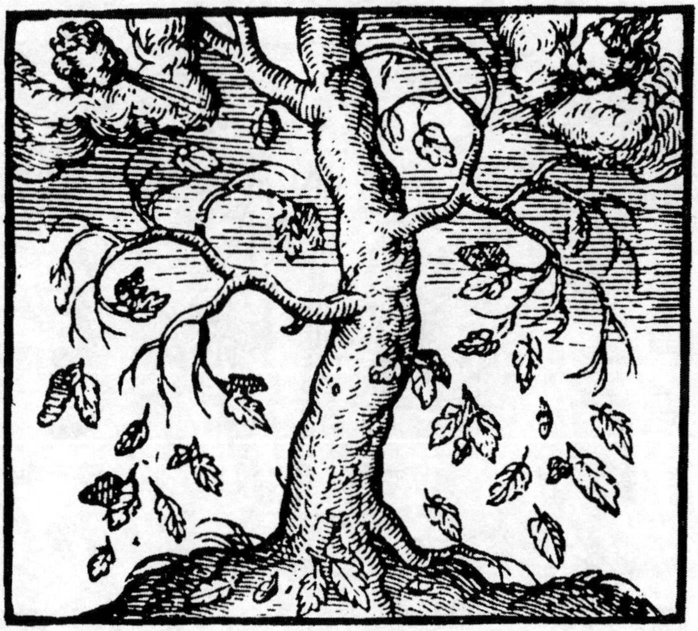

Emblema XLII

FIRMISSIMA CONVELLI NON POSSE

Oceanus quamvis fluctus pater excitet omnes;
Danubiumque omnem, barbare Turca, bibas:
Non tamen irrumpes perfracto limite, Caesar
Dum Carolus populis bellica signa dabit.
Sic sacrae quercus firmis radicibus adstant,
Sicca licet venti concutiant folia.

Emblem 42

THE FIRMEST CAN'T BE UPROOTED

Even though Father Ocean [Neptune] stirs up all his waves, and even if you, oh barbarous Turk, drink up all the Danube, you shall still never cross over the shattered [Christian] frontiers as long as the Emperor Charles [V] gives the sign leading his peoples to war. Likewise, firmly rooted, the sacred live-oaks will stand upright, even though the winds may bang together their dry leaves.

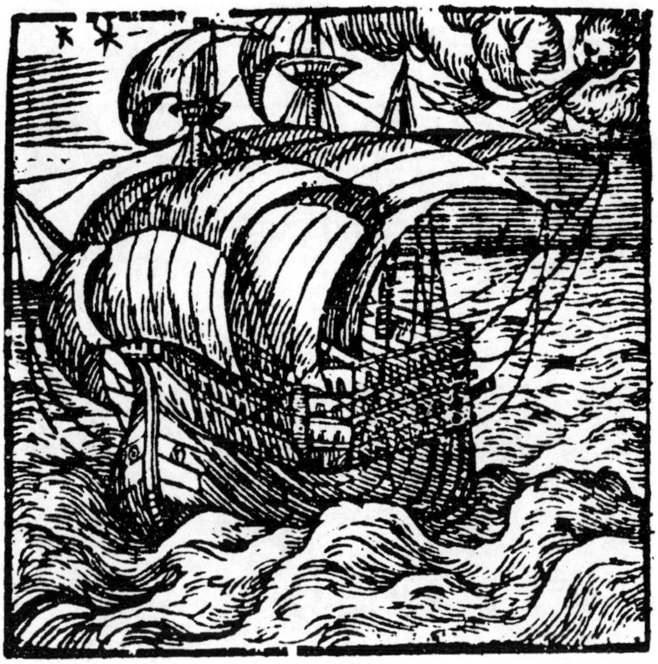

Emblema XLIII
SPES PROXIMA

Innumeris agitur Respublica nostra procellis.
Et spes venturae sola salutis adest:
Non secus ac navis medio circum aequore, venti
Quam rapiunt; salsis iamque fatiscit aquis.
Quod si Helenae adveniant lucentia sidera fratres:
Amissos animos spes bona restituit.

Emblem 43
HOPE IS NEAR

Our [Christian] Republic is blown about by numberless gusts, and the only hope remaining is that for its future safety. Not otherwise is the ship [pictured] being dragged about by the winds in the midst of the sea and already breaking up in the salty waters. But if the shining stars [Castor and Pollux], which are the brothers of Helen, are espied, then good hope revives the sinking spirits.

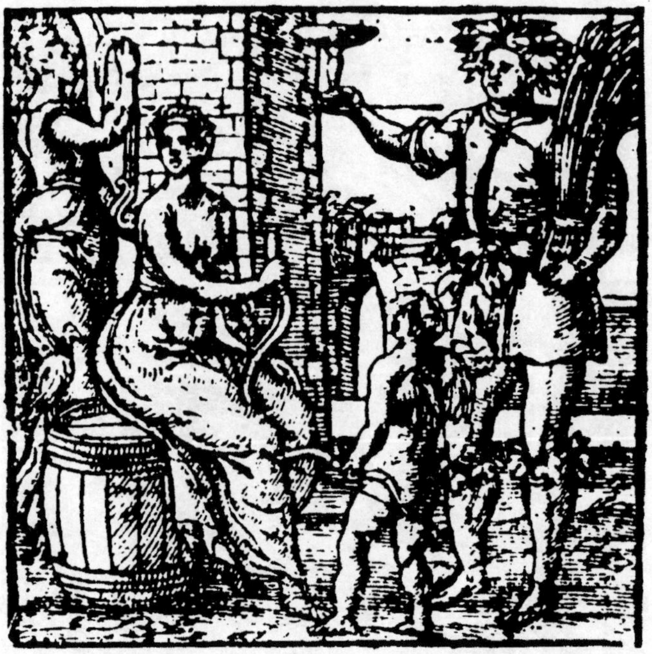

Emblema XLIV

IN SIMULACRUM SPEI

Quae Dea tam laeto suspectans sidera vultu?
Cuius peniculis reddita imago fuit?
Elpidii fecere manus. Ego nominor illa,
Quae miseris promptam Spes bona praestat opem.
Cur viridis tibi palla? Quod omnia me duce vernent.
Quid manibus Mortis tela refracta geris?
Quod vivos sperare decet, praecido sepultis.
Cur in dolioli tegmine pigra sedes?
Sola domi mansi volitantibus undique noxis,
Ascraei ut docuit Musa verenda senis.
Quae tibi adest volucris? Cornix fidissimus oscen;
Est bene cum nequeat dicere, dicit, erit.
Qui comites? Bonus Eventus, praecepsque Cupido.
Qui praeeunt? Vigilum somnia vana vocant.
Quae tibi iuncta astat? Scelerum Rhamnusia vindex,
Scilicet ut speres nil, nisi quod liceat.

Emblem 44

ABOUT THE PICTURE OF HOPE

(a dialogue)

"Which goddess are you, who looks to the stars with such a joyous face? Whose brush made her portrait?" "It was made by the hands of Elpidius [from *Elpis*, Hope]. I call myself Hope, that which seeks quick help for the unfortunate." "Why are your garments so green?" "Because under my leadership everything becomes green again." "Why do you carry in your hands the broken arrows of Death?" "Because, although hope is allowed to the living, it is cut short for the buried." "Why do you sit idly upon the lid of a small cask?" "I alone stayed at home, while evils [released by Pandora] were flying all about, just as is taught by the awesome Muse venerated by old Ascraeus [Hesiod]." "Which bird is that [shown] next to you?" "It is the hooded crow, the most faithful in augers: when it can't be said whether something is going well, it says [nonetheless] that it shall." "Who are your companions?" "Good Outcome and heedless Cupid." "How do they precede you?" "They evoke the empty dreams of the wakeful." "Who is that who is standing beside you?" "Rhamnusia [Nemesis], the avenger of crimes, showing that you may not hope for anything unless it is lawful."

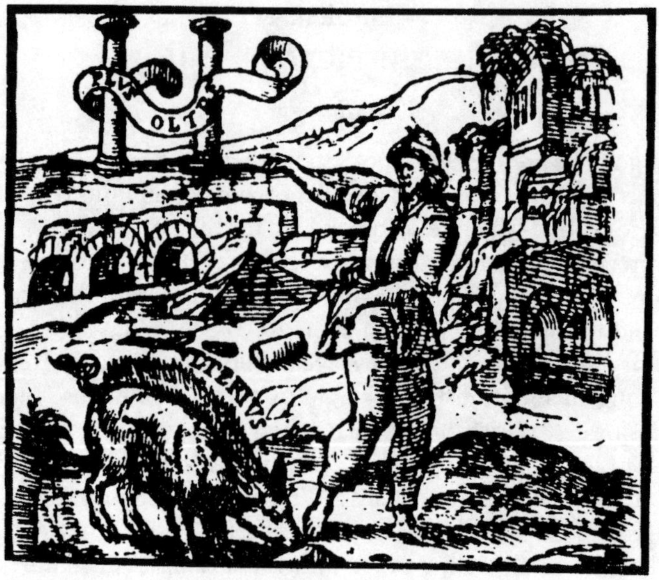

Emblema XLV

IN DIES MELIORA

Rostra novo mihi setigeri suis obtulit anno,
Haecque cliens ventri xenia, dixit, habe.
Progreditur semper, nec retro respicit unquam,
Gramina cum pando proruit ore vorax.
Cura viris cadem est, ne spes sublapsa retrorsum
Cedat, et ut melius sit, quod et ulterius.

Emblem 45

BETTER DAYS AHEAD

On new year's day, a client presented me with the head of a bristly boar, saying to me, "Take this gift for your stomach." The animal always goes forward, never looking back, when it voraciously tears up the grasses with its mouth wide open. A man must take care to see that hope never falls behind and disappears, and he must consider that what lies beyond must be better.

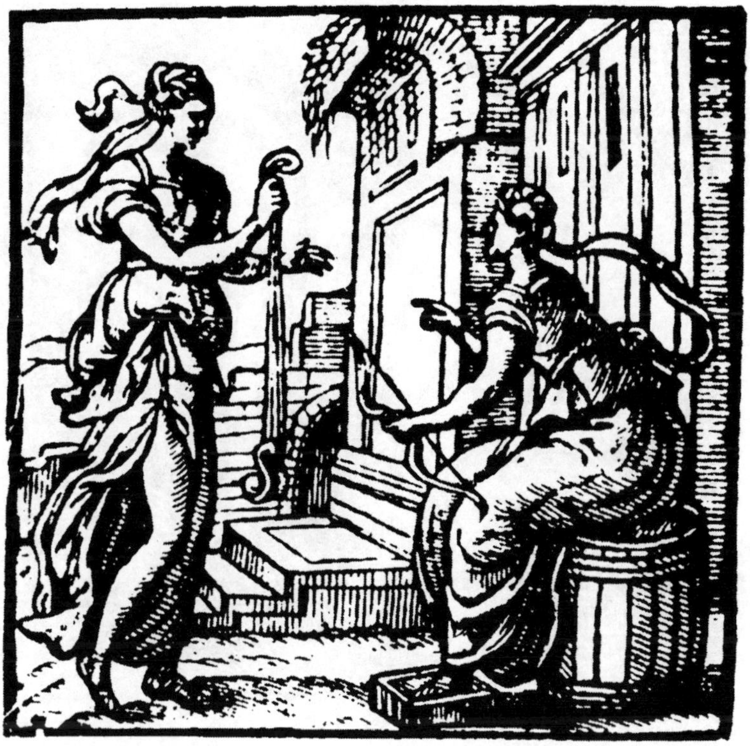

Emblema XLVI

ILLICITUM NON SPERANDUM

Spes simul et Nemesis nostris altaribus adsunt.
Scilicet ut speres non nisi quod liceat.

Emblem 46

HOPE NOT FOR THE ILLICIT

Hope and Nemesis [Fate] are placed together upon our altars. This means that you may not hope for anything unless it is lawful.

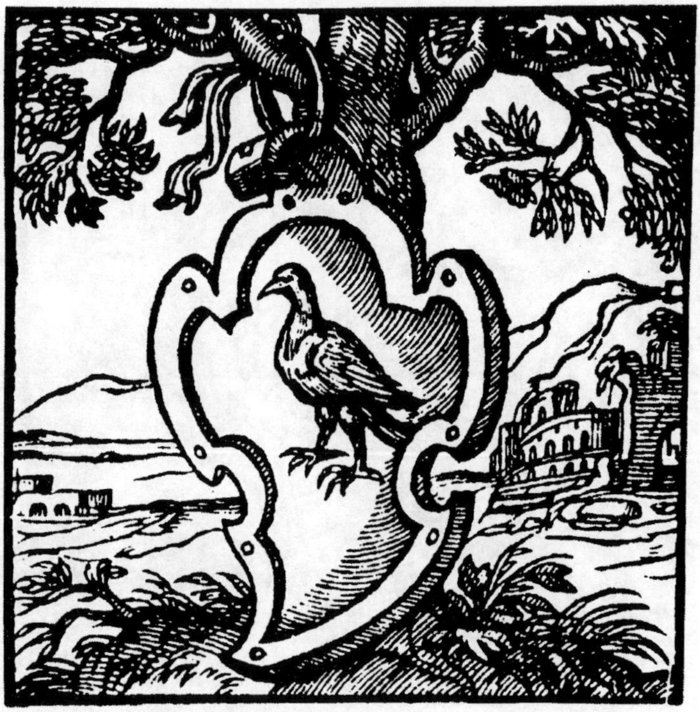

Emblema XLVII

PUDICITIA

Porphyrio, domini si incestet in aedibus uxor,
Despondetque animum, praeque dolore perit.
Abdita in arcanis naturae est causa: sit index
Sincerae haec volucris certa pudicitiae.

Emblem 47

CHASTITY

If its wife profanes with her adultery the household of her lord, the turtledove is left despondent and he dies from grief. The cause is hidden in the secrets of Nature: may this bird serve as the clear symbol of a sincere chastity.

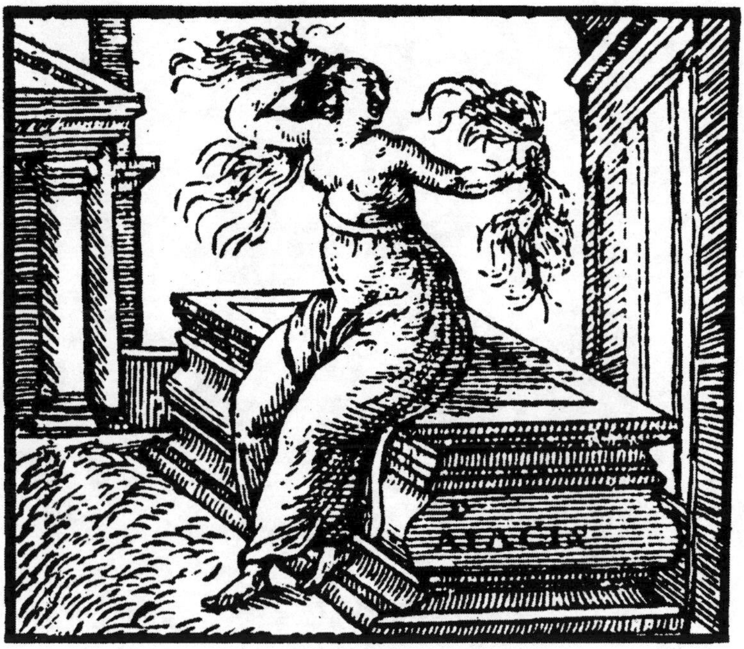

Emblema XLVIII

IN VICTORIAM DOLO PARTAM

Aiacis tumulum lacrimis ego perluo Virtus,
Heu, misera albentes dilacerata comas!
Scilicet hoc restabat adhuc, ut iudice Graeco
Vincerer: et causa stet potiore dolus.

Emblem 48

ABOUT VICTORY BORN FROM TRICKERY

Bathing the tomb of Ajax with my tears, I am Virtue; wretched, alas, I am pulling out my whitened tresses! Naturally, it had to turn out in this way, so that I am overturned by a Greek judge, and deceit now stands on the winning side of the law-suit [the distribution of the Ajax's weapons].

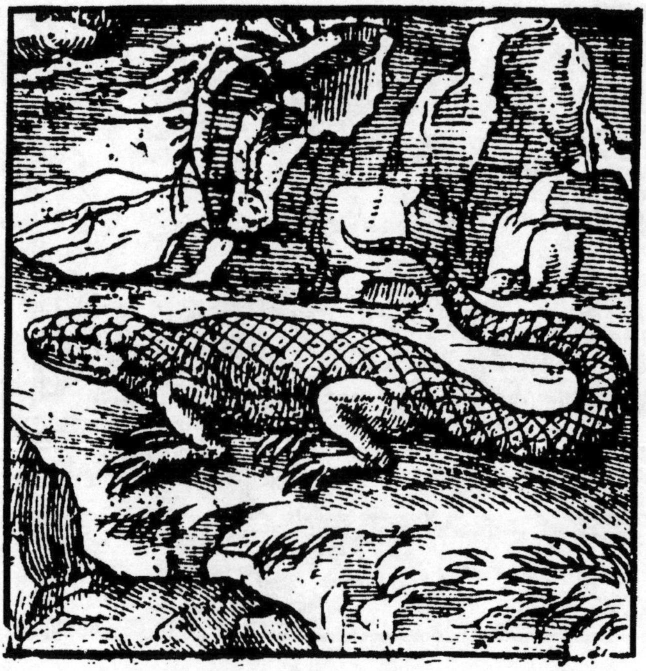

Emblema XLIX
IN FRAUDULENTOS

Parva lacertae, atris stellatus corpora guttis
Stellio, qui latebras, et cava busta colit,
Invidiae, pravique doli fert simbola pictus.
Heu nimium nuribus cognita zelotypis!
Nam turpi obtegitur faciem lentigine quisquis,
Sit quibus immersus stellio, vina bibat.
Hinc vindicta frequens decepta pellice vino,
Quam formae amisso flore relinquit amans.

Emblem 49
AGAINST DECEIVERS

A little lizard, its body patterned with black star-shaped spots, is the newt, who dwells in a hideaway and prays at empty tombs. As pictured here, it becomes a symbolic harbinger of jealousy and crooked deceit. It represents, alas, a situation all too well known to jealous young brides. Whoever drinks wine in which this lizard has been dipped now finds his face covered with ugly spots. This [poisoned] wine is frequently employed as a means of revenge by a deceived mistress, she whom the lover abandons, once the flower of her beauty has faded away.

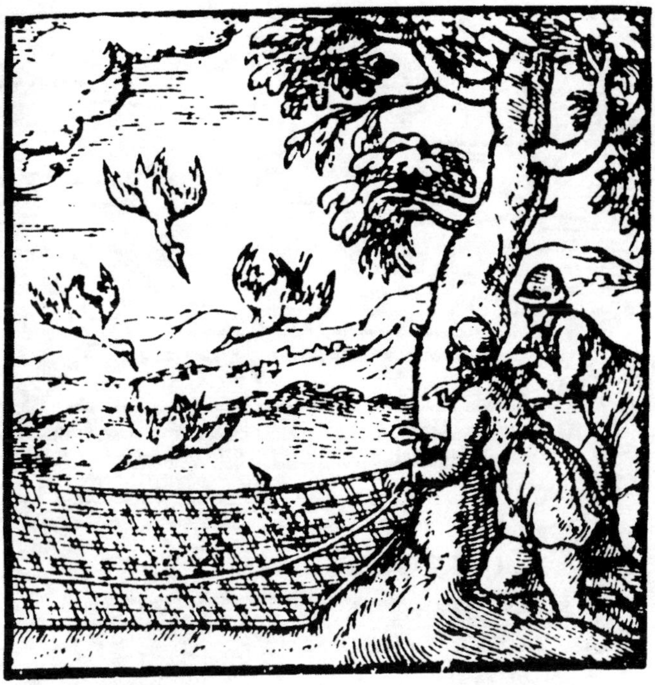

Emblema L
DOLUS IN SUOS

Altilis allectator anas, et caerula pennis,
Assueta ad dominos ire redire suos,
Congeneres cernens volitare per aera turmas,
Garrit, in illarum se recipitque gregem,
Praetensa incautas donec sub retia ducat:
Obstrepitant captae, conscia at ipsa silet.
Perfida cognato se sangine polluit ales,
Officiosa aliis, exitiosa suis.

Emblem 50
TREACHERY AGAINST ONE'S OWN KIND

Fattened as a lure, the trained duck with seductive azure plumage has been made accustomed to fly away and then return to his [human] masters. When he sees flocks of its own kind flying through the air, he quacks and places itself among their flock. He does this to lead them deceitfully into the outstretched net. The prisoners make an uproar, but he, because he knows what the game is about, keeps silent. Perfidious, he dirties his wings with the blood of his own breed: useful for others, he is a catastrophe for his own kind.

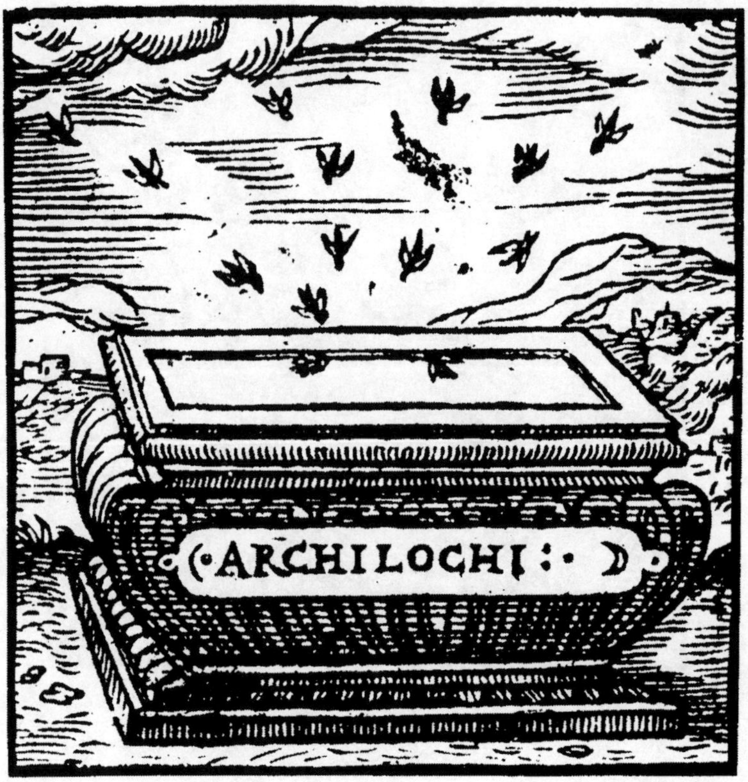

Emblema LI

MALEDICENTIA

Archilochi tumulo insculptas de marmore vespas
Esse ferunt, linguae certa sigilla malae.

Emblem 51

SLANDER

On the tomb of Archilochus wasps had been sculpted in marble: these, as it is said, provide dependable symbols for evil tongues.

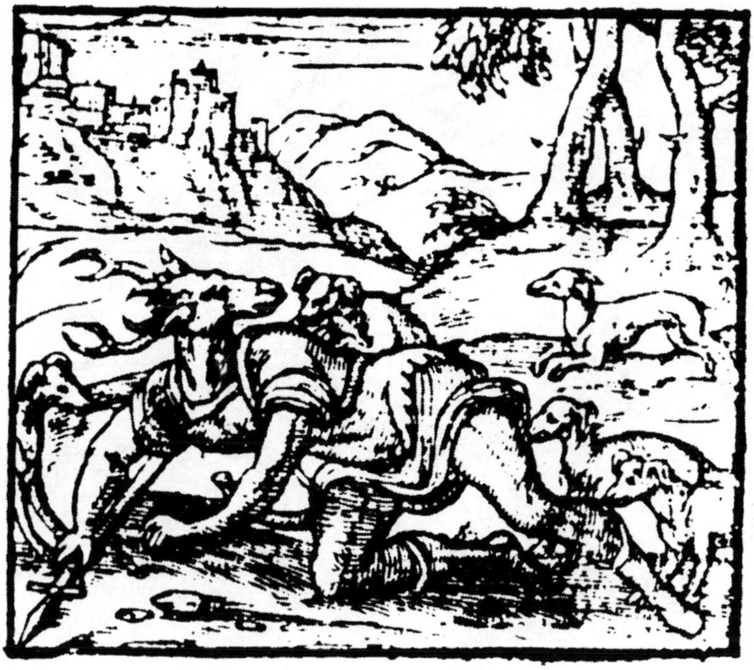

Emblema LII

IN RECEPTATORES SICARIORUM

Latronum furumque manus tibi Scaeva, per urbem
It comes, et diris cincta cohors gladiis:
Atque ita te mentis generosum prodige censes,
Quod tua complures allicit olla malos.
En novus Actaeon, qui postquam cornua sumpsit,
In praedam canibus se dedit ipse suis.

Emblem 52

ABOUT THOSE WHO SHELTER MURDERERS

Going through the city, oh Scaeva, you are accompanied by a troop of muggers and thieves and a cohort armed with fearsome swords. And so, oh profligate one, you think yourself open-minded because your pot now feeds so many evildoers. Here we have a new Actaeon, one who, having succeeded in growing horns, then gives himself up to his own dogs like prey.

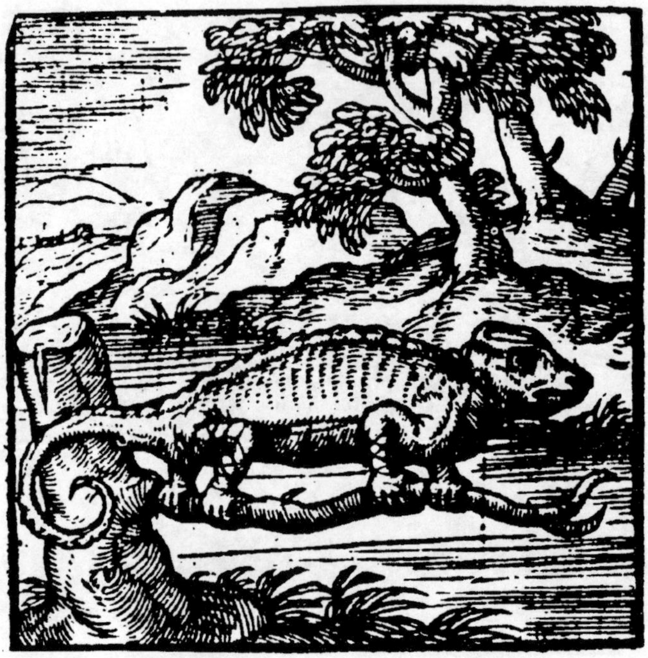

Emblema LIII

IN ADULATORES

Semper hiat, semper tenuem, qua vescitur, auram
Reciprocat Chamaleon:
Et mutat faciem, varios sumitque colores,
Praeter rubrum vel candidum.
Sic et adulator populari vescitur aura,
Hiansque cuncta devorat:
Et solum mores imitatur Principis atros;
Albi et pudici nescius.

Emblem 53

AGAINST FLATTERERS

The chameleon always yawns, always breathing in and out the gentle breezes from which he feeds himself. He changes his appearance and assumes many different colors—except for red [blushing] and white [purity]. The flatterer likewise feeds upon popular favor and, gaping, he devours it whole. He only imitates from the Prince his darker customs, for he is ignorant of all that which is pure and chaste.

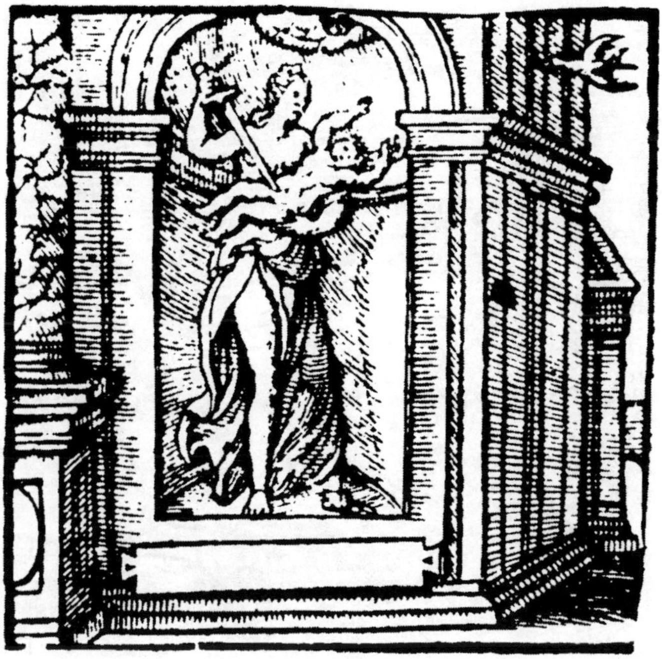

Emblema LIV

EI QUI SEMEL SUA PRODEGERIT, ALIENA CREDI NON OPORTERE

Colchidos in gremio nidum quid congeris? Eheu,
Nescia cur pullos tam male credis avis?
Dira parens Medea suos saevissima natos
Perdit; et speras parcat ut illa tuis?

Emblem 54

WASTEFUL WITH HER OWN BELONGINGS, SHE SHOULD NEVER BE ENTRUSTED WITH THOSE OF ANOTHER

Why do you make your nest upon the bosom of the woman from Colchos [Medea]? Oh my! Why do you, oh unknowing bird, entrust your chicks so badly? A most savage woman, Medea, the evil parent, killed her own offspring. So why do you think she will respect yours?

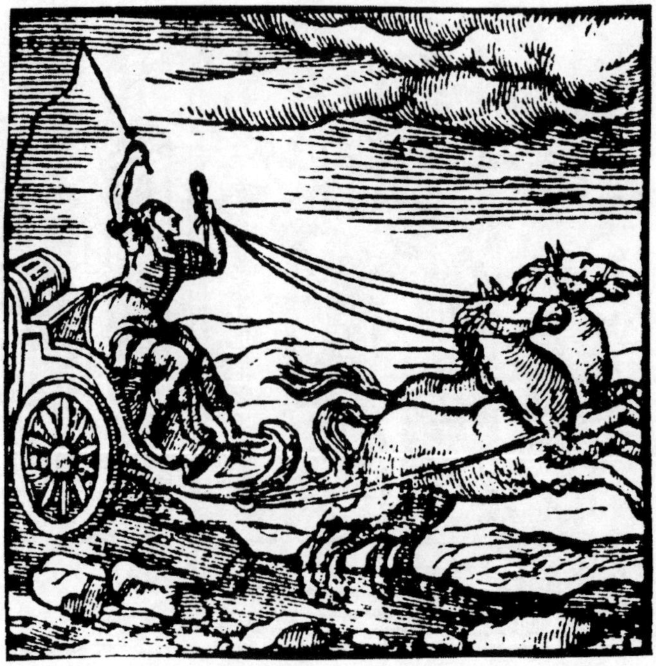

Emblema LV

TEMERITAS

In praeceps rapitur, frustra quoque tendit habenas
Auriga, effreni quem vehit oris equus.
Haud facile huic credas, ratio quem nulla gubernat,
Et temere proprio ducitur arbitrio.

Emblem 55

RECKLESSNESS

Carried away precipitously, in vain a charioteer pulls upon the reins of a horse dragging him along with an unbridled mouth. Never rush to believe in one who is not governed by reason, and who recklessly lets himself be carried away by his own willfulness.

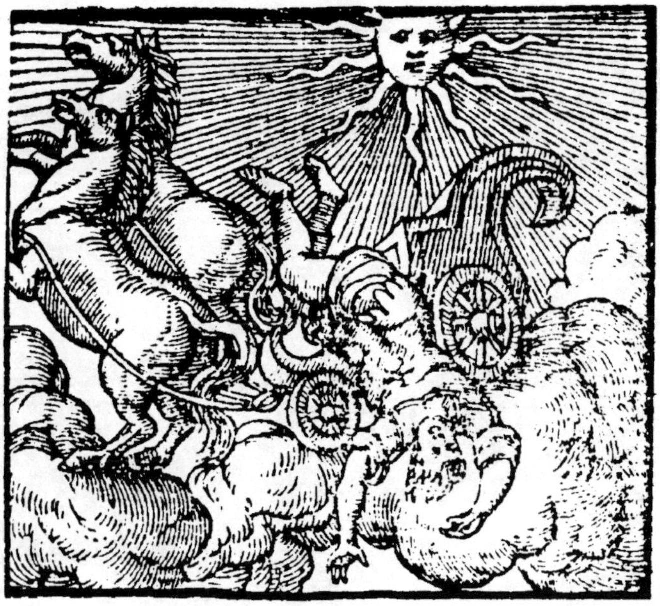

Emblema LVI

IN TEMERARIOS

Aspicis aurigam currus Phaetonta paterni
Ignivomus ausum flectere Solis equos;
Maxima qui postquam terris incendia sparsit,
Est temere insesso lapsus ab axe miser.
Sic plerique rotis fortunae ad sidera Reges
Evecti, ambitio quos iuvenilis agit;
Post magnam humani generis clademque suamque,
Cunctorum poenas denique dant scelerum.

Emblem 56

ABOUT RECKLESS PEOPLE

Here you see Phaeton; driver of the paternal chariot; he dared to guide the fire-vomiting horses of the Sun. After scattering enormous conflagrations all over the Earth, he fell disgraced from the vehicle which he had so recklessly mounted. Much the same happens to many kings who, driven by adolescent ambition, are carried toward the stars upon the wheels of Fortune. After having provoked much misfortune among the human race, they bring ruin upon themselves and, finally, they pay the penalties due for their crimes.

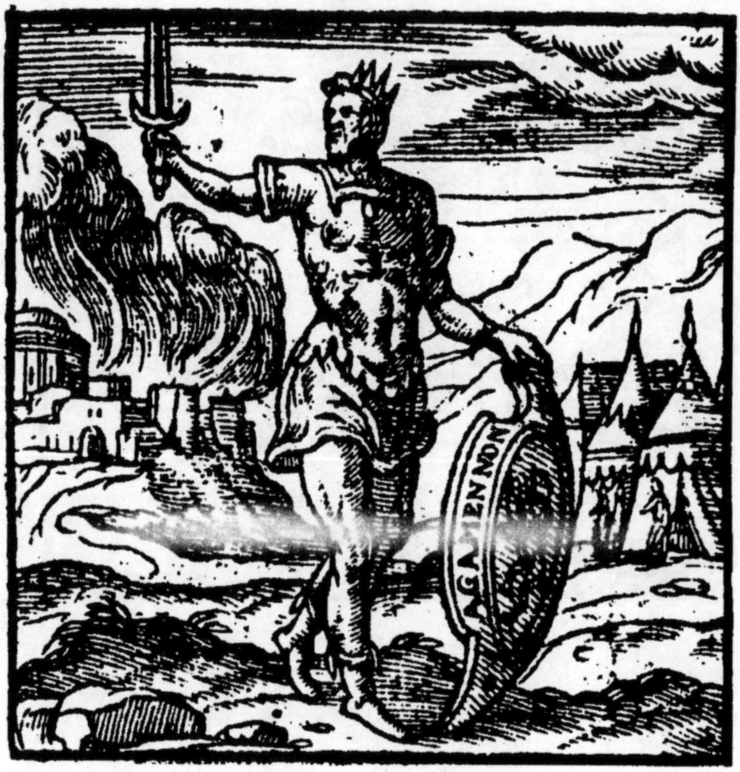

Emblema LVII

FUROR ET RABIES

Ora gerit clypeus rabiosi picta leonis,
Et scriptum in summo margine carmen habet:
Hic hominum est terror, cuius possessor Atrida:
Talia magnanimus signa Agamemno tulit.

Emblem 57

FURY AND ANGER

The shield bears the painted face of an enraged lion, and a verse is inscribed along the border: "This is the terror of men, and its master is the son of Atreus [Agamemnon]." Such was the badge worn by magnanimous Agamemnon.

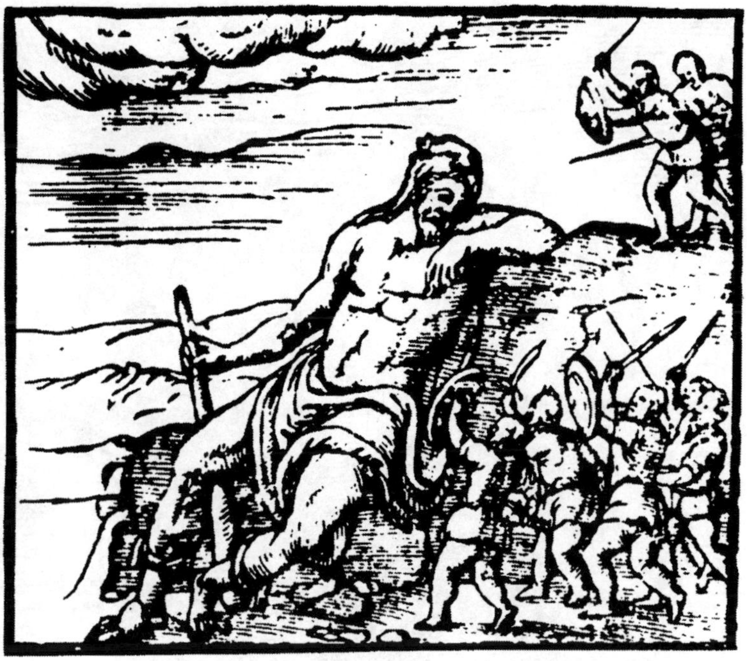

Emblema LVIII

IN EOS QUI SUPRA VIRES QUICQUAM AUDENT

Dum dormit, dulci recreat dum corpora somno
Sub picea, et clavam caeteraque arma tenet.
Alciden Pygmea manus prosternere letho
Posse putat, vires non bene docta suas.
Excitus ipse, velut pulices, sic proterit hostem,
Et saevi implicitum pelle leonis agit.

Emblem 58

ABOUT THOSE WHO DARE TO GO BEYOND THEIR POWERS

When Alcides [Hercules] is sleeping, and while he is refreshing his body in sweet sleep beneath a pine-tree and has near him his club and other weapons, a troop of Pygmies believe that they can overcome him — but without recognizing the limits of their powers. When he awakens, he crushes his enemies like fleas and carries them off, caught in the skin of the fierce lion.

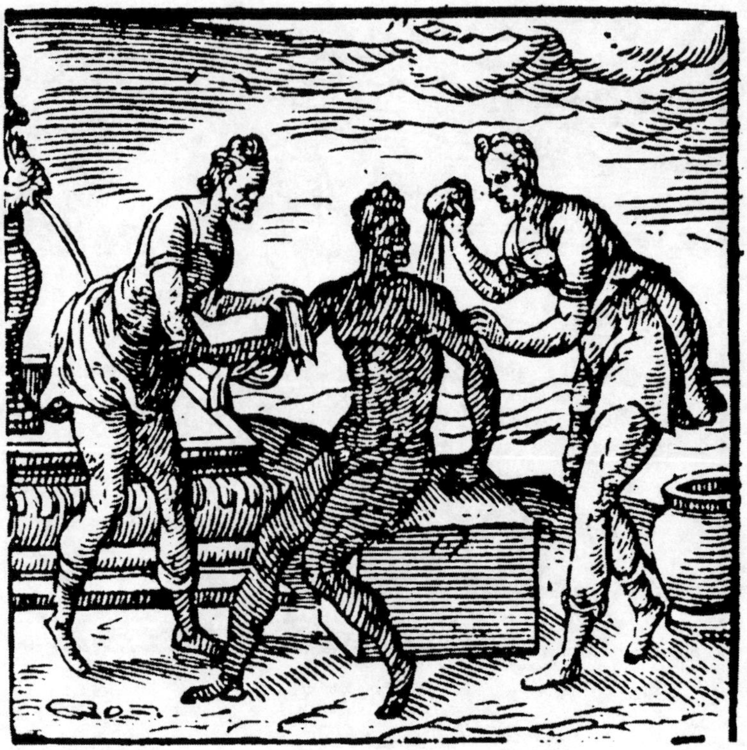

Emblema LIX

IMPOSSIBILE

Abluis Aethiopem quid frustra? Ah desine: noctis
Illustrare nigrae nemo potest tenebras.

Emblem 59

AN IMPOSSIBLE TASK

Why do you vainly set about washing off the Ethiopian? Ha, ha! Give it up: nobody can ever enlighten the shadows of blackest night.

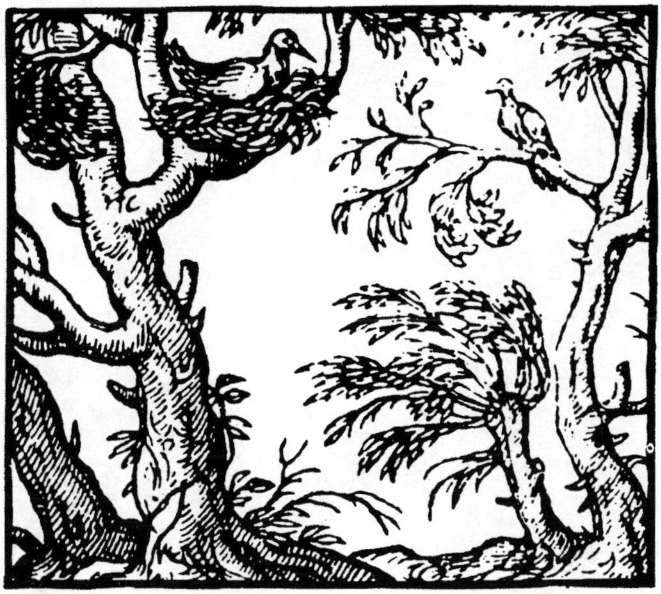

Emblema LX
CUCULI

Ruricolas agreste genus plerique cucullos
Cur vocitent, quaenam prodita causa fuit?
Vere novo cantat Coccyx, quo tempore vites
Qui non absolvit, iure vocatur iners.
Fert ova in nidos alienos, qualiter ille
Cui thalamum prodit uxor adulterio.

Emblem 60
CUCKOO BIRDS

What is the reason why many people call boorish country folk "cuckoos"? Coccyx [the cuckoo] sings in early summer, and who ever hasn't finished tending his vines by this time is rightly called a sluggish dolt. The cuckoo places its eggs in the nests of other birds, and the same happens to him [the cuckold] whose adulterous wife betrays him in the bridal bedroom.

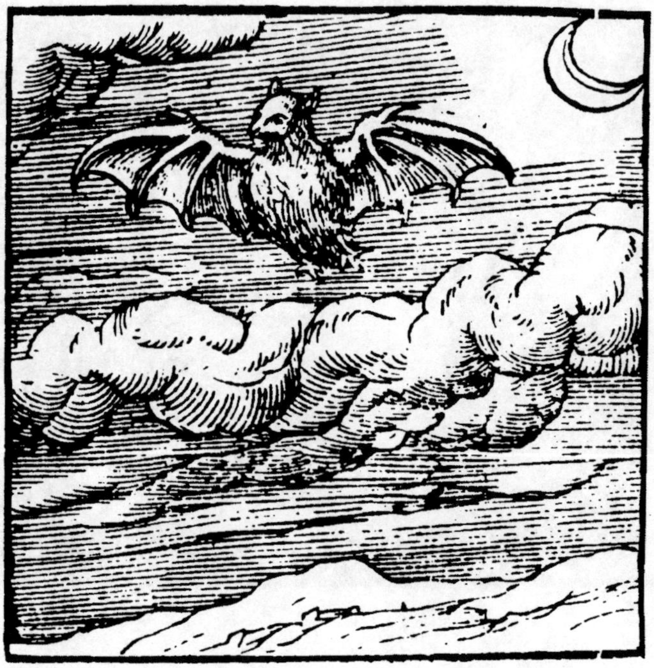

Emblema LXI

VESPERTILIO

Asumpsisse suum volucri ex Meneide nomen,
Socraticum auctores Chaerophoonta ferunt.
Fusca viro facies, et stridens vocula, tali
Hunc hominem potuit commaculare nota.

Emblem 61

THE BAT

Authors state that Chaerophon the Socratic took his name from the bird called *Meneides* [bat]. His swarthy face and strident voice could have branded this man with such a nickname.

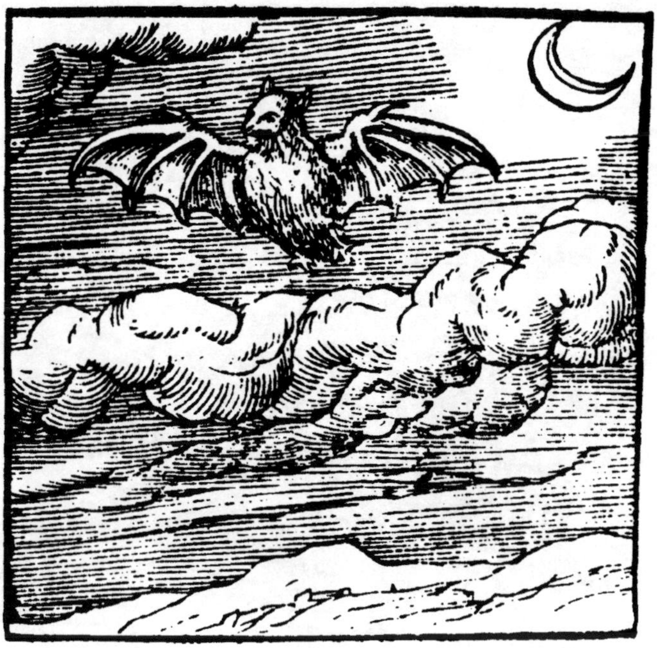

Emblema LXII

ALIUD DE VESPERTILIONE

Vespere quae tantum volitat, quae lumine lusca est,
Quae cum alas gestet, caetera muris habet;
Ad res diversas trahitur. Mala nomina primun
Signat, quae latitant, iudiciumque timent.
Inde et Philosophos, qui dum caelestia quaerunt.
Caligant oculis, falsaque sola vident.
Tandem et versutos, cum clam sectentur utrumque.
Acquirunt neutra qui sibi parte fidem.

Emblem 62

MORE ABOUT THE BAT

Since it is half-blinded by daylight, this bird only flies after dusk; even though it has wings, it shares many traits with mice. It is used to symbolize various things. In the first place, it symbolizes infamous people [like debtors], who, fearing impending justice, hide out. It serves in the same way for philosophers who, while they are investigating the things in heaven, remain with their eyes befogged and they only see false things. Finally, it symbolizes crafty folk who, secretly trailing after either party, have no credibility, neither here nor there.

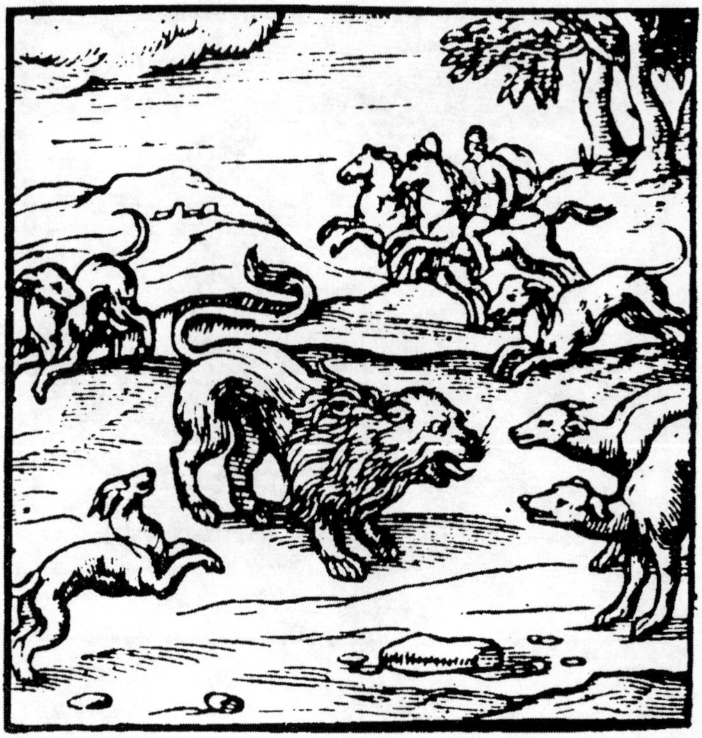

Emblema LXIII

IRA

Alcaeam veteres caudam dixere leonis,
Qua stimulare iras concipit ille graves.
Lutea cum surgit bilis, crudescit et atro
Felle dolor, furias excitat indomitas.

Emblem 63

IRE

The ancients called the lion's tail Mars-like; whipping himself with it, the animal provokes in himself great anger. When yellow bile arises, and when the pain is aggravated by black gall, uncontrollable fury is awakened.

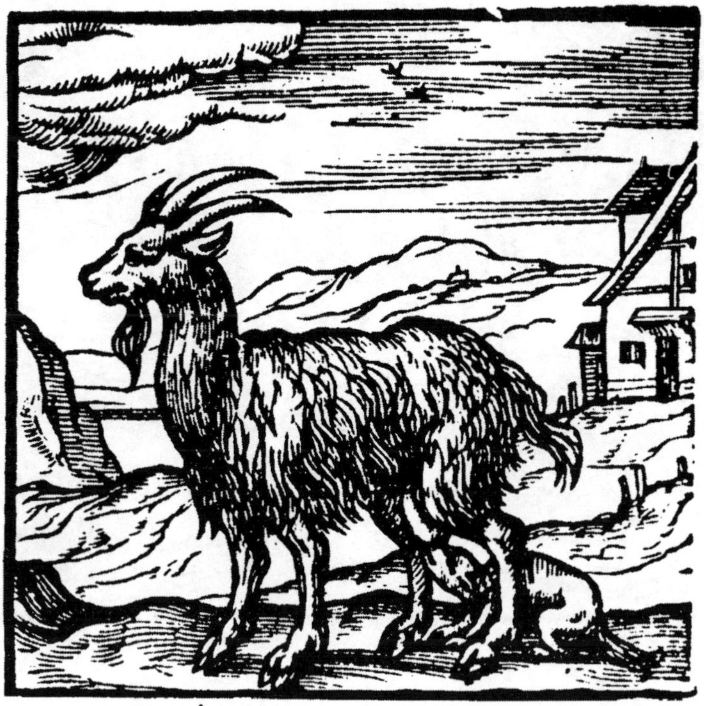

Emblema LXIV

IN EUM QUI SIBI IPSI DAMNUM APPARAT

Capra lupum non sponte meo nunc ubere lacto,
Quod male pastoris provida cura iubet.
Creverit ille simul, mea me post ubera pascet:
Improbitas nullo flectitur obsequio.

Emblem 64

ABOUT ONE WHO INCURS ITS OWN DESTRUCTION

Because my imprudent shepherd lacking in foresight so orders, I — a she-goat — am now forced, and quite against my will, to let the wolf-cub suckle milk from my udder. Having been nourished at my tit, once he has grown, I shall similarly become his food. Wickedness is never softened by any indulgence.

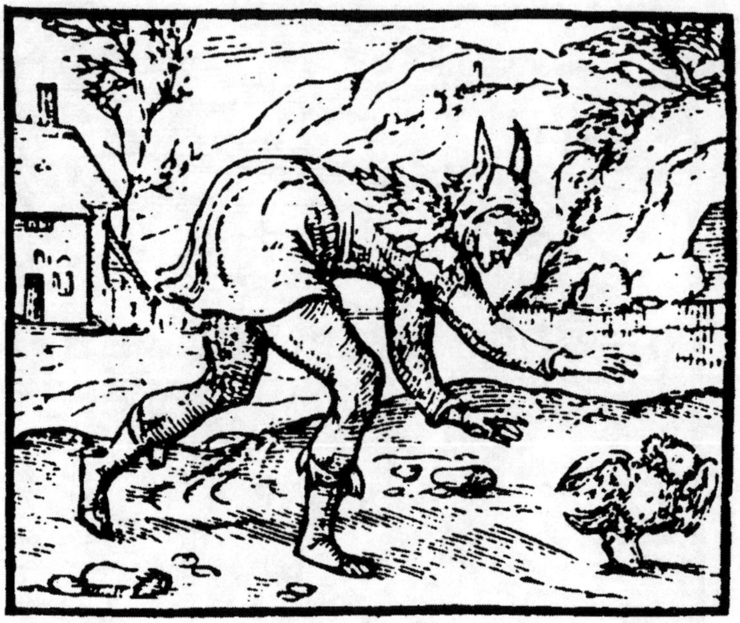

Emblema LXV
FATUITAS

Miraris nostro quod carmine diceris Otus,
Sit vetus a proavis cum tibi nomen Otho.
Aurita est, similes et habeat ceu noctua plumas,
Saltantemque auceps mancipat aptus avem.
Hinc fatuos, captu et faciles, nos dicimus otos:
Hoc tibi conveniens tu quoque nomen habe.

Emblem 65
FOOLISHNESS

Since your forefathers gave you the name of Otho [a Roman emperor who ruled for only three months], you are astonished to be called *Otus* [red-owl] in our poem. The red-owl is horned and has feathers like those of the barn-owl, and the smart fowler can capture this bird while it hops about. Therefore, fools and the easily trapped are called "red-owls": hence, it is fitting that you, too, take this name.

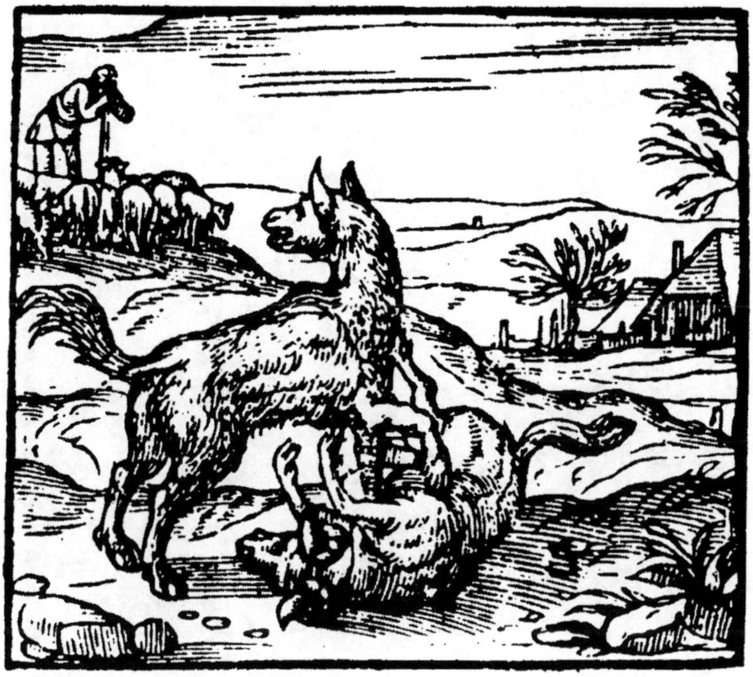

Emblema LXVI

OBLIVIO PAUPERTATIS PARENS

Cum lupus esuriens mandit cervarius escam
Praeque fame captum devorat hinnuleum,
Respiciat si forte alio, vel lumina vertat,
Praesentem oblitus quem tenet ore cibum,
Quaeritat incertam (tanta est oblivio) praedam.
Qui sua neglexit, stulte aliena petit.

Emblem 66

FORGETFULNESS IS THE FATHER OF POVERTY

While the famished deer-seeking wolf chews its pittance, devouring a fawn which its hunger had earlier caused it to chase down, if it turns around, and perchance diverting its glance, sees something else, so great is its forgetfulness that, ignoring the food which it presently has in its mouth, it goes off in search of an uncertain prey. Whoever neglects what is [already] his own, foolishly seeks what belongs to someone else.

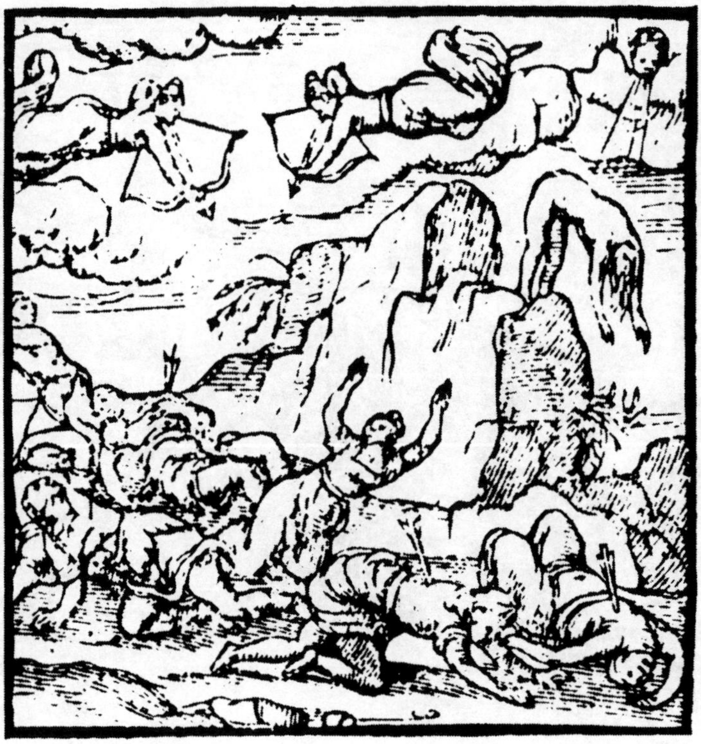

Emblema LXVII

SUPERBIA

En statuae statua, et ductum de marmore marmor,
Se conferre Deis ausa procax Niobe.
Est vitium muliebre superbia, et arguit oris
Duritiem, ac sensus, qualis inest lapidi.

Emblem 67

PRIDE

Here is [pictured] the statue of a statue, and marble taken from marble: it depicts insolent Niobe, who dared to compare herself to the Gods. Pride is a feminine vice and it denotes hardened speech and feelings, hard like rocks.

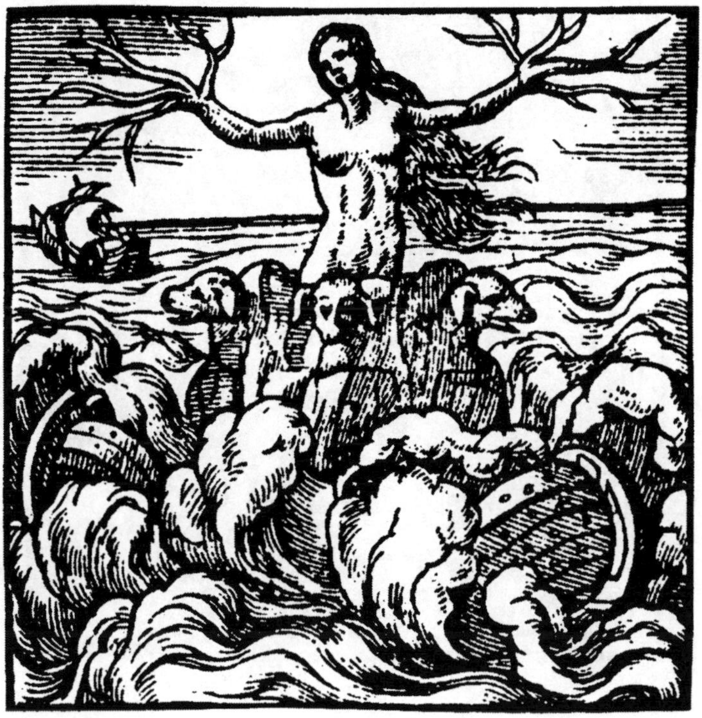

Emblema LXVIII

IMPUDENTIA

Pube tenus mulier, succincta latrantibus infra
Monstrorum catulis Scylla biformis erat.
Monstra putantur avarities, audacia, raptus:
At Scylla est, nullus cui sit in ore pudor.

Emblem 68

IMMODESTY

A woman down to the crotch, and with her lower part girted with her monstrous barking pups, Scylla was two-formed. It is thought that the monsters are avarice, audacity, and plunder, and surely she is a Scylla, one who has no shame whatsoever in her speech.

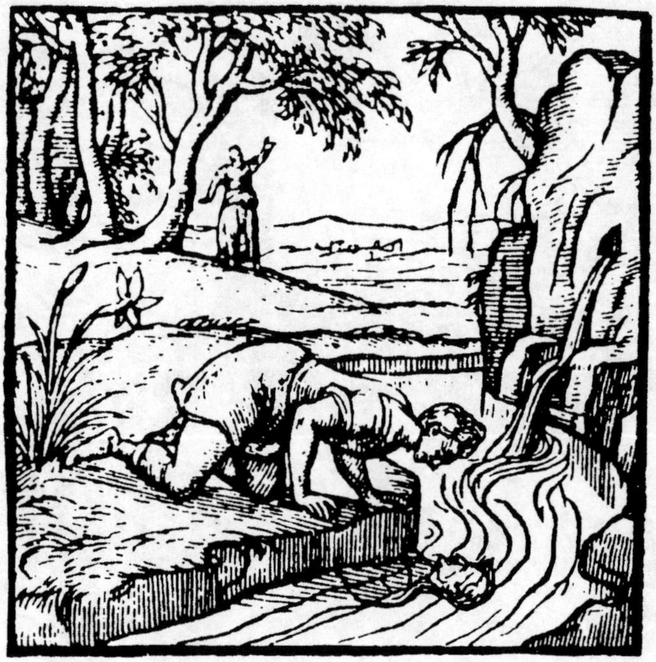

Emblema LXIX

PHILAUTIA

Quod nimium tua forma tibi, Narcisse, placebat,
In florem, et noti est versa stuporis holus.
Ingenii est marcor, cladesque *philautia*, doctos
Quae pessum plures datque, deditque viros:
Qui veterum abiecta methodo, nova dogmata quaerunt,
Nilque suas praeter tradere phantasias.

Emblem 69

SELF-LOVE

Due to the excessive pleasure that you took, oh Narcissus, in your own beauty, it was changed into a flower, and that became the well-known plant designating stupor. *Philautia* [self-love] is the decay and scourge of genius, and it has ruined many learned men: unappreciative of the ways of the ancients, and questing for new dogmas, they pass on nothing but their own fantasies.

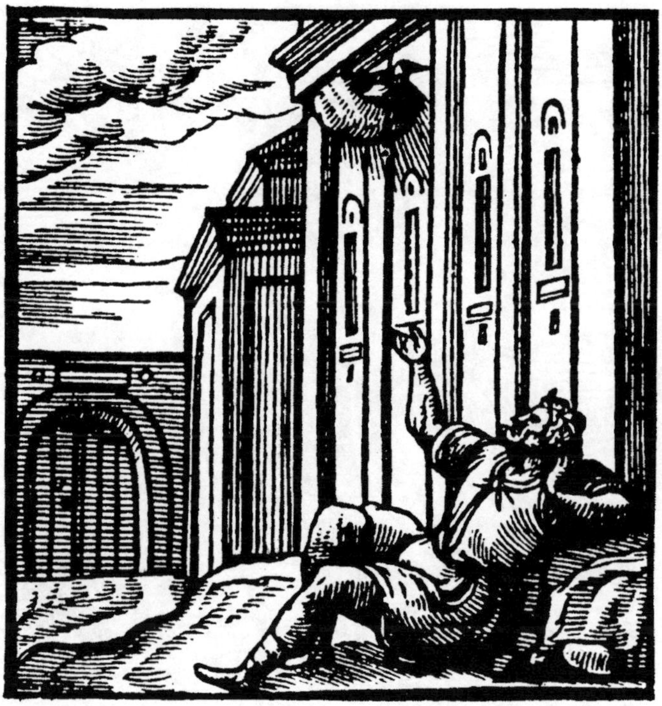

Emblema LXX

GARRULITAS

Quid matutinos Progne mihi garrula somnos
Rumpis, et obstrepero Daulias ore canis?
Dignus Epops Tereus, qui maluit ense putare,
Quam linguam immodicam stirpitus eruere.

Emblem 70

CHATTERING

Why, oh chattering Progne from Daulis [who was changed into a swallow], do you interrupt my morning sleep and sing with such an obstreperous mouth? Tereus deserved to become [changed into] a hoopoe bird since he preferred to prune your tongue with his sword rather than rippping it out by the roots.

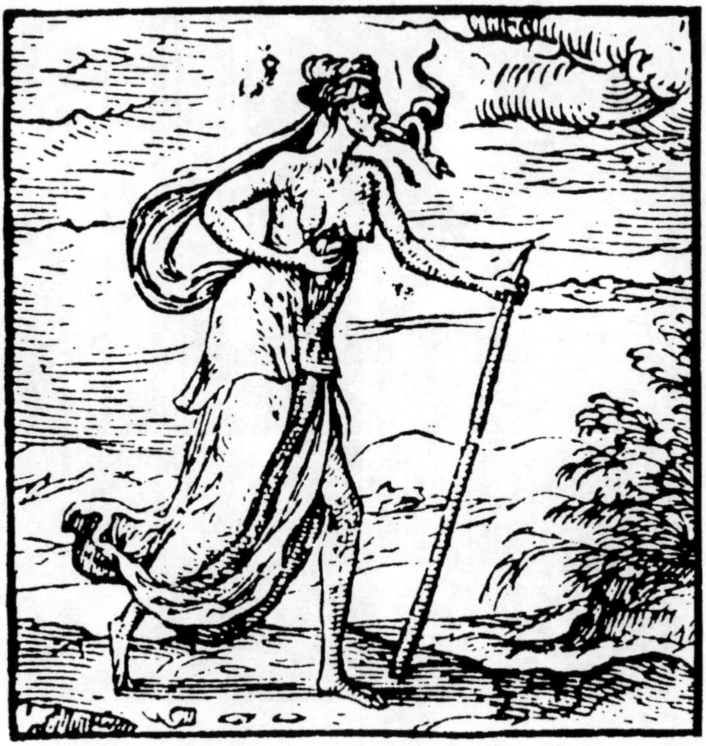

Emblema LXXI

INVIDIA

Squallida vipereas manducans femina carnes,
Cuique dolent oculi, quaeque suum cor edit,
Quam macies et pallor habent, spinosaque gestat
Tela manu: talis pingitur Invidia.

Emblem 71

ENVY

A filthy woman who chews the flesh of vipers, whose eyes hurt, and who devours her own heart; emaciated and grayish, she carries a thorny staff in her hand: this is how Envy is to be pictured.

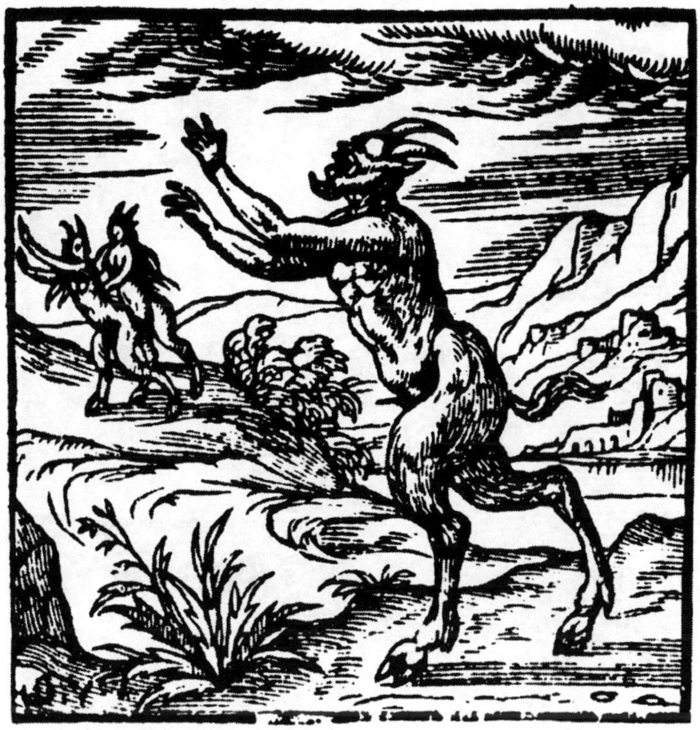

Emblema LXXII

LUXURIA

Eruca capripes redimitus tempora Faunus
Immodicae Veneris symbola certa refert.
Est eruca salax, indexque libidinis hircus:
Et Satyri Nymphas semper amare solent.

Emblem 72

LUST

A goat-footed Faun, his temples covered with colewort, provides a proper symbol for immoderate acts [sexual intercouse provoked] by Venus. Colewort is an aphrodisiac, and the male goat is the symbol of lust, and Satyrs are accustomed to make love to their Nymphs continuously.

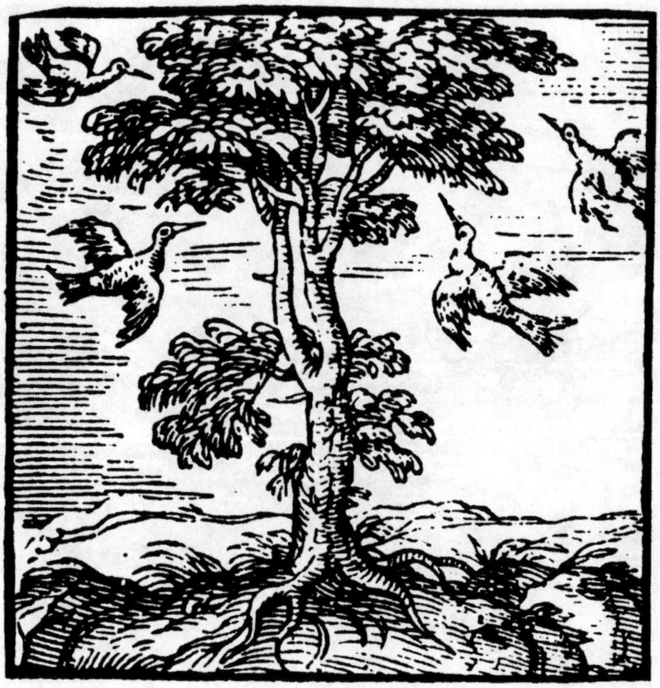

Emblema LXXIII

LUXURIOSORUM OPES

Rupibus aeriis, sumique crepidine saxi
Immites fructus ficus acerba parit:
Quos corvi comedunt, quos devorat improba cornix,
Qui nihil humanae commoditatis habent:
Sic fatuorum opibus parasiti et scorta fruuntur,
Et nulla iustos utilitate iuvant.

Emblem 73

THE RICHES OF THE LUSTFUL

The unripe fig-tree drops its bitter fruits upon the rocks on the edge of lofty crags: these are fed upon by ravens and devoured by the shameless crows, and they serve no use for men. In the same way, parasites and whores benefit from the wealth of the fatuous, who are of no use to the just.

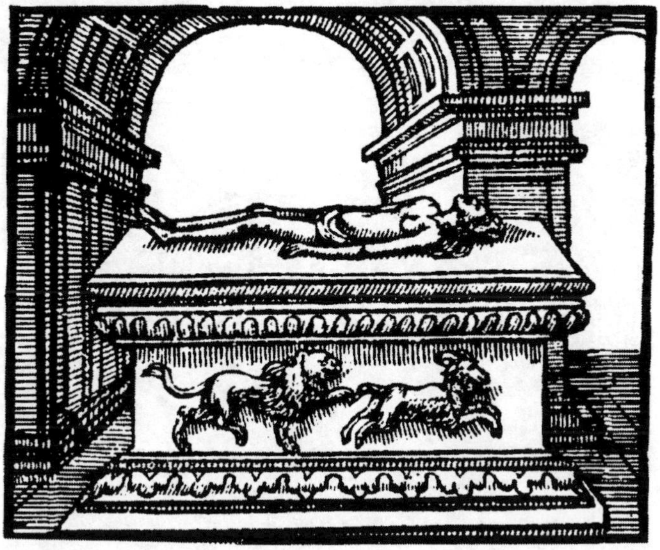

Emblema LXXIV
TUMULUS MERETRICIS

Quis tumulus? Cuia urna? Ephyraeae est Laidos. Ah!, non
Erubuit tantum perdere Parca decus?
Nulla fuit tum forma, illam iam carpserat aetas,
Iam speculum Veneri cauta dicaverat anus.
Quid scalptus sibi vult aries, quem parte leaena
Unguibus apprehensum posteriore tenet?
Non aliter captos quod et ipsa teneret amantes:
Vir gregis est aries, clune tenetur amans.

Emblem 74
THE WHORE'S TOMB

(a dialogue)

"Whose tomb is this? Whose urn is that?" "It belongs to Lais of Ephyrea [Corinth]." "Oh! Didn't the Parca [Fate] blush after ruining such beauty?" "There was no such beauty then, for age had already reaped it. The old lady had already shrewdly dedicated her mirror to Venus." "What is the meaning of the sculpted ram being clawed by a lioness on its hind quarters?" "Nothing, if not to show how she had kept her customers captive: a man is a ram taken from the fold, and the lover is clawed on his buttocks."

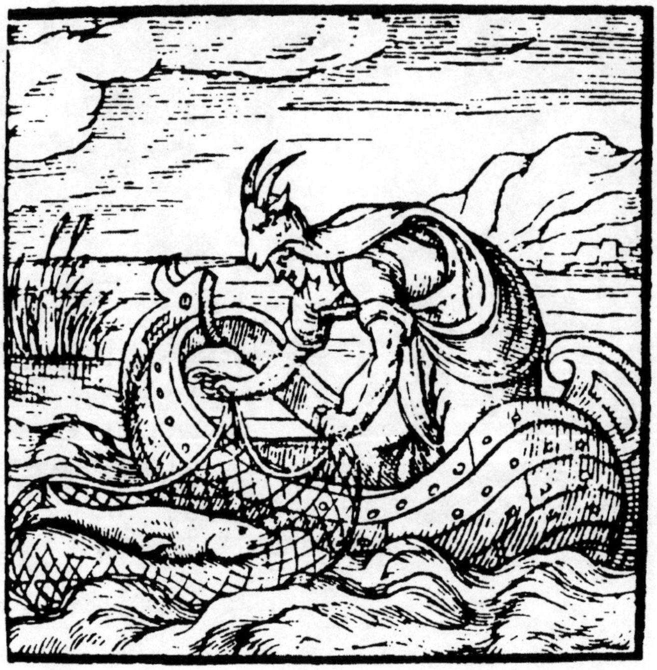

Emblema LXXV

IN AMATORES MERETRICUM

Villosae indutus piscator tegmina caprae,
Addidit ut capiti cornua bina suo;
Fallit amatorem stans summo in littore sargum,
In laqueos simi quem gregis ardor agit.
Capra refert scortum: similis sit sargus amanti,
Qui miser obsceno captus amore perit.

Emblem 75

AGAINST THOSE WHO LOVE WHORES

Dressed in the skin of a hairy she-goat, the fisherman has placed two horns upon his head; standing on the bank, he tricks an enamored bream-fish, whose passion for like company has driven it into the net. The goat refers to the whore, and the bream resembles the lover who, trapped by an obscene love, wretchedly perishes.

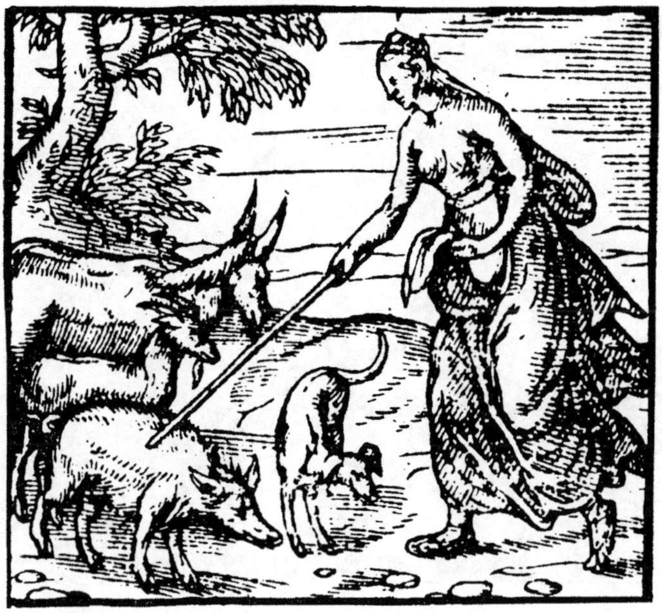

Emblema LXXVI

CAVENDUM A MERETRICIBUS

Sole satae Circes tam magna potentia fertur,
Verterit ut multos in nova monstra viros.
Testis equum domitor Picus, tum Scylla biformis,
Atque Ithaci postquam vina bibere sues.
Indicat illustri meretricem nomine Circe,
Et rationem animi perdere, quisquis amat.

Emblem 76

WATCH OUT FOR WHORES

So great was the power of Circe, the daughter of the Sun, that she changed many men into unheard of monsters. The horse-tamer Picus provides proof of this, and so does two-form Scylla, and also the Ithacans, who were turned into pigs after drinking her wine. With her illustrious name, Circe symbolizes the whore, and whoever falls in love with any of these loses control of his reason and soul.

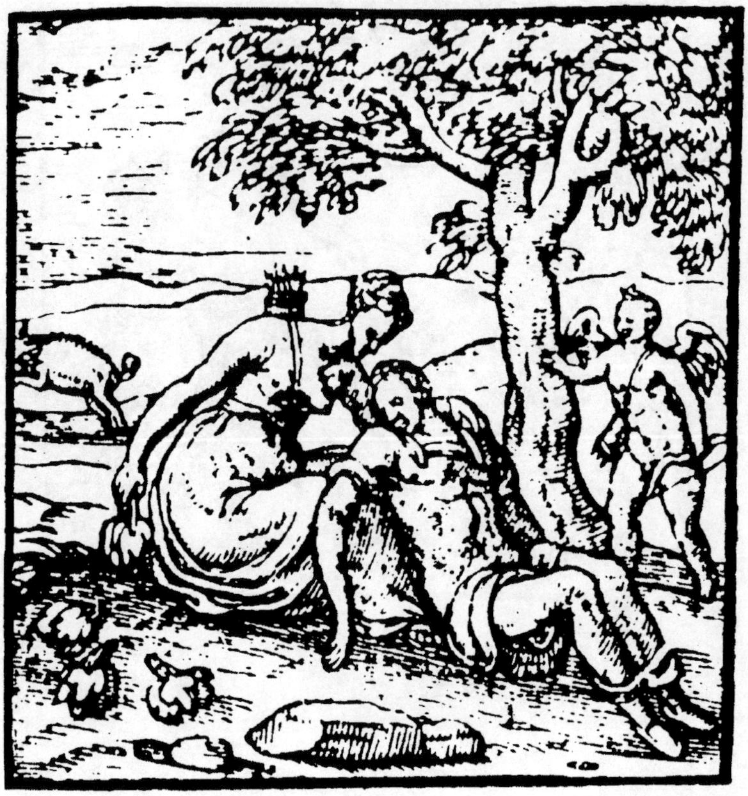

Emblema LXXVII

AMULETUM VENERIS

Inguina dente fero suffossum Cypris Adonin
Lactucae foliis condidit exanimem.
Hinc genitali arvo tantum lactuca resistit,
Quantum eruca salax vix stimulate potest.

Emblem 77

THE AMULET OF VENUS

After he was wounded in the groin by the boar's tusk, Cypris [Venus] covered the lifeless Adonis with lettuce leaves. Accordingly, just as lettuce curbs genital ardor, so does the lubricious colewort stimulate it.

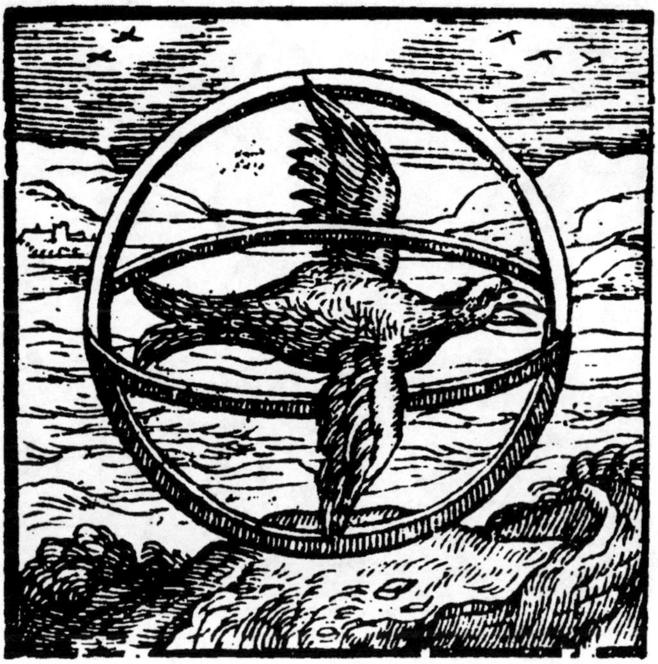

Emblema LXXVIII

INVIOLABILES TELO CUPIDINIS

Ne dirus te vincat amor, neu femina mentem
Diripiat magicis artibus ulla tuam:
Bacchica avis praesto tibi motacilla paretur,
Quam quadriradiam circuli in orbe loces:
Ore crucem et cauda, et geminis ut complices alis,
Tale amuletum carminis omnis erit.
Dicitur hoc Veneris signo Pagasaeus Iason
Phasiacis laedi non potuisse dolis.

Emblem 78

SAFE FROM CUPID'S DART

So that you won't become a victim to cruel love, and so that no woman will ever devastate your mind with her magical arts, I advise you forthwith to get a wagtail, the bird sacred to Bacchus, and this you will place as a four-spoked form set within a circle. It forms a cross with its head and tail and the two wings spread out. Such an amulet works as a charm against every enchantment. With this seal of Venus it is said that Jason the Pagaesaean became immune to the bewitchments of the woman from Phasis [Medea].

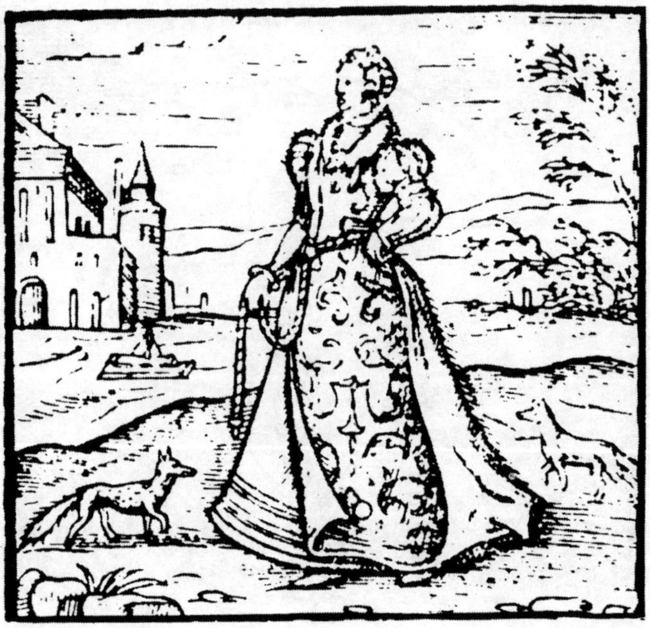

Emblema LXXIX
LASCIVIA

Delicias et mollitiem mus creditur albus
Arguere, at ratio non sat aperta mihi est.
An quod ei natura salax et multa libido est?
Ornat Romanas an quia pelle nurus?
Sarmaticum murem vocitant plerique Zibellum,
Et celebris suavi est inguine muscus Arabs.

Emblem 79
LEWDNESS

It is believed that the ermine (a sort of white mouse) denotes sensual pleasures and voluptuousness, but the reason remains unclear to me. Could it be because the animal is salacious by nature and full of lust? Or is it because its fur adorns Roman matrons? Many call the Sarmatian mouse a Zibellan [sable], and Arabic musk is famed for being the perfume to apply to the crotch.

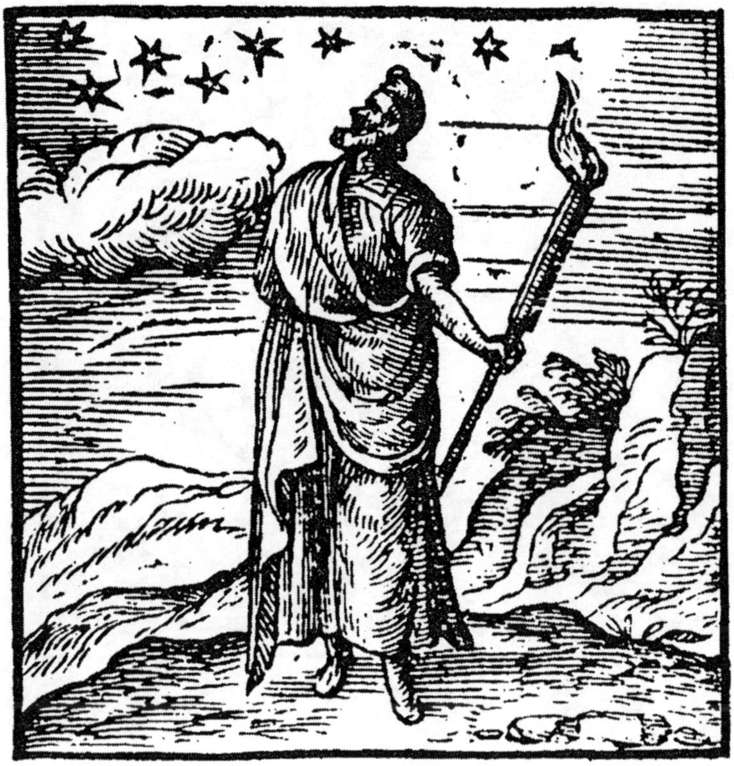

Emblema LXXX

DESIDIA

Desidet in modio Essaeus, speculator et astra,
Subtus et accensam contegit igne facem.
Segnities specie recti velata cucullo,
Non se non alios utilitate iuvat.

Emblem 80

SLOTH

An Essene sits upon a bushel and idly contemplates the stars, and beneath him he conceals a lighted torch. Veiled with a hood in the guise of the righteous, sloth is of no use to itself nor to anybody else.

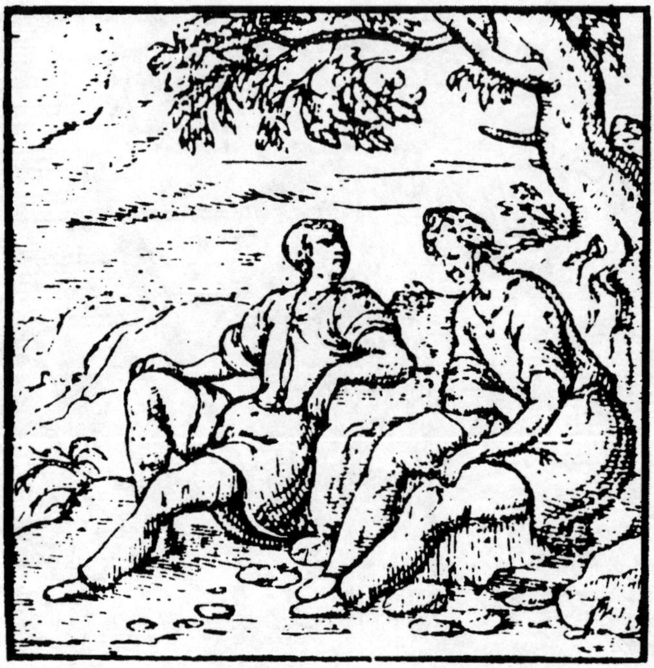

Emblema LXXXI

DESIDIAM ABJICIENDAM

Quisquis iners, abeat. Nam in choenice figere sedem
Nos prohibent Samii dogmata sancta senis.
Surge igitur, duroque manus assuesce labori;
Det tibi dimensos crastina ut hora cibos.

Emblem 81

SLOTH MUST BE CAST ASIDE

Send packing anyone who is inactive. The holy precepts of the aged Samnian [Pythagoras] prohibit us from squatting upon a food dish [to defecate]. So, get up: get your hands accustomed to hard labor, so that the morrow will provide you with your measure of food.

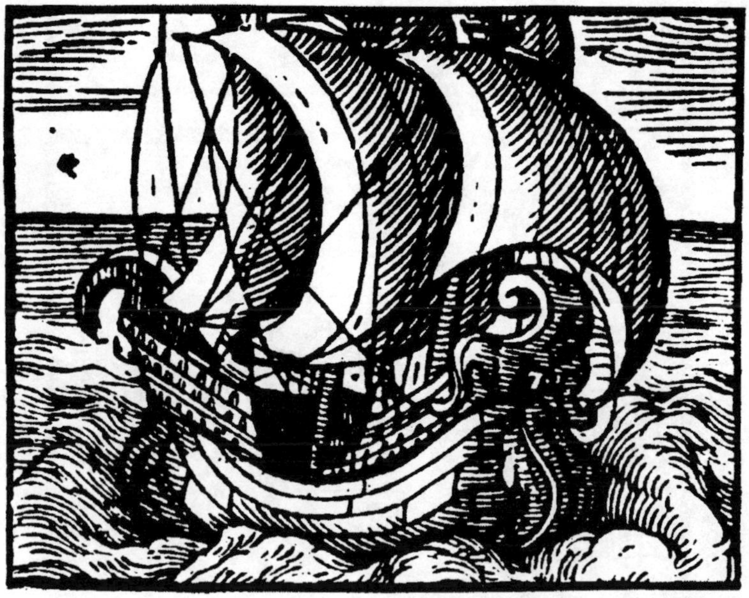

Emblema LXXXII

IN FACILE A VIRTUTE DESCISCENTES

Parva velut limax spreto Remora impete venti,
Remorumque, ratem sistere sola potest:
Sic quosdam ingenio et virtute ad sidera vectos
Detinet in medio tramite causa levis.
Anxia lis veluti est, vel qui meretricius ardor
Egregiis iuvenes sevocat a studiis.

Emblem 82

ABOUT THOSE EASILY SEPARATED FROM VIRTUE

A remora as small as a snail can, by itself, stop a ship, and in spite of the force of the winds and the impulse of its oars. Similarly, in the midst of their journey, an insignificant reason detains those drawn by their talent and virtue towards the stars. This is like a worrisome litigation, or like the passion for a whore, seducing exceptional youth from their studies.

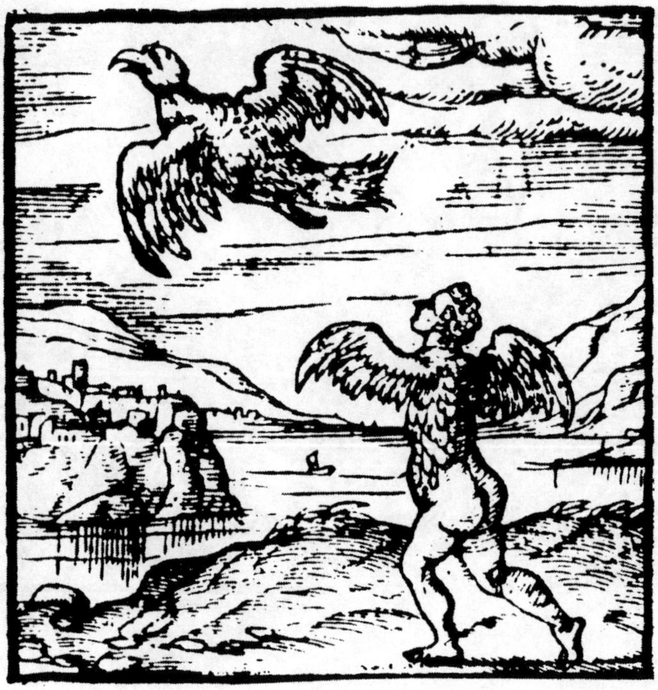

Emblema LXXXIII

IGNAVI

Ignavi ardeolam stellarem effingere servi
Et studia, et mores, fabula prisca fuit:
Quae famulum Asteriam volucris sumpsisse figuram
Est commenta: fides sit penes historicos.
Degener hic veluti qui cevet in aere falco est,
Dictus ab antiquis vatibus ardelio.

Emblem 83

SLUGGARTS

According to an ancient fable, the starred night-heron symbolizes the enthusiasms and habits of a sluggish servant, and it is alleged that the slave Asterias took on the appearance of this bird: we must place our confidence in the historians. This degenerate is like the kestrel who wags its butt in the air, and it was called by the ancient poets an *ardelion*, a busybody.

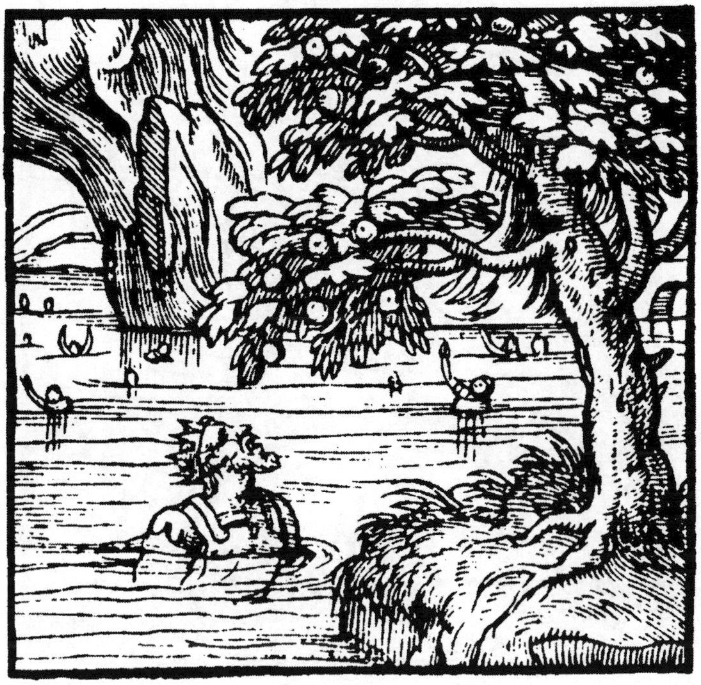

Emblema LXXXIV

AVARITIA

Heu miser, in mediis sitiens stat Tantalus undis,
Et poma esuriens proxima habere nequit.
Nomine mutato de te id dicetur, avare,
Qui, quasi non habeas, non frueris quod habes.

Emblem 84

AVARICE

Oh my, the misfortunate Tantalus is thirsting in the middle of the waves and hungering because he is unable to reach the nearby fruits. Changing your name, oh miser, the same applies to you; because you don't enjoy what you have, it is as though you didn't have it.

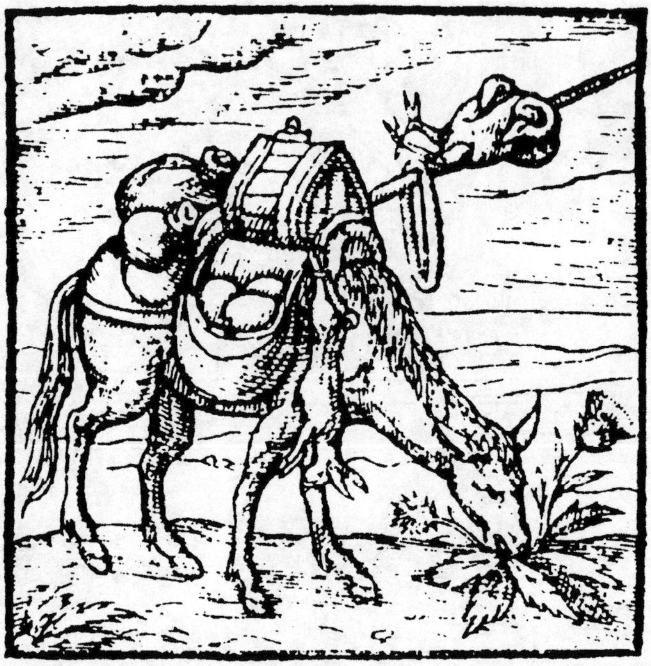

Emblema LXXXV

IN AVAROS

Septitius populos inter ditissimus omnes,
Arva senex nullus quo magis ampla tenet,
Defraudans geniumque suum, mensasque paratas,
Nil praeter betas duraque rapa vorat.
Cui similem dicam hunc, inopem quem copia reddit?
Anne asino? Sic est: instar hic eius habet.
Namque asinus, dorso pretiosa obsonia gestat,
Seque rubo aut dura carice pauper alit.

Emblem 85

ABOUT MISERS

Septitius is the richest among the population and no other old man has estates more extensive than his. Defrauding his own appetite for the well-furnished banquet tables, he feeds instead upon no more than beets and hard turnips. What can I compare to this one, whose wealth becomes poverty? Can I not liken him to the ass? That's it: he does resemble the animal. Just so; the ass carries upon his back costly groceries and, nonetheless, the impoverished beast grazes upon brambles and tough reed-grass.

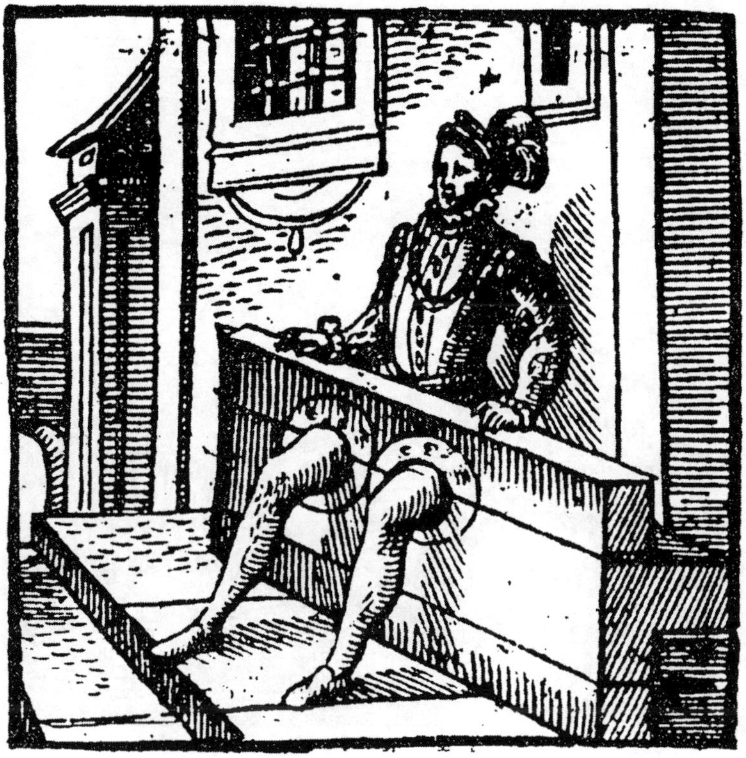

Emblema LXXXVI

IN AULICOS

Vana Palatinos, quos educat aula, clientes;
Dicitur auratis nectere compedibus.

Emblem 86

ABOUT COURTIERS

The palace summons its palatine favorites to its frivolous court; it is said that these are tied to it with golden shackles.

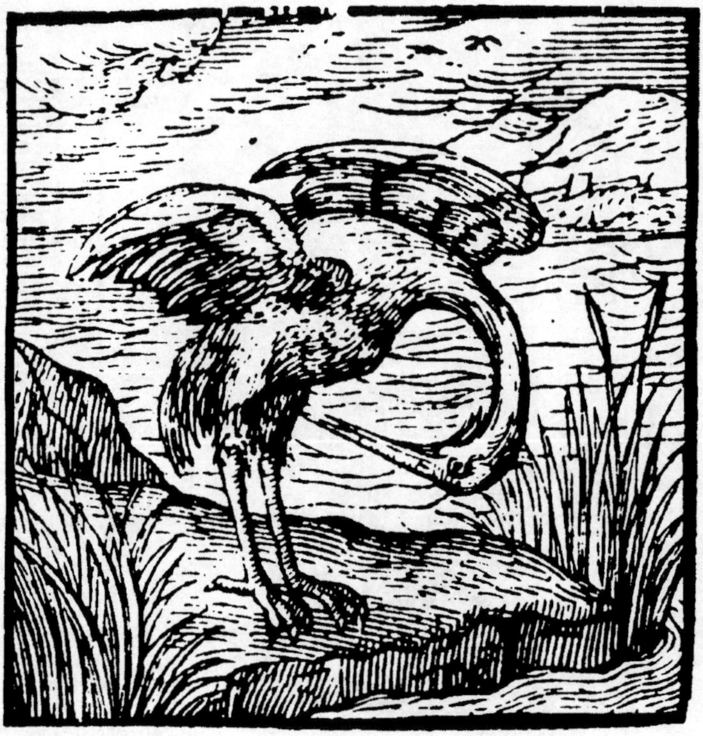

Emblema LXXXVII

IN SORDIDOS

Quae rostro, clystere velut, sibi proluit alvum
Ibis, Niliacis cognita littoribus,
Transiit opprobrii in nomen: quo Publius hostem
Naso suum appellat, Battiadesque suum.

Emblem 87

ABOUT THE FILTHY

The name of the ibis is well known along the banks of the Nile; since it cleans out its belly using its beak as a syringe, it has become a term of opprobrium: Publius Naso [Ovid] applied it [*naso* = nose] to name his enemy, and Battiades [Callimachus] used it for his.

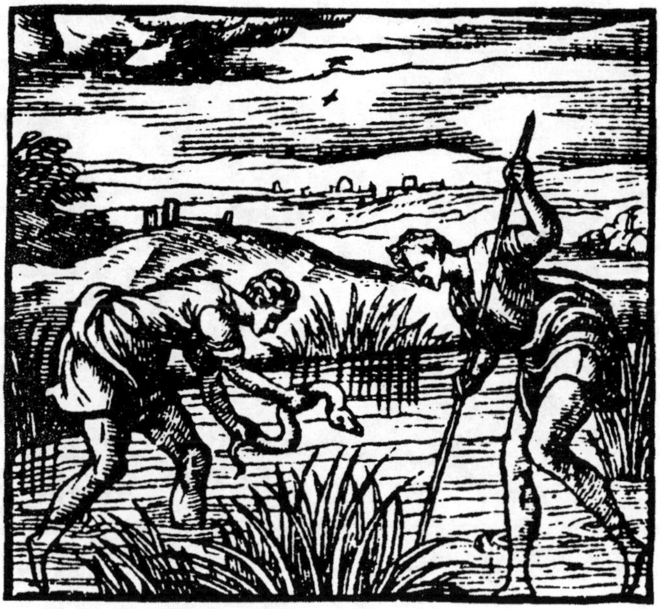

Emblema LXXXVIII

IN DIVITES PUBLICO MALO

Anguillas quisquis captat, si limpida verrat
Flumina. Si illimes ausit adire lacus,
Cassus erit, ludetque operam: multum excitet ergo
Si cretae, et vitres palmula turbet aquas;
Dives erit: sic iis res publica turbida lucro est,
Qui pace, arctati legibus, esuriunt.

Emblem 88

THOSE ENRICHED BY PUBLIC MISFORTUNE

Anybody can catch eels if he stirs up the limpid rivers. If, however, he dares to venture into an unmuddied pool, he will come back empty-handed and will have wasted his time. Accordingly, if the mud is stirred up, and if he agitates the crystalline waters with an oar, he will become rich. In the same way, a republic in disorder becomes the source of benefit for those who, restrained by the law, starve in [the preceding] times of peace.

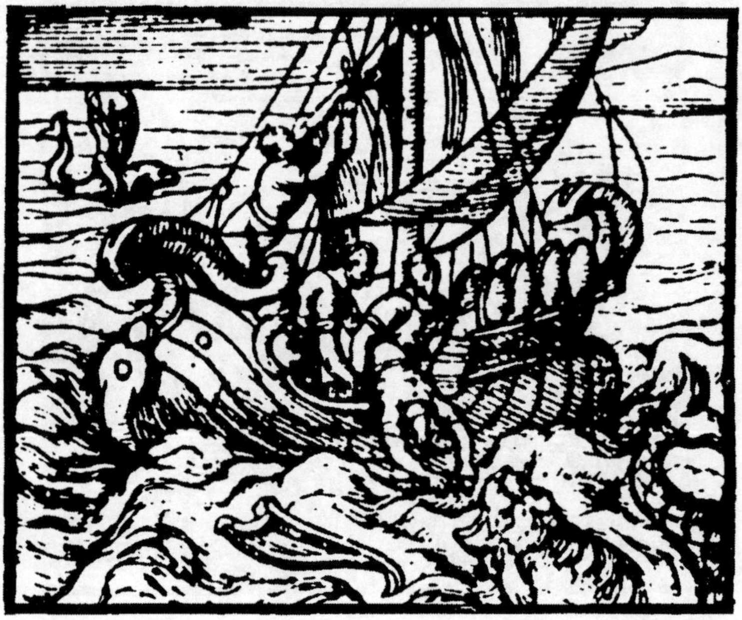

Emblema LXXXIX

IN AVAROS, VEL QUIBUS MELIOR CONDITIO AB EXTRANEIS OFFERTUR

Delphini insidens vada caerula sulcat Arion,
Hocque aures mulcet, frenat et ora sono.
Quam sit avari hominis, non tam mens dira ferarum est:
Quique viris rapimur, piscibus eripimur.

Emblem 89

ABOUT MISERS, OR HOW STRANGERS OFTEN OFFER A BETTER SITUATION

Mounted upon a dolphin, Arion [the winged horse] breasts the azure waves caressing its ears, and he puts the bridle into its mouth with this song: "The mind of any beast is not as cruel as are the minds of miserly men; those who are robbed by men are rescued by the fish [dolphins]."

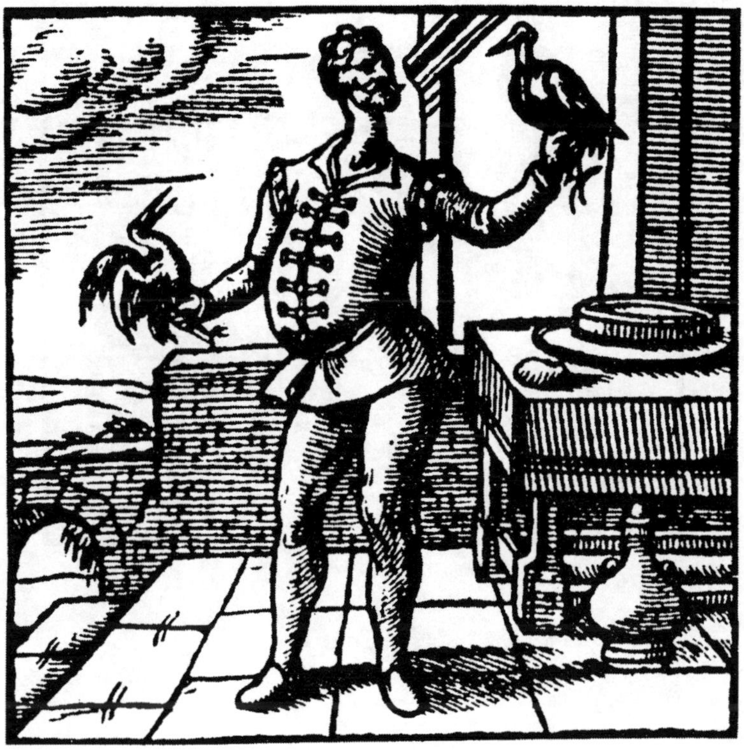

Emblema XC

GULA

Gurgulione gruis, tumida vir pingitur alvo,
Qui Laron, aut manibus gestat Onocrotalum;
Talis forma fuit Dionysii, et talis Apicii,
Et gula quos celebres deliciosa facit.

Emblem 90

GLUTTONY

A man is painted with the neck of a crane and a swollen belly; he carries in his hands a seagull or a pelican. Such was the shape of Dionysius [the tyrant of Syracuse] and Apicius, and those who make themselves famous by their gluttony for pleasure.

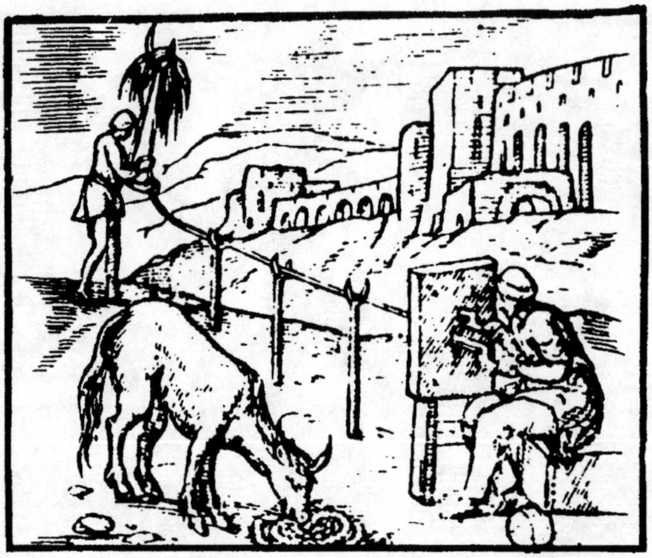

Emblema XCI

OCNI EFFIGIES, DE IIS QUI MERETRICIBUS DONANT, QUOD IN BONOS USUS VERTI DEBEAT

Impiger haud cessat funem contexere sparto,
Humidaque artifici iungere fila manu.
Sed quantum multis vix torquet strenuus horis,
Protinus ignavi ventris asella vorat.
Femina iners animal, facili congesta marito
Lucra rapit, mundum prodigit inque suum.

Emblem 91

THE PICTURE OF OCNUS, OR ABOUT THOSE WHO GIVE TO WHORES WHAT SHOULD BE TURNED TO BETTER USES

Industrious, he won't cease weaving his rope with esparto grasses, and [Ocnus] joins the wet strands with a skillful hand. Yet all that which has been twisted during many hours, and with so much difficulty, is immediately devoured by a female jackass with a sterile belly. Woman, an indolent animal, snatches up the accumulated earnings of a compliant husband and squanders it on her own adornment.

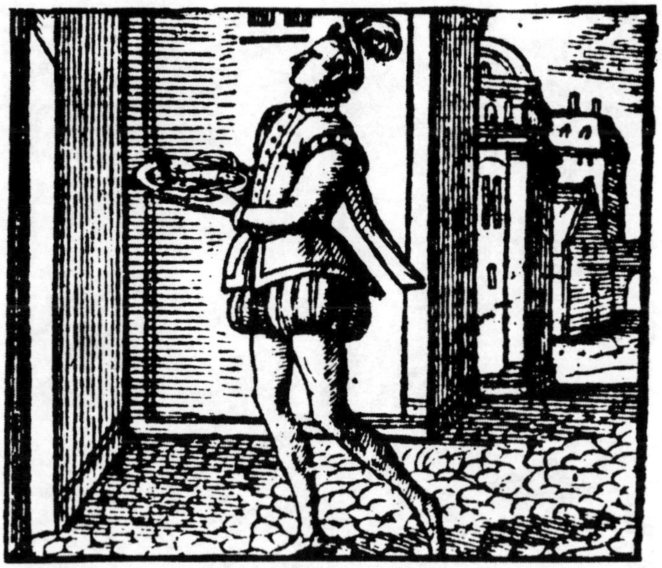

Emblema XCII

IN PARASITOS

Quos tibi donamus, fluviales accipe cancros;
Munera conveniunt moribus ista tuis.
His oculi vigiles, et forfice plurimus ordo
Chelarum armatus, maximaque alvus adest:
Sic tibi propensus stat pingui abdomine venter,
Pernicesque pedes, spiculaque apta pedi.
Cum vagus in triviis, mensaeque sedilibus erras,
Inque alios mordax scommatta salsa iacis.

Emblem 92

ABOUT PARASITES

Accept these crabs that we give to you, for such presents are appropriate to your character. They have vigilant eyes and several rows of feet armed with claws and their belly is enormous. Similar is your belly, with its fat, hanging abdomen, and your nimble feet, with stings tied to them. While you wander aimlessly through the streets or among the tables of the diners, you also toss at the others the briny barbs of your stinging taunting.

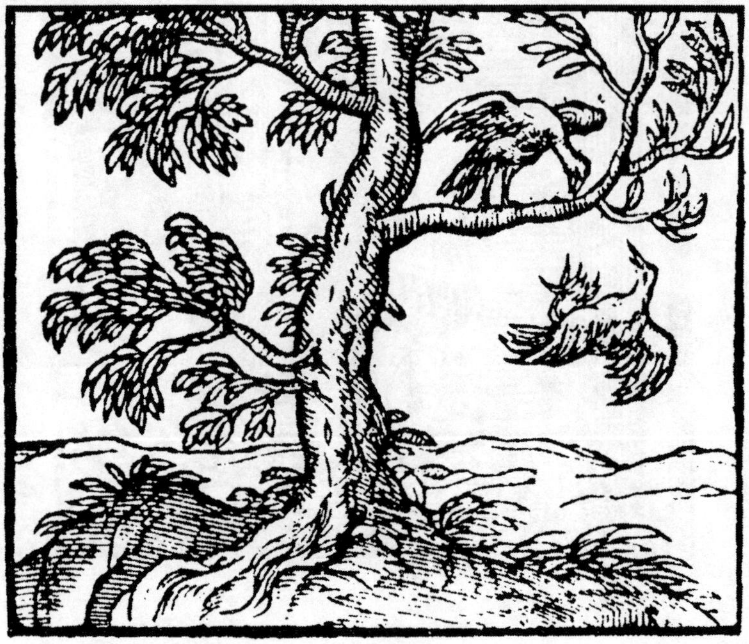

Emblema XCIII

PARVAM CULINAM DUOBUS GANEONIBUS NON SUFFICERE

In modicis nihil est quod quis lucreatur: et unum
Arbustum geminos non alit erithacos.
Aliud
In tenui spes nulla lucri est: unoque residunt
Arbusto geminae non bene ficedulae.

Emblem 93

A SMALL LARDER IS INSUFFICIENT FOR TWO GLUTTONS

In moderate circumstances there is nothing for anyone to profit from, and one orchard cannot support two red crows. (Otherwise) In trifling matters there is no hope whatsoever of profit: two jays are not comfortable within one orchard.

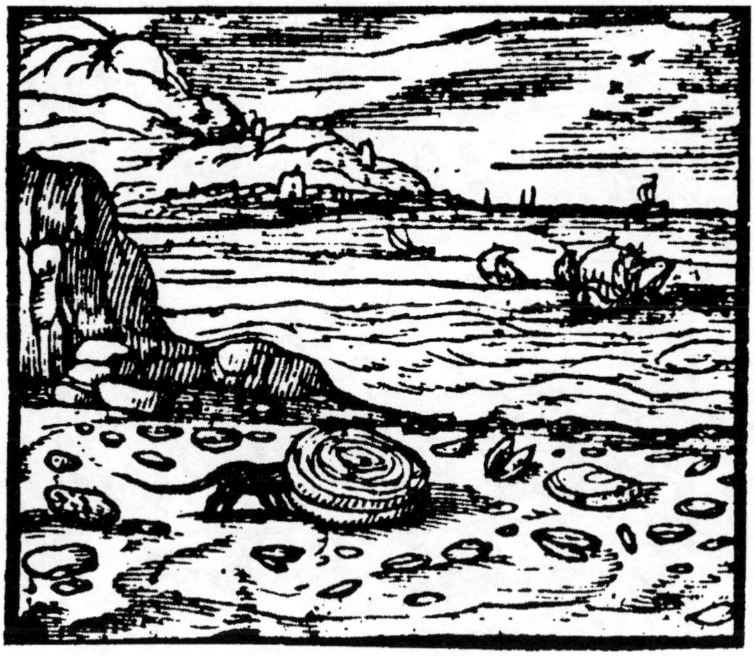

Emblema XCIV

CAPTIVUS OB GULAM

Regnatorque penus, mensaeque arrosor herilis
Ostrea mus summis vidit hiulca labris.
Queis teneram apponens barbam, falsa ossa momordit:
Ast ea clauserunt tacta repente domum;
Deprensum et tetro tenuerunt carcere furem,
Semet in obscurum qui dederat tumulum.

Emblem 94

CAPTURED BY GLUTTONY

A mouse, the king of the cupboard and vacuum-cleaner of the master's tables, saw the opened lips of an oyster. Drawing his tender muzzle to it, he munched upon the deceptive bones; but, once touched, the oyster suddenly shut up its house and trapped the thief within a horrid prison, he who had given himself a dark tomb.

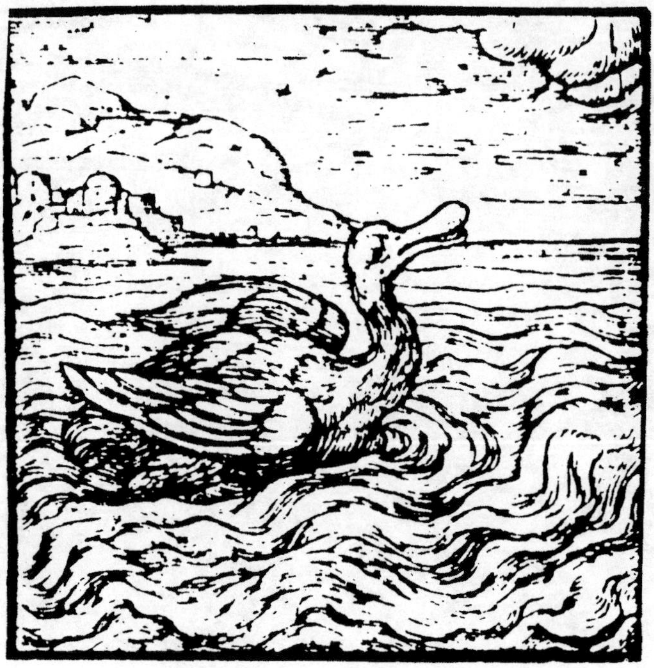

Emblema XCV

IN GARRULUM ET GULOSUM

Voce boat torva, praelargo est gutture, rostrum
Instar habet nasi, multiformisque tubae.
Deformem rabulam, addictum ventrique gulaeque
Signabit, volucer cum Truo pictus erit.

Emblem 95

ABOUT A CHATTERER AND A GLUTTON

He squawks with a piercing voice; his gullet is very long; he has a beak instead of a nose, and this is shaped like a many-valved trumpet. The picture of a bird like the pelican will represent the deformed, ranting lawyer, addicted to his belly and his gluttony.

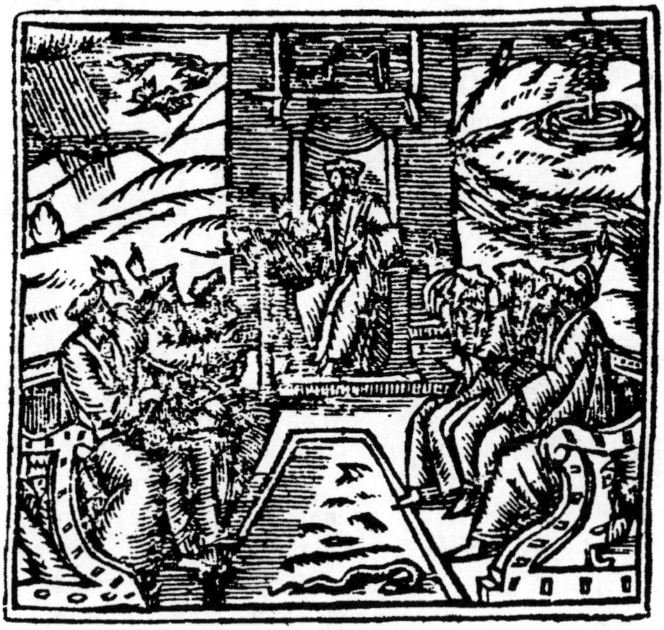

Emblema XCVI
DOCTORUM AGNOMINA

Moris vetusti est, aliqua professoribus
Superadiici cognomina.
Faciles apertosque explicans tantum locos,
Canon vocatur Curtius.
Revolvitur qui eodem, et iterat qui nimis
Maenander, ut Parisius.
Obscurus et confusus, ut Pictus fuit,
Labyrinthus appellabitur.
Nimis brevis, multa amputans, ut Claudius,
Mucronis agnomen feret.
Qui vel columnas voce erumpit, Parpalus,
Dictus Truo est scholasticis.
Contra est vocatus, tenuis esset Albius
Quod voce, Vespertilio.
At ultimas mutilans colobotes syllabas,
Hirundo Crassus dicitur.
Qui surdus aliis solus ipse vult loqui,
Ut sturnus in proverbio est.
Hic blaesus, ille raucus, iste garriens:
Hic sibilat ceu vipera.
Tumultuatur ille rictu et naribus,

Huic lingua terebellam facit.
Singultit alius, atque tussit haesitans.
At conspuit alius, ut psecas.
Quam multa rebus vitia in humanis agunt,
Tam multa surgunt nomina.

Emblem 96
THE PROFESSORS' NICKNAMES

It is an ancient custom to give nicknames to professors. Curtius was called "the Canon" because he could only explain accessible and standard citations. The one who goes in circles and excessively repeats himself is called "Meander," just as happened to Parisius. The obscure and confused one, like Pictus was, is called "Labyrinth." The one who is too brief, who cuts out a lot, like Claudius, is nicknamed "Sword." The one who makes columns collapse with his voice, like Parpalus, is called "Pelican" by his students. By way of contrast, Albius, who had a soft voice, is called "Bat." Crassus became "Swallow" because he swallowed his final syllables. Another who, deaf to all the rest, and only allowing himself to speak, becomes the proverbial "Starling." This one lisps, that one is hoarse; the former is garrulous, and the latter hisses like a viper; that one there raises a ruckus, slobbering and blowing his nose; this one uses his tongue as a drill; another gasps and, perplexed, coughs; and yet another spits like a rainstorm. So many such nicknames will arise as there are vices in human affairs.

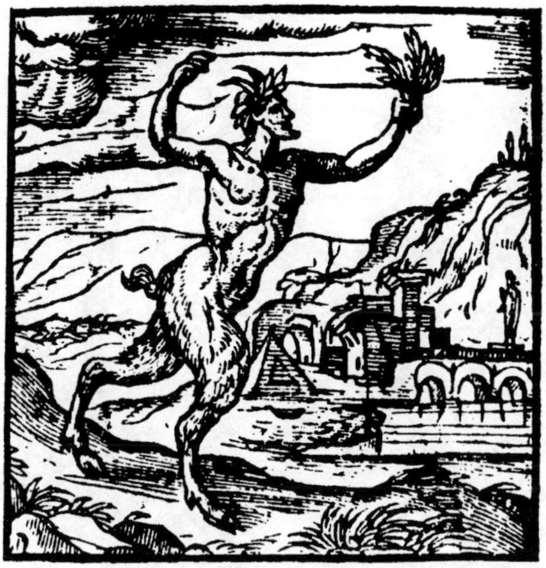

Emblema XCVII

NATURA

Pana colunt gentes (naturam hoc dicere rerum est)
Semicaprumque hominem, semivirumque Deum.
Est vir pube tenus, quod nobis insita virtus
Corde oriens, celsa verticis arce sedet.
Hinc caper est, quia nos natura in secla propagat
Concubitu, ut volucres, squamea, bruta, feras.
Quod commune aliis animantibus, est caper index
Luxuriae, Veneris signaque aperta gerit.
Cordi alii sophian, alii tribuere cerebro:
Inferiora modus, nec ratio ulla tenet.

Emblem 97

NATURE

People worship Pan — meaning the nature of things— and he is a man half-goat and a god half-man. He is a man down to his groin, and this is because our virtue, which is implanted in our heart at birth, has its seat in the lofty citadel of the head. Below the crotch he is a goat, and this is because Nature has propagated us through the ages by means of coitus, just as occurs with birds, fish, brutes and beasts. Because this [sexual intercourse] is common to all living things, the goat becomes the symbol of lust, and it clearly bears the signs of Venus. Some have attributed wisdom to the heart, others to the mind: but neither moderation nor reason will ever rule over the lower parts.

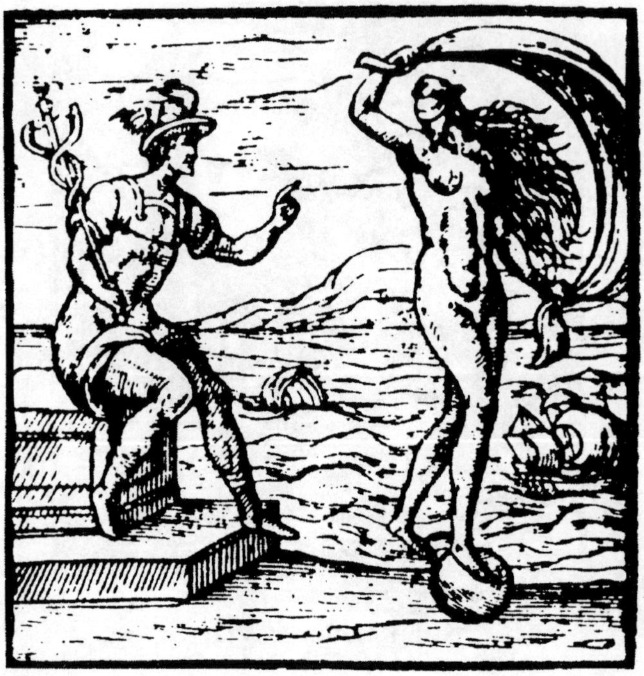

Emblema XCVIII

ARS NATURAM ADIUVANS

Ut sphaerae Fortuna, cubo sic insidet Hermes:
Artibus hic variis, casibus illa praeest:
Adversus vim fortunae est ars facta: sed artis
Cum fortuna mala est, saepe requirit opem.
Disce bonas artes igitur studiosa iuventus,
Quae certae secum commoda sortis habent.

Emblem 98

ART TO THE AID OF NATURE

Just as [blind] Fortune [precariously] stands upon a sphere, so Mercury [the God of the arts and crafts] sits [securely] upon a cube. He presides over diverse arts; she is the mistress of [random] acts of chance. Art is made to counter the power of fortune, but when fortune turns out badly, often she requires the aid of art. Learn then, oh studious youth, the useful arts, for these have in themselves the advantage of an assured fate.

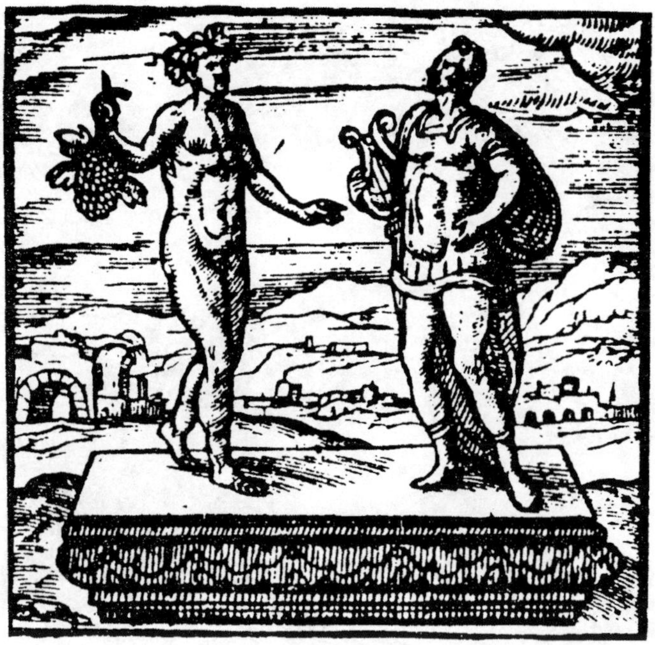

Emblema XCIX

IN IUVENTAM

Natus uterque Iovis, tener atque imberbis uterque,
Quem Latona tulit, quem tulit et Semele,
Salvete, aeterna simul et florete iuventa,
Numine sit vestro quae diuturna mihi.
Tu vino curas, tu victu dilue morbos,
Ut lento accedat curva senecta pede.

Emblem 99

ABOUT YOUTH

Both youths are the children of Jupiter, one and the other are soft and beardless; one [Apollo] sprang from Latona and the other [Bacchus] from Semele. Good health to you, and may you flower together in eternal youth, and may mine last for me a long time by your divine will. You [Bacchus] wash away cares with your wine, and you [Apollo] overcome illnesses, so that bent old age may approach me with a slowed foot.

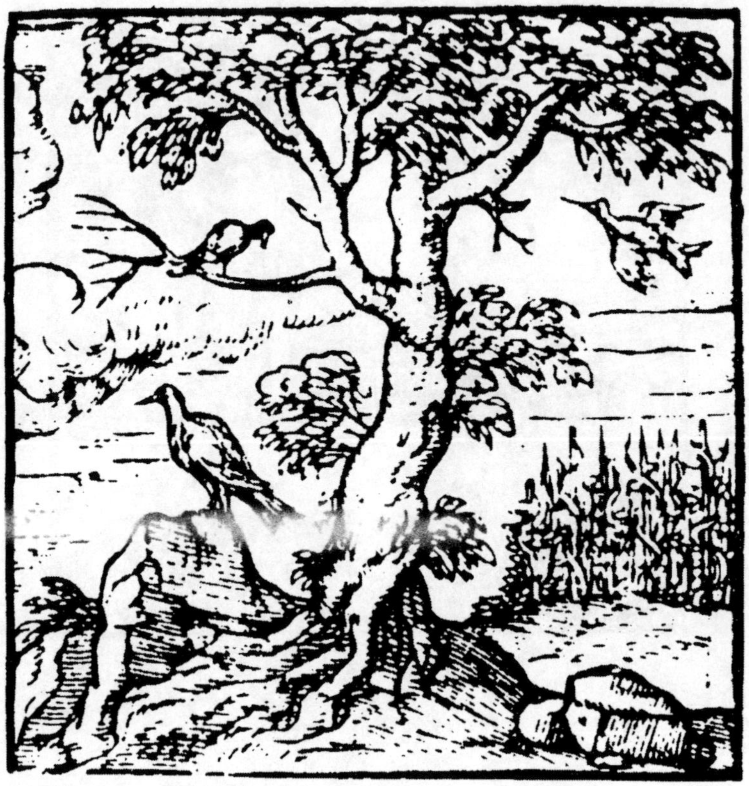

Emblema C

IN QUATTUOR ANNI TEMPORA

Advenisse hiemem frigilla renunciat ales:
Ad nos vere novo garrula hirundo redit.
Indicat aestatem sese exspectare cucullus:
Autumno est tantum cernere ficedulas.

Emblem 100

ABOUT THE FOUR SEASONS OF THE YEAR

The robin announces the arrival of Winter. The warbling swallow returns to us in early Spring. The cuckoo indicates that Summer is awaited. In Autumn, only jays are seen.

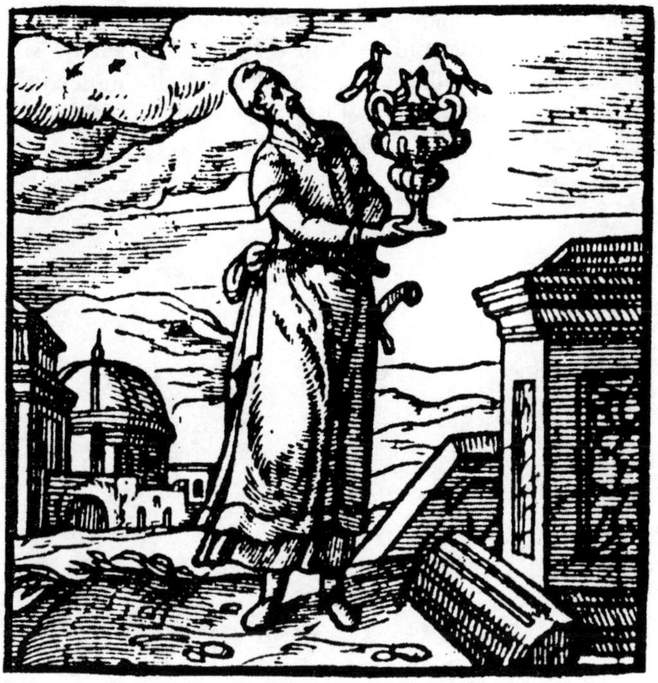

Emblema CI

SCYPHUS NESTORIS

Nestoreum geminis cratera hunc accipe fundis,
Quod gravis argenti massa profundit opus.
Claviculi ex auro, stant circum quatuor ansae:
Unamquamque super fulva colomba sedet.
Solus eum potuit longaevus tollere Nestor.
Maeonidae doceas quid sibi Musa velit?
Est caelum, scyphus ipse: colorque argenteus illi,
Aurea sunt caeli sidera claviculi.
Pleiadas esse putant, quas dixerit ille columbas.
Umbilici gemini magna minorque fera est.
Haec Nestor longo sapiens intelligit usu:
Bella gerunt fortes: callidus astra tenet.

Emblem 101

THE CUP OF NESTOR

Receive Nestor's double-bottomed crater, a work cast from a mass of heavy silver. Golden studs cover the four handles at the top, and upon each of these sits a tawny dove. Only long-lived Nestor was able to lift it. Can you teach us about the intention of the Muse of the Maeonidan [Homer]? With its silver color, the cup itself represents the sky, and the little studs become the golden stars in the sky. It is thought that the Pleiades are the [constellations] called doves. The doubled belly [of the cup] represents the great twin and its little sibling [the Big Bear and the Little Bear constellations]. Wise Nestor came to understand this after long practice: the powerful wage war, and the experienced man is the master of the stars.

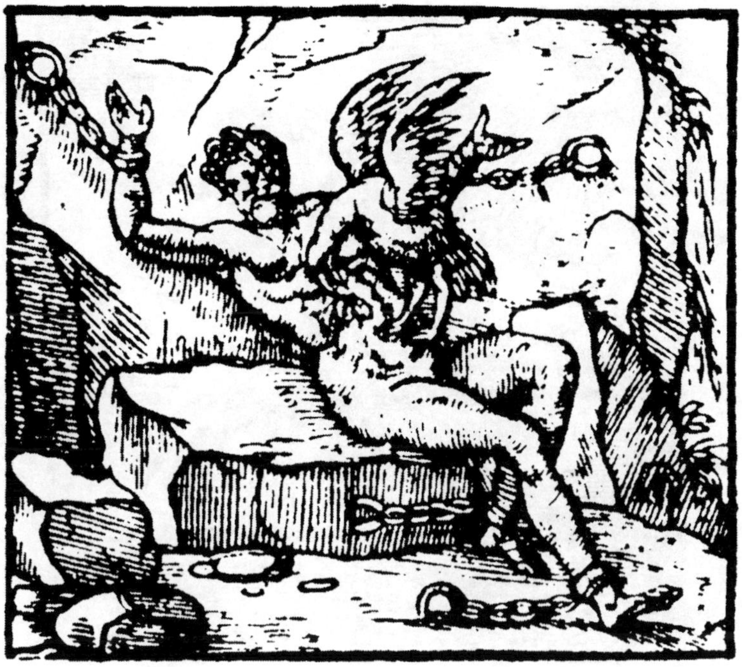

Emblema CII

QUAE SUPRA NOS, NIHIL AD NOS

Caucasia aeternum pendens in rupe Prometheus
Diripitur sacri praepetis ungue iecur.
Et nollet fecisse hominem: figulosaque perosus
Accensam rapto damnat ab igne facem.
Roduntur variis prudentum pectora curis,
Qui caeli affectant scire, deumque vices.

Emblem 102

WHAT LIES ABOVE US IS NOT OUR CONCERN

Hanging eternally from the crags of the Caucasus, Prometheus watches his liver ripped by the claws of the sacred bird. And he would prefer not to have fashioned man [from clay]; he renounces the hateful potters and damns the torch lighted with stolen fire. Aspiring to know the changing fortunes of heaven and the gods, [formerly] prudent men shall have their breasts tormented by various worries.

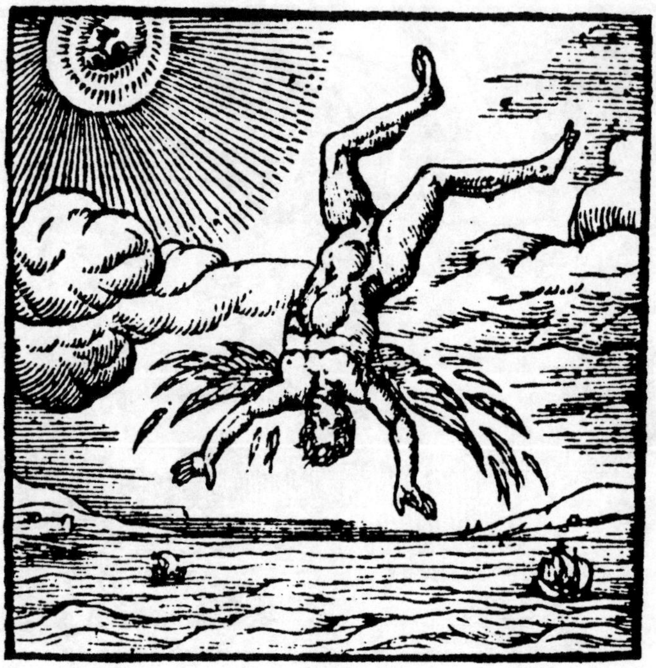

Emblema CIII
IN ASTROLOGOS

Icare, per superos qui raptus et aera, donec
In mare praecipitem cera liquata daret,
Nunc te cera eadem, fervensque resuscitat ignis,
Exemplo ut doceas dogmata certa tuo.
Astrologus caveat quicquam praedicere: praeceps
Nam cadet impostor dum super astra volat.

Emblem 103
ABOUT ASTROLOGERS

Oh Icarus, you who ascended through air up into the heaven, until the melting wax pitched you into the sea, now this same wax and the same burning fire bring you back to life as an example by which you will teach us your resolved doctrine. The astrologer must be careful with what he predicts, since the impostor falls head down when he flies above the stars.

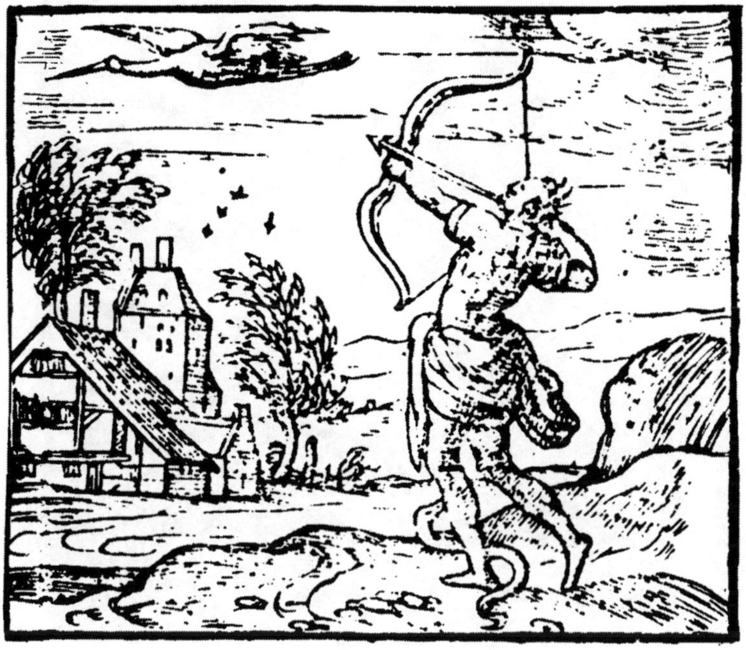

Emblema CIV

QUI ALTA CONTEMPLANTUR, CADERE

Dum turdos visco, pedica dum fallit alaudas,
Et iacta altivolam figit arundo gruem,
Dipsada non prudens auceps pede perculit: ultrix
Illa mali, emissum virus ab ore iacit.
Sic abit, extento qui sidera respicit arcu,
Securus fati quod tacet ante pedes.

Emblem 104

HE WHO CONTEMPLATES THINGS ON HIGH, FALLS DOWN

While he is busy deceiving the thrushes with the birdlime, and trapping the larks with a snare, and pierceing the flying crane with an arrow, the imprudent fowler steps upon a viper. Revenging this unlucky act, it injects its poison through its mouth. This is what happens to one who looks at the stars with a stretched bow, and who is heedless of fate, his escort, lying silently before his feet.

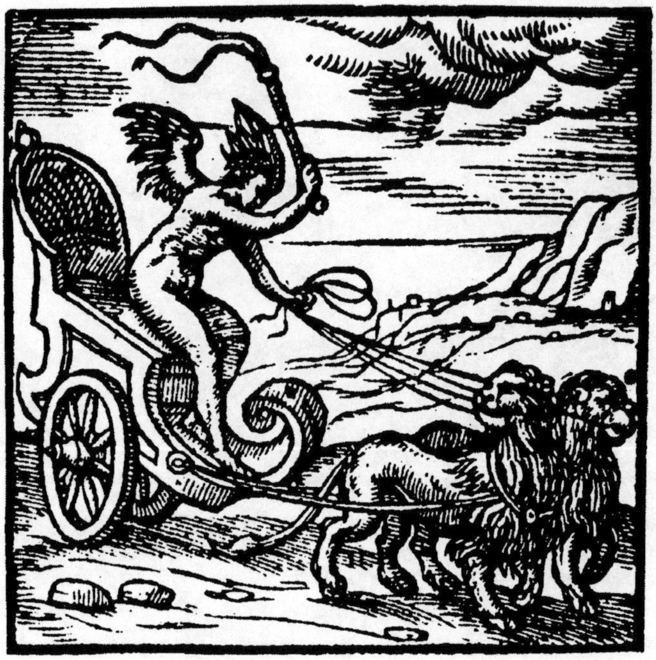

Emblema CV

POTENTISSIMUS AFFECTUS AMOR

Aspice ut invictus vires auriga leonis,
Expressus gemma pusio vincat Amor.
Utque manu hac scuticam tenet, hac ut flectit habenas,
Utque est in pueri plurimus ore decor.
Dira lues procul esto: feram qui vincere talem
Est potis, a nobis temperet anne manus?

Emblem 105

LOVE IS A MOST POWERFUL EMOTION

See how Love is shown engraved upon this gem as a little boy and as an invincible charioteer overcoming the might of a lion. Note also how Cupid holds a whip in one hand and pulls upon the reins with the other, and how great is the beauty in his childish face. Go away, oh cruel pestilence! Could one who is able to best such a beast be expected to keep his hands off us?

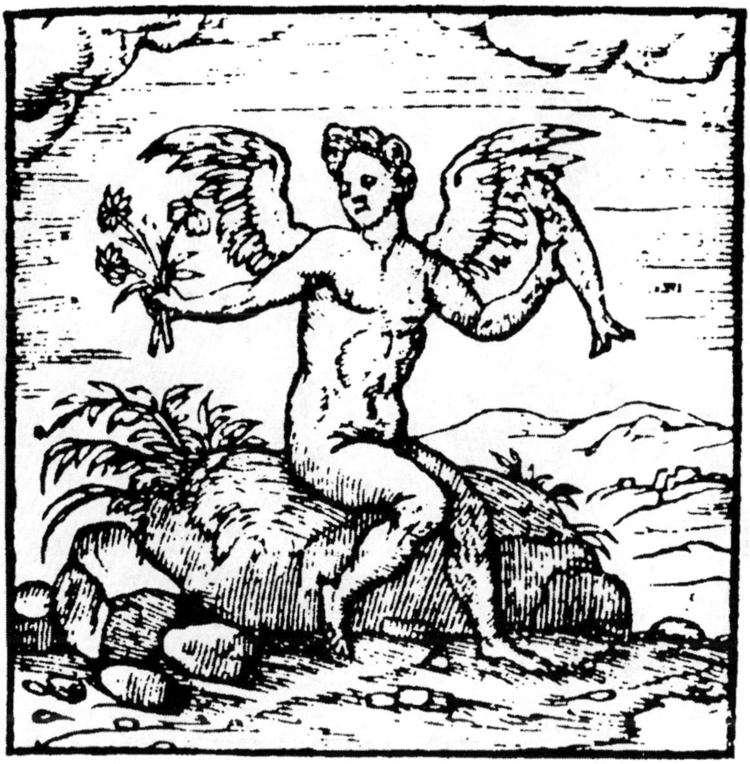

Emblema CVI

POTENTIA AMORIS

Nudus Amor viden ut ridet placidumque tuetur?
Nec faculas, nec quae cornua flectat, habet:
Altera sed manuum flores gerit, altera piscem,
Scilicet ut terrae iura det atque mari.

Emblem 106

THE POWER OF LOVE

Do you see how naked Love laughs, and how placidly he looks about? He has neither torches nor bows to bend. To the contrary, in one hand he holds flowers and in the other a fish. This shows that he lays down the law, both on land and at sea.

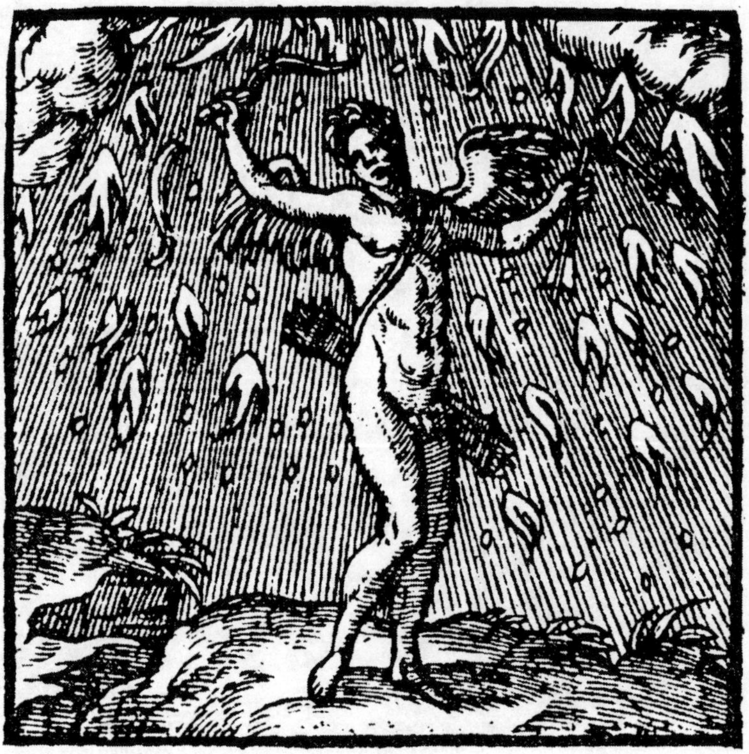

Emblema CVII

VIS AMORIS

Aligerum fulmen fregit Deus aliger, igne
Dum demonstrat uti est fortior ignis Amor.

Emblem 107

THE FORCE OF LOVE

The winged god broke the winged lightening-bolt, and this is to show how the fire of Love is mightier than fire.

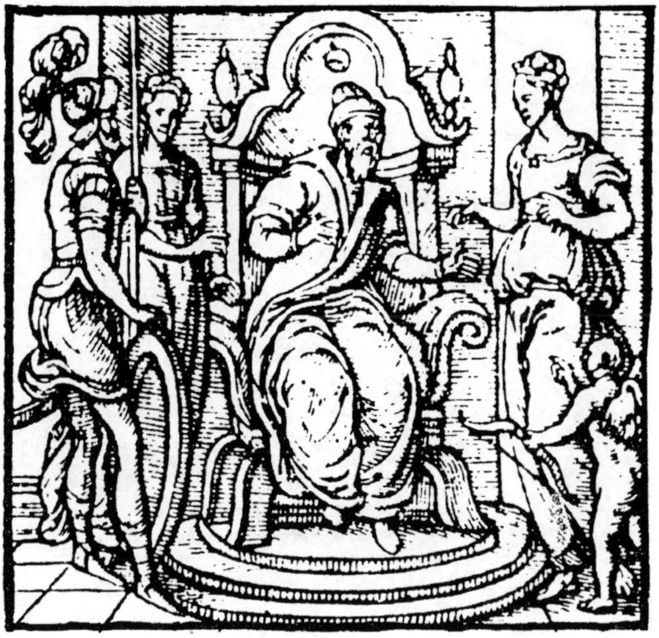

Emblema CVIII

IN STUDIOSUM CAPTUM AMORE

Immersus studiis, dicundo et iure peritus,
Et maximus libellio,
Helianiram amat, quantum nec Thracius umquam
Princeps sororis paelicem.
Pallada cur alio superasti iudice, Cypri?
Num sat sub Ida est vincere?

Emblem 108

ABOUT THE SCHOLAR TRAPPED BY LOVE

Immersed in his studies, expert in rhetoric and the law and, above all, very well read, he falls in love with Helianira, and even more so than the Thracean prince [Tereus] was enamored of his concubine [Philomena], the sister [of Procne, his wife]. Oh Cyprian [Venus], why do you wish to conquer Pallas with yet another judge? Isn't it enough that you beat her beneath Mount Ida [in the Judgment of Paris, where Venus won over Pallas and Juno]?

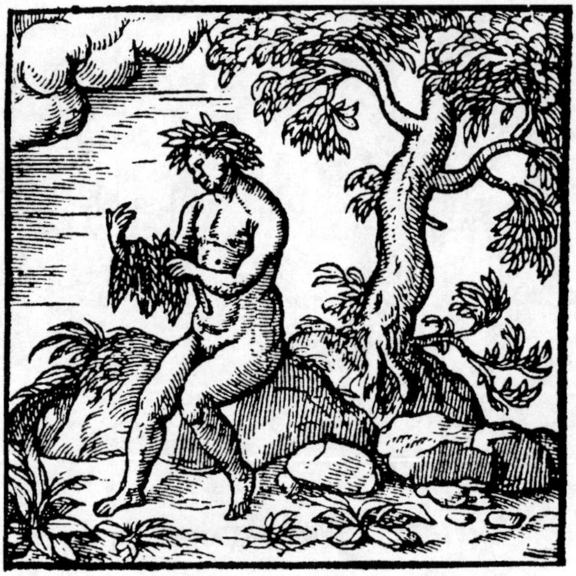

Emblema CIX

ANTEROS, ID EST, AMOR VIRTUTIS

Dic ubi sunt incurvi arcus? Ubi tela, Cupido?
Mollia queis iuvenum figere corda soles?
Fax ubi tristis? Ubi pennae? Tres unde corollas
Fert manus? Unde aliam tempora cincta gerunt?
Haud mihi vulgari est hospes cum Cypride quicquam,
Ulla voluptatis nos neque forma tulit.
Sed puris hominum succendo mentibus ignes
Disciplinae, animos astraque ad alta traho.
Quarttuor ecce ipsa texo virtute corollas:
Quarum, quae Sophia est, tempora prima tegit.

Emblem 109

ANTEROS, THAT IS, THE LOVE OF VIRTUE

(a dialogue)

"Tell me, where is your curved bow? Where, oh Cupid, are the arrows which you are accustomed to bury in the tender hearts of adolescents. Where is the torch of sadness? Where are your wings? Why are you holding three crowns? Why is another placed upon your brow?" "I am [Anteros and] not [Cupid,] the companion of the common Cyprian [Venus], and I am not moved by any kind of sensuality. Instead, I light within the pure minds of men the fires of learning, and thus I carry their souls away to the highest stars. These four crowns I am weaving out of virtue itself: the first of these, which is Wisdom, now covers my head."

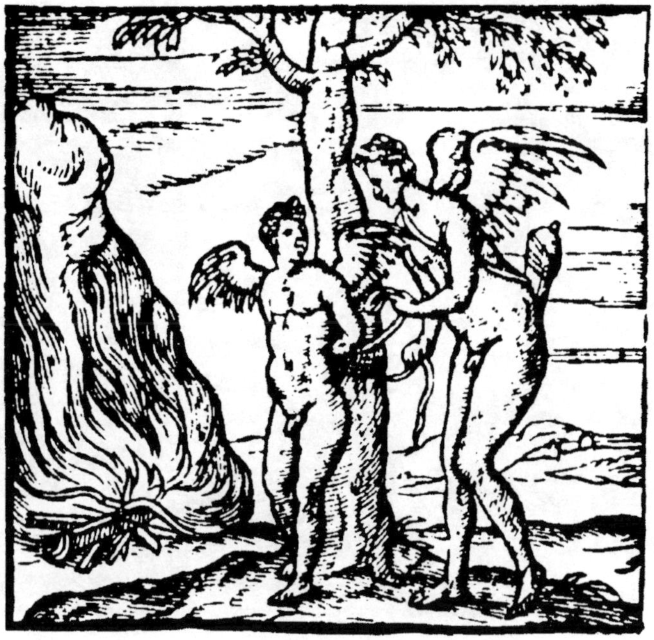

Emblema CX

ANTEROS, AMOR VIRTUTIS ALIUM CUPIDINEM SUPERANS

Aligerum, aligeroque inimicum pinxit Amori,
Arcu arcum, atque ignes igne domans Nemesis.
Ut qua diis fecit, patiatur: at hic puer olim
Intrepidus gestans tela, miser lacrimat.
Ter spuit inque sinus imos: res mira, crematur
Igne ignis, furias odit Amoris amor.

Emblem 110

ANTEROS, THE LOVE OF VIRTUE, DEFEATS THE OTHER CUPID

Nemesis [Vengeance] has painted winged Love [Cupid] as the enemy to the other winged one [Anteros]; he is punishing him, bow against bow, fire with fire, so that he suffers the same pain that he causes in others. Previously intrepid when he brandished his arrows, miserable, now this child [Cupid] weeps and spits three times upon his breast. It is an wondrous thing, when fire is consumed by fire, and [virtuous] Love abhors the madness of [sensual] love.

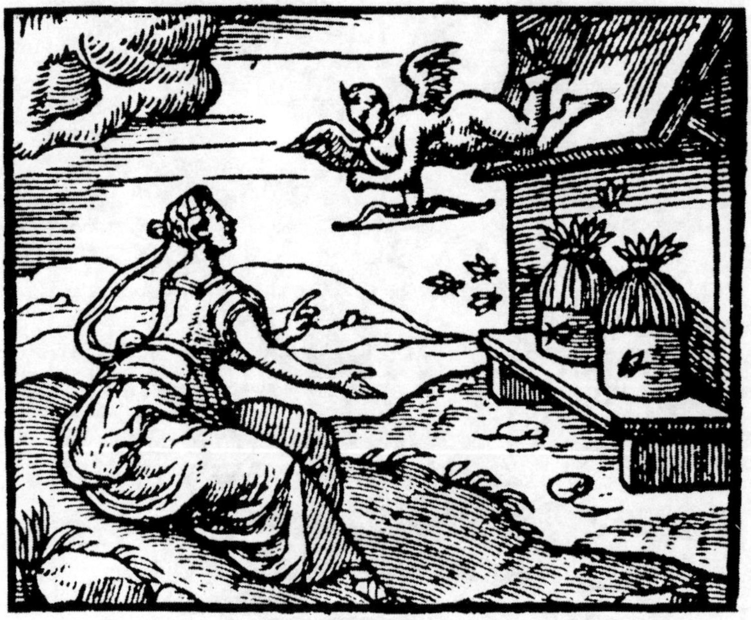

Emblema CXI

DULCIA QUANDOQUE AMARA FIERI

Matre procul licta, paullum secesserat infans
Lydius: hunc dirae sed rapuistis apes.
Venerat hic ad vos placidas ratus esse volucres,
Cum nec ita immitis vipera saeva foret.
Quae datis, ah, dulci stimulos pro munere mellis;
Pro dolor, heu, sine te gratia nulla datur!

Emblem 111

SOMETIMES SWEET THINGS TURN BITTER

Leaving behind his mother, the Lydian child [Cupid] has gone off a way on his own. And then, oh cruel bees, you attacked him. Thinking you were gentle birds, he came to you, but a viscious viper would not be not so cruel. Ah-ha! So you [bees] give stings in exchange for your a sweet gift of honey. Oh my, oh pain, nothing pleasant is ever granted without you!

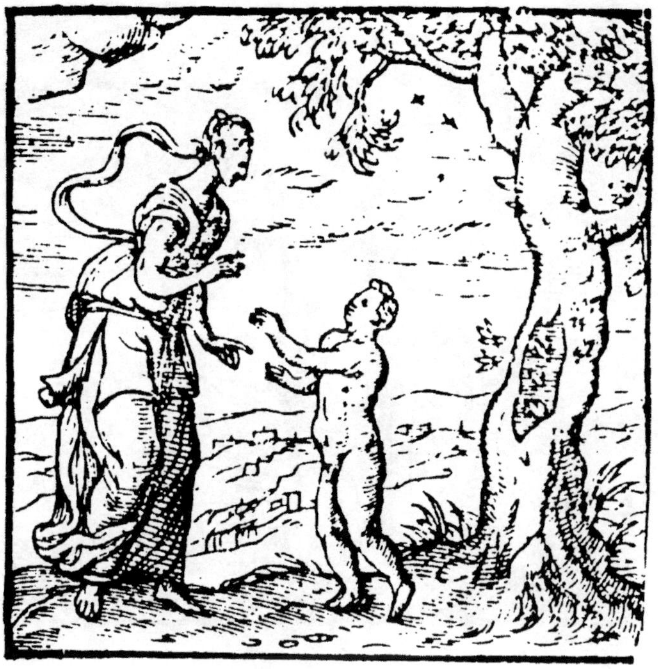

Emblema CXII

FERE SIMILE EX THEOCRITO

Alveolis dum mella legit, percussit Amorem
Furacem mala apes, et summis spicula liquit
In digitis: tumido gemit at puer anxius ungue,
Et quatit errabundus humum, Venerique dolorem
Indicat, et gravitur queritur, quod apicula parvum
Ipsa inferre animal tam noxia vulnera possit.
Cui ridens Venus, Hanc imitaris tu quoque, dixit,
Nate, feram, qui das tot noxia vulnera parvus.

Emblem 112

ALMOST LIKE IN THEOCRITUS

While Amor-Cupid, that little thief, was gathering honey from the hive, the wicked bee attacked him and stuck its stinger into his finger-tip. Tormented by the swelling under his nails, the child whined and ran about beating upon the ground. Telling Venus about his pain, he bitterly complained about how a tiny creature like the bee can cause such worrying wounds. Smiling at him, Venus says to him: "Son, you yourself imitate this creature; even though you are but small, you also inflict noxious wounds."

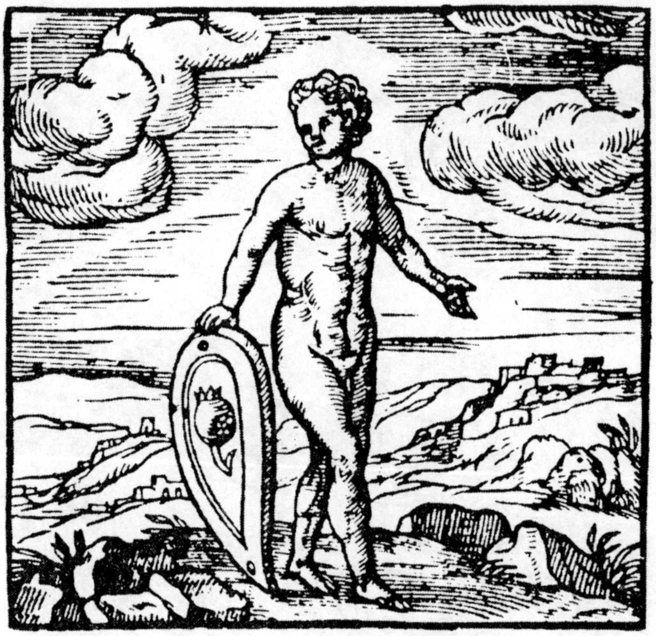

Emblema CXIII
IN STATUAM AMORIS

Quis sit Amor, plures olim cecinere Poetae,
Eius qui vario nomine gesta ferunt.
Convenit hoc, quod veste caret, quod corpore parvus,
Tela alasque ferens, lumina nulla tenet.
Haec ora hic habitusque Dei est. Sed dicere tantos
Si licet in vates, falsa subesse reor.
Et cur nudus agat? Divo quasi pallia desint,
Qui cunctas domiti possidet orbis opes?
Aut qui quaeso nives boreamque evadere nudus
Alpinum potuit, strictaque prata gelu?
Si puer est, puerumne vocas qui Nestora vincit?
An nosti Ascraei carmina docta senis?
Inconstans puer hic obdurans pectora, quae iam
Transadiit, numquam linquere sponte potest.
At pharetras et tela gerit, quid inutile pondus?
An curvare infans cornua dira valet?
Alas curve tenet quas nescit in aethera ferre?
Inscius in volucrum flectere tela iecur.
Serpit humi, semperque virum mortalia corda
Laedit, et haud alas saxeus inde movet.
Si caecus, vittamque gerit, quid taenia caeco

Utilis est? Ideo num minus ille videt?
Quisve sagittiferum credat qui lumine captus?
Hic certa, at caeci spicula vana movent.
Igneus est, aiunt, versatque in pectore flammas.
Cur age vivit adhuc? Omnia flamma vorat.
Quinetiam tumidis cur non extinguitur undis
Naiadum, quoties, mollia corda subit?
At tu ne tantis capiare erroribus, audi.
Verus quid sit Amor, carmina nostra ferent.
Iucundus labor est, lasciva per otia: signum
Illius est nigro punica glans clypeo.

Emblem 113

A STATUE OF CUPID

In former times, many poets sang about who and what Cupid might be, and they spoke of his deeds with various terminology. They are in agreement about this: he lacks clothing, he has a small body, he carries darts, and he is winged and blind. Such is the appearance and the attributes of the god. However, if it is permitted to me to speak against so many poets, I accuse them of falsehood. Why must he be shown naked? Is the god who possesses all the riches of the world really going to be lacking in clothing? Or, as I question, how could he, naked, break through the snows and winds of the Alps and across meadows frozen solid? If he is a child, how can you call a boy the one who conquered Nestor? Don't you know the learned songs of the old Ascraean [Hesiod]? This child, being fickle and inconstant, can never willfully leave those hearts into which he has already entered. But he is carrying a quiver and arrows: so why this useless weight? Is a child perhaps capable of bending a stout bow? Why does he have arched wings if he doesn't know how to use these to fly in the air? Not knowing how to shoot his arrows at the livers of birds, he instead slithers across the ground, and always wounds the mortal hearts of men. He doesn't move his wings because he is made of stone. If he is [supposedly] blind, and if he wears a rag over his eyes, then what use is a blindfold for a blind person? Does he perhaps see less because of it? And who would believe that an archer would be deprived of sight? His arrows are unerring, but the arrows of the blind miss their mark. They say that he is fiery and that he sets hearts on fire. Come on, so how can he still live? Fire devours everything. Then why was his fire not extinguished by the swollen waves of the Naiads, since he so often subdued their tender hearts? Don't let yourself get misled by so many errors. Listen: our songs tell who and what may be the true Cupid. This is a diverting task, playfulness for the leisurely: their symbol is a pomegranate on a black shield.

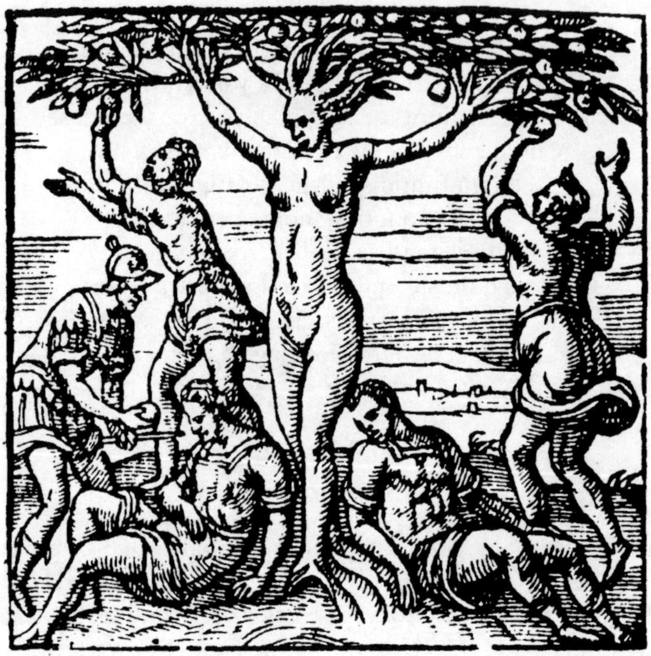

Emblema CXIV

IN OBLIVIONEM PATRIAE

Iamdudum missa patria, oblitusque tuorum,
Quos tibi seu sanguis, sive paravit amor;
Romam habitas, nec cura domum subit ulla reverti,
Aeternae tantum te capit urbis honos.
Sic Ithacum praemissa manus dulcedine loti
Liquerat et patriam, liquerat atque ducem.

Emblem 114

FORGETFUL OF THE FATHERLAND

Having abandoned the fatherland long ago, you have since forgotten about all those who had provided for you because of blood-ties or from love. Now, you now live in Rome, and have no desire to return home, so much do the charms of the Eternal City make you its captive. In the same way, a group of Ithacans sent ahead as a scouting party left behind not only their fatherland but also their leader [Ulysses], all due to the delights of the [intoxicating] lotus.

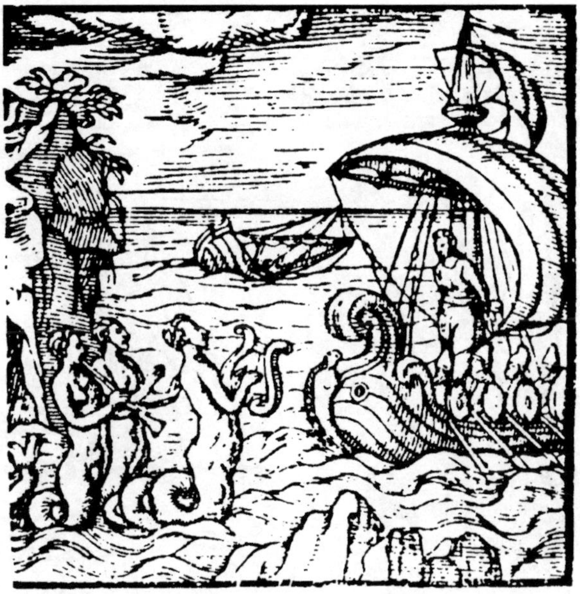

Emblema CXV

SIRENES

Absque alis volucres, et cruribus absque puellas,
Rostro absque et pisces, qui tamen ore canant,
Quis putat esse ullos? Iungi haec Natura negavit:
Sirenes fieri sed potuisse docent.
Illicium est mulier quae in piscem desinit atrum,
Plurima quod secum monstra libido vehit.
Aspectu, verbis, animi candore trahuntur,
Parthenope, Ligia, Leucosiaque viri.
Has Musae explumant, has atque illudit Ulysses:
Scilicet est doctis cum meretrice nihil.

Emblem 115

THE SIRENS

Who would ever have believed that there are such things as birds without wings, and girls without legs, and fish without a face that, nonetheless, sing through their lips? Nature refused to join together such things, but the Sirens teach that it is possible. This is a seductive woman whose lower part is a grayish fish, and that is because lust brings along with it many monsters. Men are attracted [to women] by beauty, words, and a brilliant spirit, that is, Parthenope, Ligeia and Leucosia [the three Sirens]. The Muses rip out their feathers, and Ulysses ridicules them. This signifies that learned men should have nothing whatsoever to do with whores.

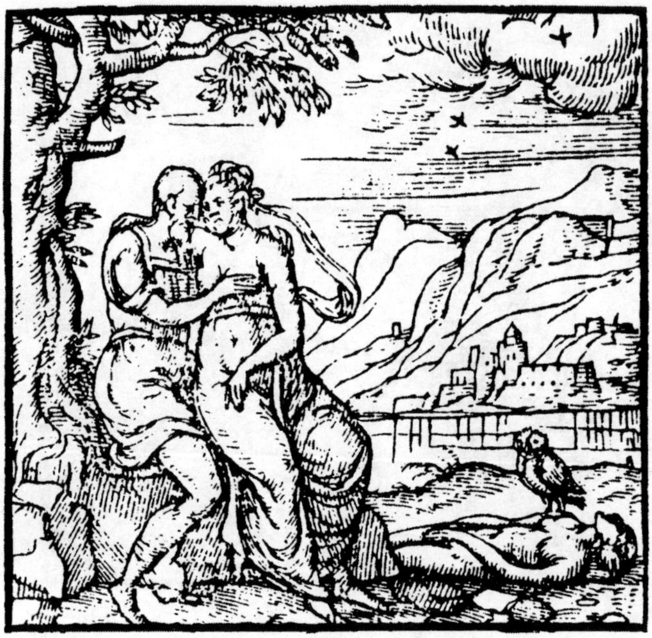

Emblema CXVI

SENEX PUELLAM AMANS

Dum Sophocles (quamvis affecta aetate) puellam
A quaestu Archippen ad sua vota trahit,
Allicit et pretio, tulit aegre insana inventus
Ob zelum, et tali carmine utrumque notat:
Noctua ut in tumulis, super utque cadavera bubo,
Talis apud Sophoclem nostra puella sedet.

Emblem 116

THE OLD MAN IN LOVE WITH A GIRL

Although advanced in years, when Sophocles enticed the girl Archippe away from prostitution to his own desires, then seducing her with money, an adolescent took it badly and, insane with jealousy, he described the couple in this poem: "Like the night-owl perched upon the tombs, and like the horned-owl standing upon cadavers, so sits our girl next to Sophocles."

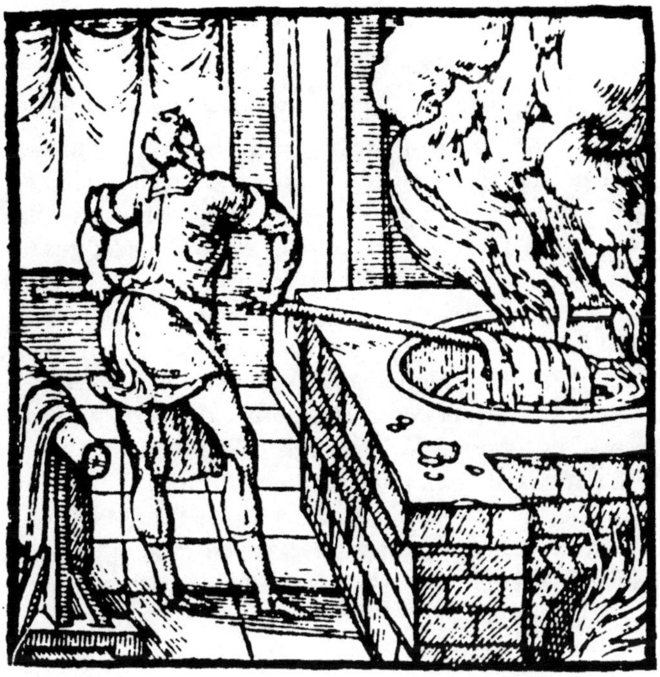

Emblema CXVII
IN COLORES

Index maestitiae est pullus color: utimur omnes
Hoc habitu, tumulis cum damus inferias:
At sinceri animi, et mentis stola candida purae:
Hinc sindon sacris linea grata viris.
Nos sperare docet viridis. Spes dicitur esse
In viridi, quoties irrita retro cadit.
Est cupidis flavus color: est et amantibus aptus,
Et scortis, et queis spes sua certa fuit.
At ruber armatos equites exornet amictus;
Indicet et pueros erubuisse pudor.
Caeruleus nautas, et qui caelestia vates
Attoniti nimia religione petunt.
Vilia sunt gilvis nativaque vellera burrhis:
Qualia lignipedes stragula habere solent.
Quem curae ingentes cruciant vel zelus amoris,
Creditur hic fulva non male veste tegi.
Quisquis sorte sua contentus ianthina gestet;
Fortunae aequanimis taedia quique ferat.
Ut varia est natura coloribus in gignendis,
Sic aliis aliud: sed sua cuique placent.

Emblem 117

ABOUT THE COLORS

The color black is a sign of sorrow: we all wear such a habit when we sacrifice at the tombs. To the contrary, white robes are the sign of the sincere soul and pure mind; hence, linen is the fabric pleasing to priests. Green teaches us to hope: it is said that hope is garbed in green, and no matter how many times hope is let down [it remains green]. Bright yellow is the color of greedy people: it is suits lovers, also whores, for their hope is assured. But let a ruby-red cloak adorn armed knights, and ruby-red also denotes the modesty which makes many boys blush. Blue is suitable for mariners and for prophets who, dazed with a surfeit of religion, seek the heavens. Low-priced are the dun-colored hoods with scarcely worked wool which cripples are accustomed to wear for cover. For those with enormous responsibilities, or to those tormented by amorous jealousy, it is believed appropriate that they cover themselves with tawny yellow clothing. Who ever may be content with his lot, he may wear violet, likewise may he who bears up to the insults of Fortune with equanimity. Just as Nature has been prodigious in the creation of colors, so do different things please different people, but what is pleasing to each is his own [color symbolism].

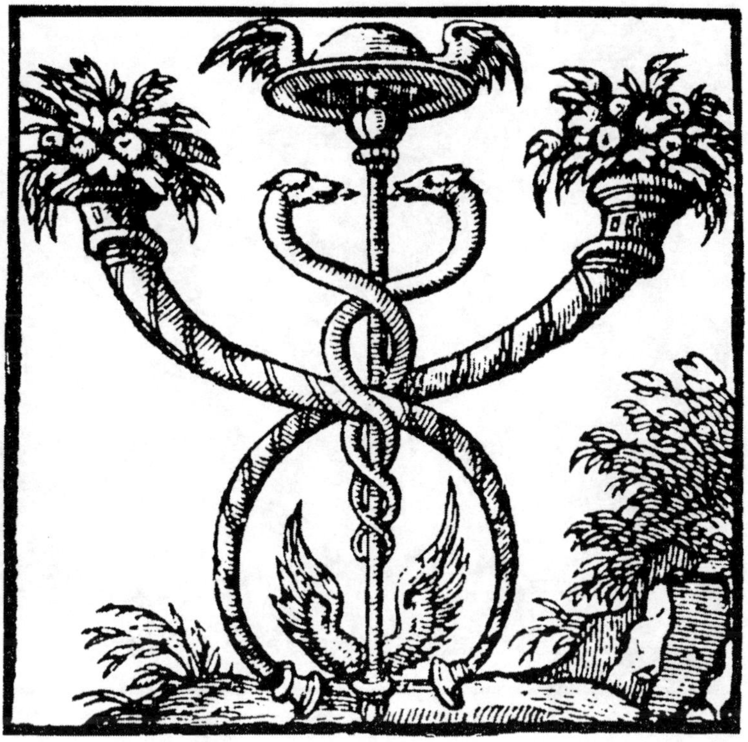

Emblema CXVIII

VIRTUTE FORTUNA COMES

Anguibus implicitis, geminis caduceus alis
Inter Amaltheae cornua rectus adest.
Pollentes sic mente viros, fandique peritos
Indicat, ut rerum copia multa beet.

Emblem 118

FORTUNE IS THE COMPANION OF VIRTUE

With its intertwined serpents and twin wings, the caduceus [or wand of Mercury] rises up between the horns [or cornucopia] of Amalthea [the goat that nursed the infant Jupiter in Crete]. This means that eloquent men with a powerful mind are favored [by Fortune] with abundance.

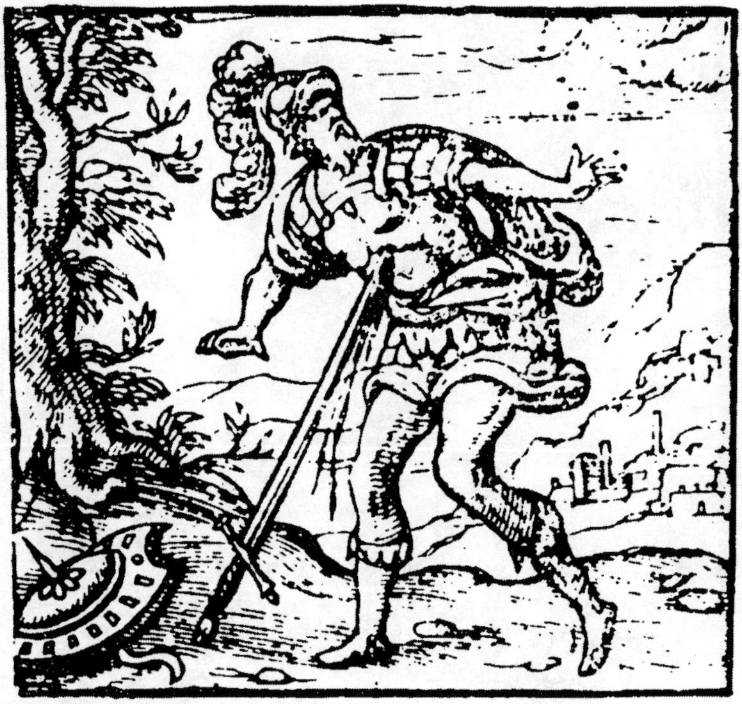

Emblema CXIX

FORTUNA VIRTUTEM SUPERANS

Caesareo postquam superatus milite, vidit
Civili undantem sanguine Pharsaliam;
Iam iam stricturus moribunda in pectora ferrum,
Audaci hos Brutus protulit ore sonos:
Infelix virtus, et solis provida verbis,
Fortunam in rebus cur sequeris dominam?

Emblem 119

FORTUNE DEFEATS VIRTUE

After being overcome by the troops of Cesar [Augustus], Brutus saw Pharsalia awash in the blood of its citizens; then drawing the steel to his moribund chest, he pronounced these words with a bold mouth: "Oh unhappy virtue, only caring for words, why do you only follow Fortune as your mistress in events?"

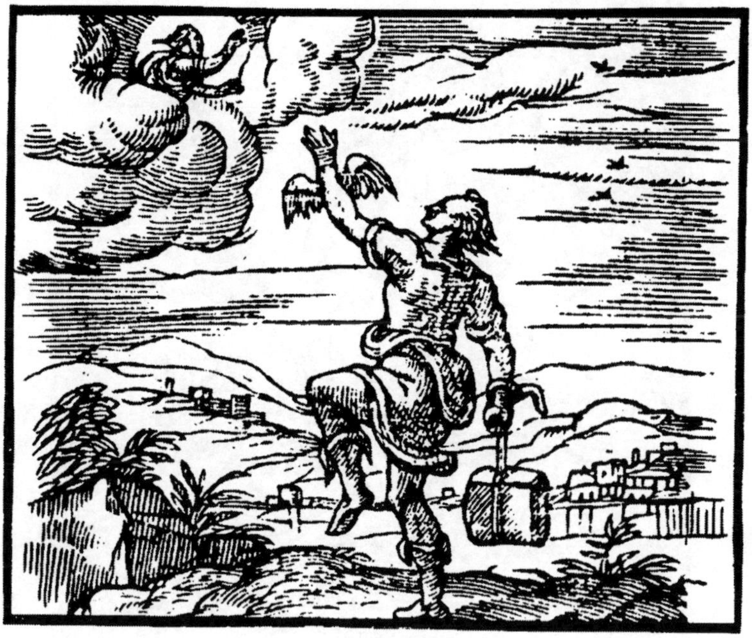

Emblema CXX

PAUPERTATEM SUMMIS INGENIIS OBESSE NE PROVEHANTUR

Dextra tenet lapidem, manus altera sustinet alas:
Ut me pluma levat, sic grave mergit onus.
Ingenio poteram superas volitare per arces,
Me nisi paupertas invida deprimeret.

Emblem 120

POVERTY BRINGS DOWN THE BEST MINDS, HINDERING THEIR PROGRESS

A stone hangs from his right hand, but the left hand is winged: [as he complains], "While the feather does lift me, so am I [also] buried by a heavy weight. By means of my innate talent I could fly around the highest citadels, that is, were I not oppressed by an inopportune poverty."

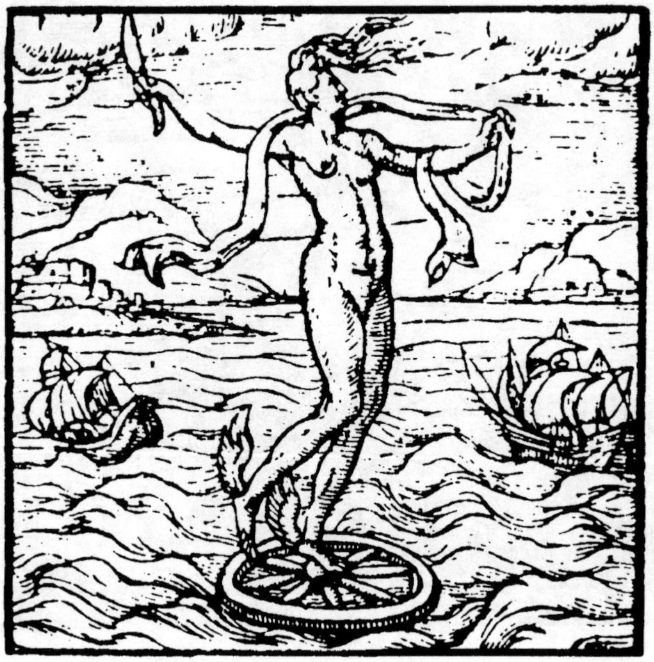

Emblema CXXI

IN OCCASIONEM

Dialogismus

Lysippi hoc opus est, Sicyon cui patria. Tu quis?
Cuncta domans capti temporis articulus.
Cur pinnis stas? Usque rotor. Talaria plantis
Cur retines? Passim me levis aura rapit.
In dextra est tenuis dic unde novacula? Acutum
Omni acie hoc signum me magis esse docet.
Cur in fronte coma? Occurrens ut prendar. At heu: tu
Dic cur pars calva est posterior capitis?
Me semel alipedem si quis permittat abire,
Ne possim apprenso postmodo crine capi.
Tali opifex nos arte, tui causa edidit, hospes:
Utque omnes moneam, pergula aperta tenet.

Emblem 121
ABOUT CHANCE
(a dialogue)

This is the work of [the sculptor] Lysippus of Sicyon. "You, who are you?" "I am that captured instant of time that dictates all things." "Why are you standing on wheels?" "Because I am continually turning around." "Why do you have [winged] sandals on your feet?" "So that even the slightest breeze may rush me about." "Tell me, why you hold in your right hand a sharpened razor?" "This sign teaches that I am sharper than all [mental] sharpness." "Why do you have a lock of hair on your forehead?" "So that I [Chance] may be seized when I [choose to] present myself." "Oh my! Tell me, why then is the back of your head bald?" "If sometime, perchance, somebody ever allows me to escape on my winged feet, then he can't catch me again by grabbing my hair. Oh stranger, know that the artist made me with such artifice, then placing me inside an open gallery, so that I might serve as a warning to all."

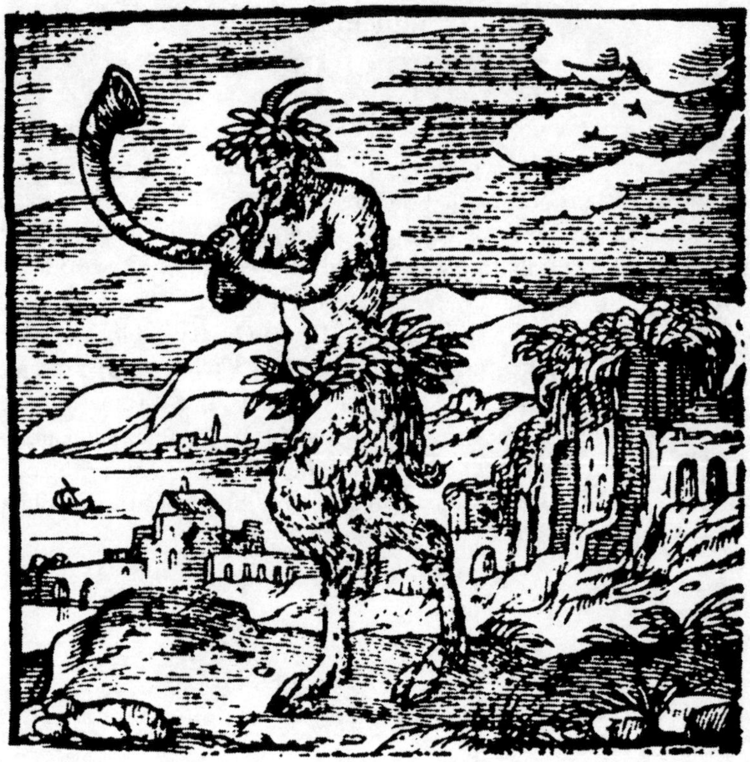

Emblema CXXII

IN SUBITUM TERROREM

Effuso cernens fugientes agmine turmas,
Quis mea nunc inflat cornua? Faunus ait.

Emblem 122

SUDDEN TERROR

Seeing troops who were fleeing in disorder, the Faun [Pan] said, "Who is now blowing my horn [of panic]?"

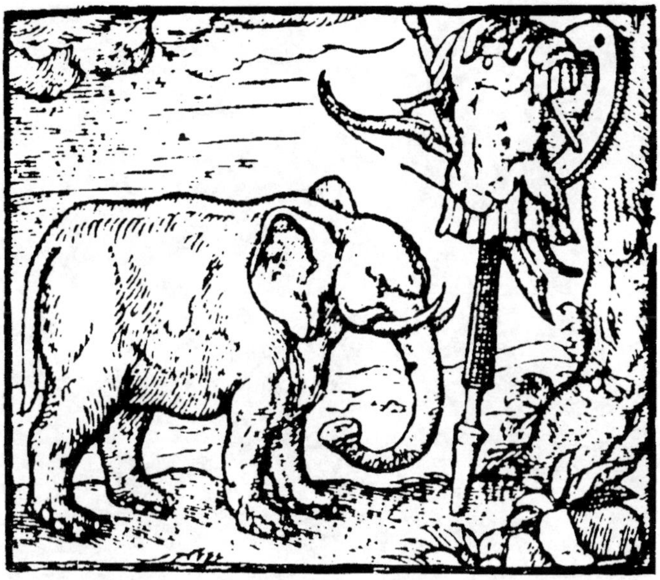

Emblema CXXIII

IN ILLAUDATA LAUDANTES

Ingentes Galatum semermi milite turmas,
Spem praeter trepidus fuderat Antiochus:
Lucarum cum saeva boum vis, ira, proboscis,
Tum primum hostiles corripuisset equos.
Ergo trophaea locans Elephantis imagine pinxit,
Insuper et sociis, Occideramus ait,
Bellua servasset ni nos foedissima barrus:
Ut superasse iuvat, sic superasse pudet.

Emblem 123

AGAINST THOSE WHO PRAISE WHAT IS NOT PRAISEWORTHY

Alarmed, and with his badly-armed army facing the overwhelming forces of the Galatians, Antiochus had abandoned all hope. At that moment, the enemy cavalry was first taken by surprise by the savage fury, the anger and the trunks of his [hidden] battle elephants. For that reason, when Antiochus set up his trophies, he had them painted with the image of an elephant, and above it is inscribed: "We and our allies would have been killed, had not an elephant, a detestable beast, saved us." While it may be pleasing to survive, to win in this way is shameful.

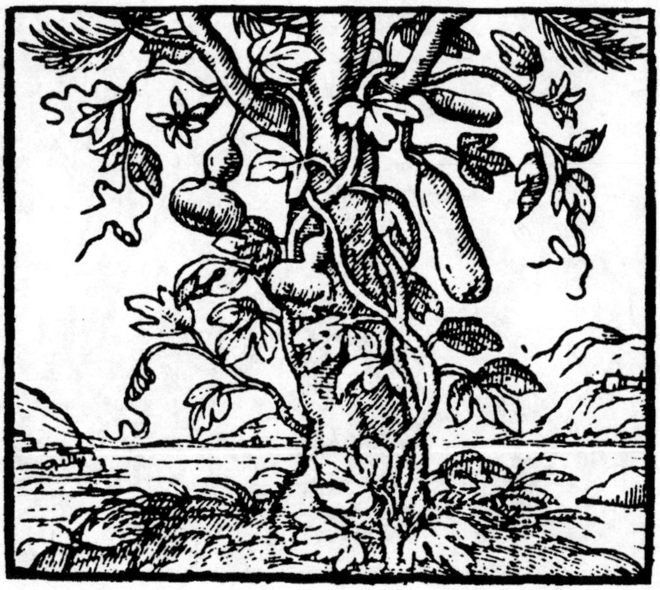

Emblema CXXIV

IN MOMENTANEAM FELICITATEM

Aeream propter crevisse cucurbita pinum
Dicitur, et grandi luxuriasse coma:
Cum ramos complexa, ipsumque egressa cacumen.
Se praestare aliis credidit arboribus.
Cui pinus, Nimium brevis est haec gloria: nam te
Protinus adveniet, quae male perdet, hiems.

Emblem 124

ABOUT FLEETING HAPPINESS

It is said that a gourd grew beside a lofty pine-tree, and that its foliage was fast-growing. Embracing the tree with its branches, it climbed to the very top, and so it believed that it was superior to all the other trees. The pine said to it, "This glory is all too brief, for winter will implacably come upon you, then causing [us] utter ruin."

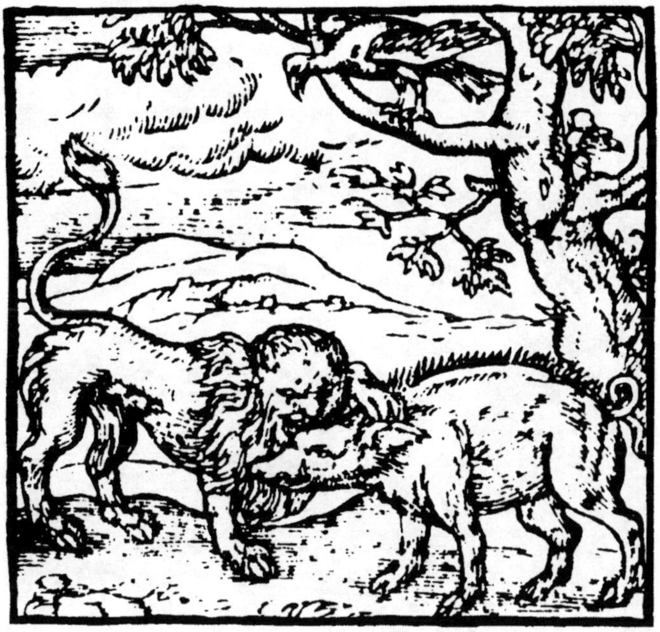

Emblema CXXV

EX DAMNO ALTERIUS, ALTERIUS UTILITAS

Dum saevis ruerent in mutua vulnere telis,
Ungue leaena ferox, dente timentius aper,
Accurrit vultur spectatum, et prandia captat.
Gloria victoris, praeda futura sua est.

Emblem 125

ONE PERSON'S LOSS IS ANOTHER'S GAIN

While they mutually wounded one another with their cruel weapons, the ferocious lion with his claws and the fearsome boar with his tusks, the vulture rushes in to watch, and so he gets his meal. Glory may go to the victor [either lion or boar], but the prey forthcoming becomes his [the vulture].

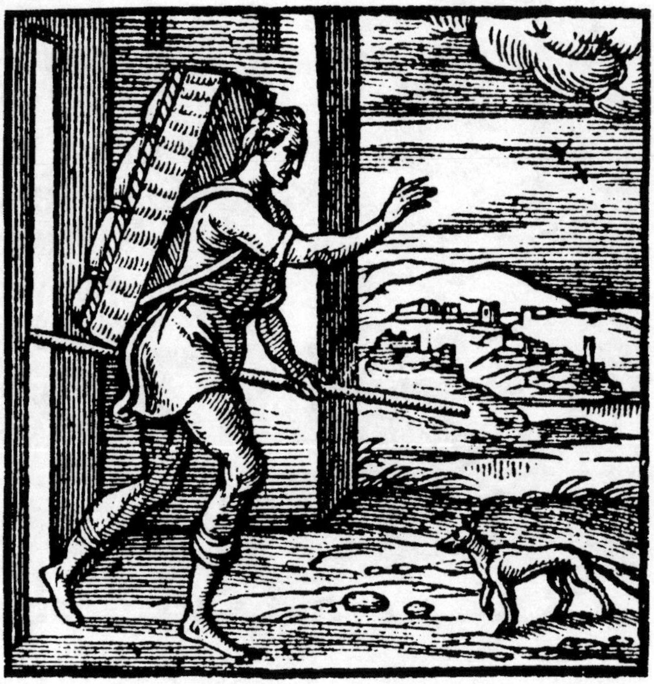

Emblema CXXVI

BONIS AUSPICIIS INCIPIENDUM

Auspiciis res coepta malis, bene cedere nescit.
Felici quae sunt omine facta, iuvant.
Quidquid agis, mustela tibi si occurrant, omitte:
Signa malae haec sortis bestia prava gerit.

Emblem 126

ONE MUST BEGIN WITH FAVORABLE AUSPICES

Something begun under bad auspices does not end well. Things done with favorable omens bring benefits. Whatever it was that you intended to do, abandon it should you come across a weasel: this vicious animal is a sign of bad luck.

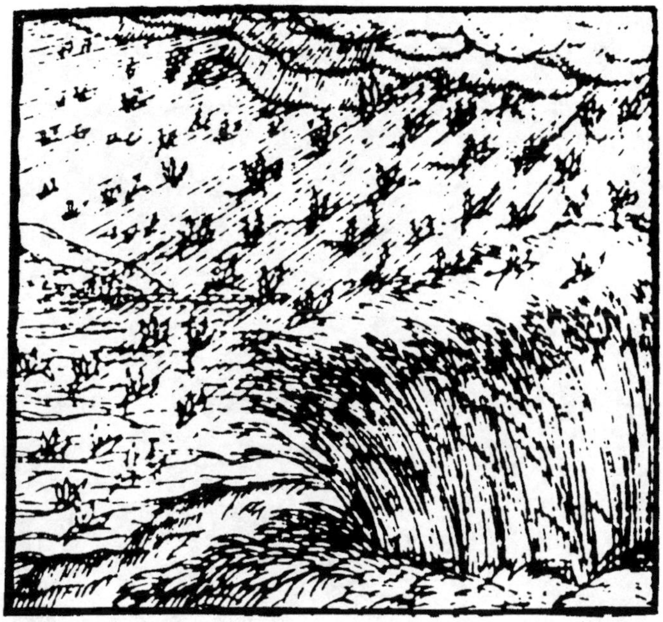

Emblema CXXVII

NIHIL RELIQUI

Scilicet hoc deerat post tot mala, denique nostris
Locusta ut raperent quicquid inesset agris.
Vidimus innumeras Euro duce tendere turmas,
Qualia non Atylae castrave Xerxis erant.
Hae faenum, milium, farra omnia consumpserunt.
Spes et in angusto est, stant nisi vota super.

Emblem 127

NOTHING IS LEFT

After so many misfortunes, this was the last thing we lacked, that the locusts would finally lay waste to what remained in our fields. Carried upon Euro [the east wind], we have seen countless swarms of these come swooping down; not such as these were the garrisons of Attila or Xerxes. They devoured it all: hay, millet and wheat. Hope finds itself reduced; only prayer remains.

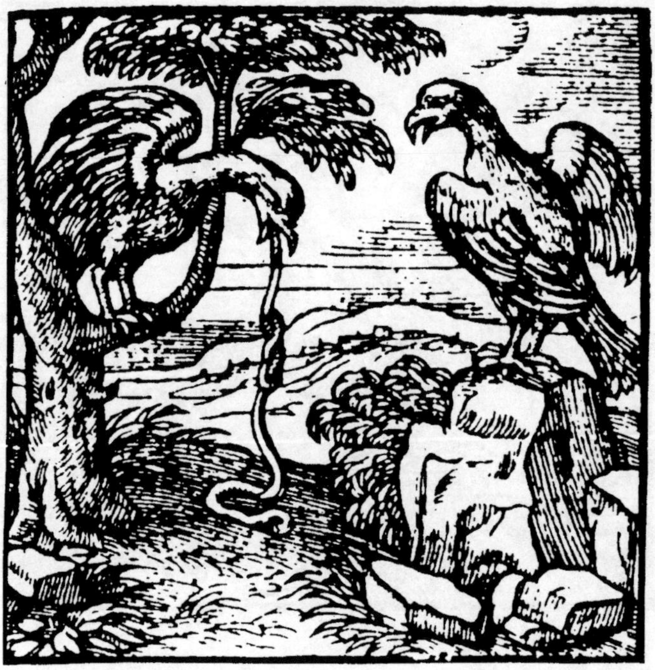

Emblema CXXVIII

MALE PARTA, MALE DILABUNTUR

Milvus edex, nimiae quem nausea torserat escae,
Hei mihi, mater, ait, viscera ab ore fluunt.
Illa autem, Quid fles? Cur haec tua viscera credas,
Qui rapto vivens sola aliena vomis?

Emblem 128

BADLY PREPARED, BADLY DISPERSED

A gluttonouos kite, nauseated from overeating, said, "Oh woe is me; oh mother, my guts are coming out of my mouth." And she responded, "What are you complaining about? Since you only live by theft, how you believe that what you are vomiting out is anything but the guts of another?"

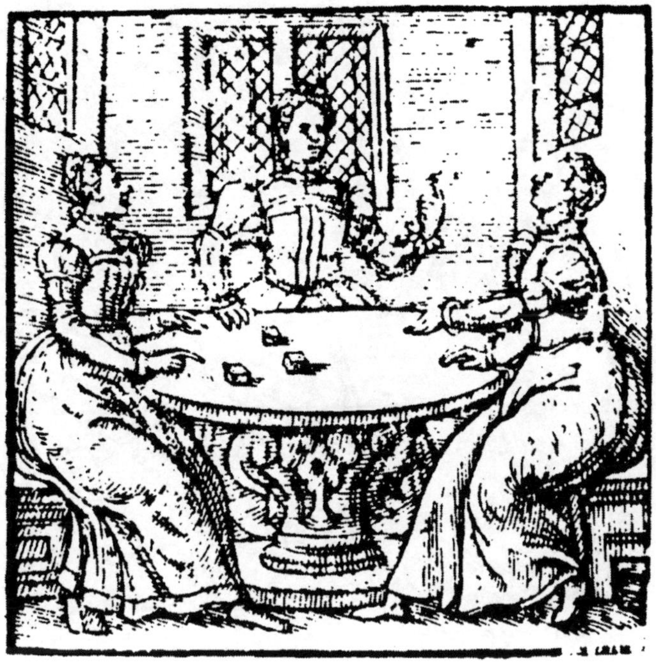

Emblema CXXIX

SEMPER PRAESTO ESSE INFORTUNIA

Ludebant parili tres olim aetate puellae
Sortibus, ad Stygias quae prior iret aquas.
At cui iactato male cesserat alea talo,
Ridebat sortis caeca puella suae:
Cum subito icta caput labente est mortua tecto,
Solvit et audacis debita fata ioci.
Rebus in adversis mala sors non fallitur: ast in
Faustis, nec precibus, nec locus est manui.

Emblem 129

MISFORTUNE IS ALWAYS AT HAND

Three girls of the same age were playing a game of chance to determine which of them would be the first to go to the Stygian waters [or to die]. Ignorant of her fate, the one indicated by the malicious throw of the dice laughed. Suddenly, struck on the head by a collapsing roof, she was struck dead, so paying fate what was due for her bold jest. In adverse affairs, bad luck is never eluded. However, in relation to auspicious events, no effort need be placed, not even prayer.

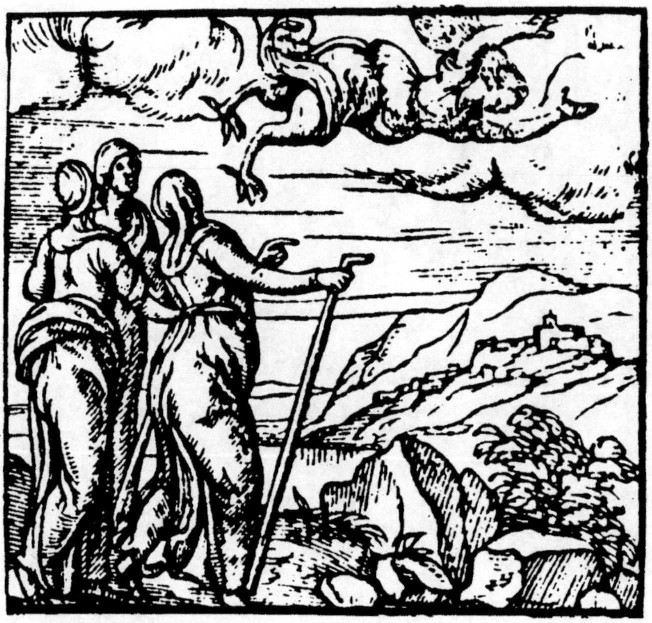

Emblema CXXX

REMEDIA, IN ARDUO, MALA IN PRONO ESSE

Aetheriis postquam deiecit sedibus Aten
Iupiter, heu, vexat quam mala noxa viros!
Evolat haec pedibus celer et pernicibus alis,
Intactumque nihil casibus esse sinit.
Ergo Litae, proles Iovis, hanc comitantur euntem,
Sarturae quidquid fecerit illa mali.
Sed quia segnipedes, luscae, lassaeque senecta,
Nil nisi post longo tempore restituunt.

Emblem 130

A REMEDY ARRIVES WITH DIFFICULTY, EVIL WITH EASE

Ever since Jupiter ejected Ate [Discord] from the heavenly throne — oh my!— how many misfortunes have vexed mankind! Ate flies with nimble feet and swift wings, and she leaves nothing untouched by misfortunate chance. Therefore, the Litae, the daughters of Jupiter, follow wherever she goes in order to mend whatever disasters she provokes. However, since they are slow-footed, half-blind and fatigued by age, they only repair things after much time has passed.

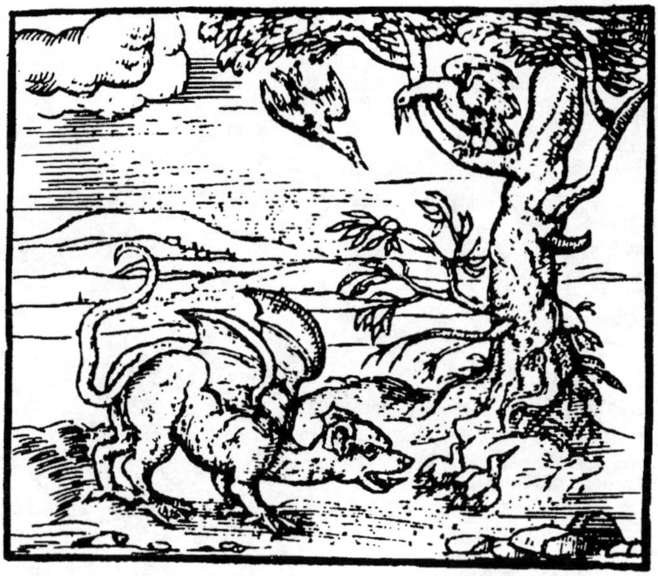

Emblema CXXXI

EX ARDUIS PERPETUUM NOMEN

Crediderat platani ramis sua pignora passer
Et bene, ni saevo visa dracone forent.
Glutiit hic pullos omnes, miseramuque parentem
Saxeus, et tali dignus obire nece.
Haec, nisi mentitur Calchas, monimenta laboris
Sunt longi, cuius fama perennis eat.

Emblem 131

PERPETUAL FAME COMES FROM ARDUOUS TASKS

A sparrow confided its offspring to the branches of the plane-tree, and that would have been well, that is, had they not have been espied by the cruel serpent. It swallowed up all the chicks and also their hapless mother. Deserving such a death, the dragon was changed into stone . Such things, if Calchas does not lie [in his predictions about the fall of Troy], are forewarnings of an extended task, the fame of which will be eternal.

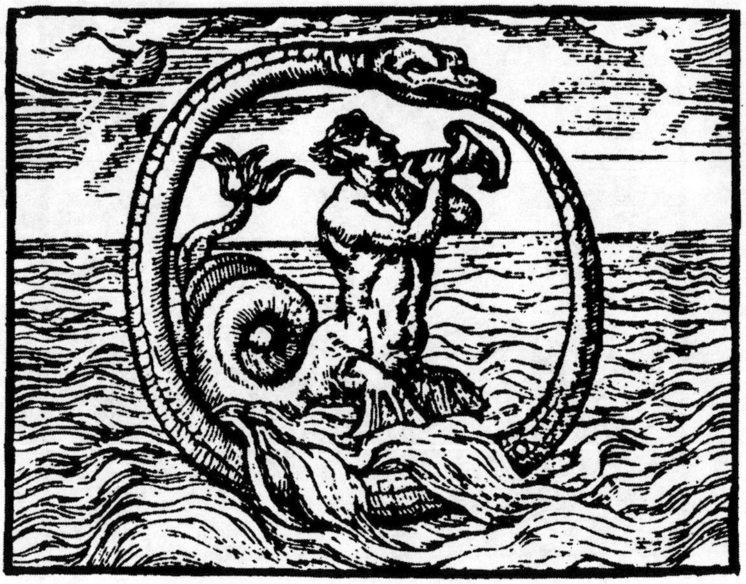

Emblema CXXXII

EX LITTERARUM STUDIIS IMMORTALITATEM ACQUIRI

Neptuni tubicen (cuius pars ultima cetum,
Aequoreum facies indicat esse deum)
Serpentis medio Triton comprenditur orbe,
Qui caudam inserto mordicus ore tenet.
Fama viros animo insignes, praeclaraque gesta
Prosequitur, toto mandat et orbe legi.

Emblem 132

IMMORTALITY IS ACQUIRED THROUGH HUMANISTIC STUDY

Triton, the trumpeter of Neptune, whose lower part is shaped like a fish, and with a countenance indicating that he is a marine god, is shown in the middle of a circle formed by a serpent which, biting, holds its tail inserted within its mouth. Fame accompanies men of outstanding talent, demanding that their illustrious deeds be read about throughout the world.

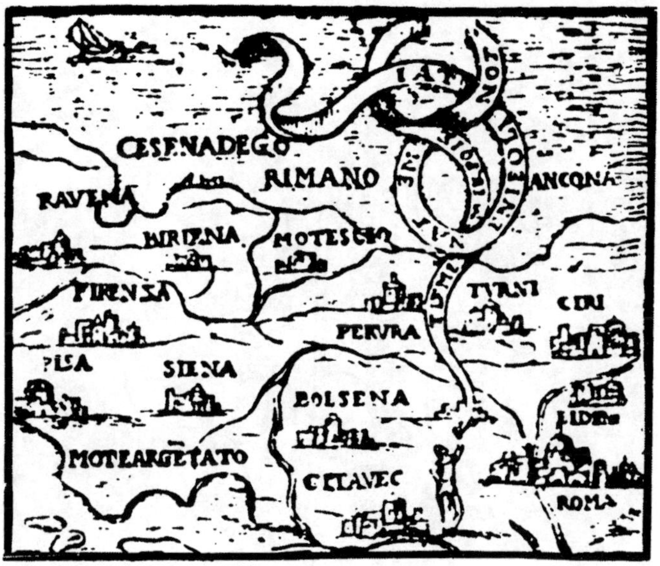

Emblema CXXXIII

TUMULUS IOANNIS GALEACII VICECOMITIS, PRIMI DUCIS MEDIOLANENSIS

Pro tumulo pone Italiam, pone arma ducesque,
Et mare, quod geminos mugit adusque sinus.
Adde his Barbariem conantem irrumpere frustra,
Et mercede emptas in fera bella manus.
Anguiger est summo sistens in culmine, dicat:
Quis parvis magnum me super imposuit?

Emblem 133

THE TOMB OF GIANGALEAZZO VISCONTI, FIRST DUKE OF MILAN

Instead of a tomb, show Italy, and the sea which roars from one gulf to the other; put upon it leaders and weapons. Add to these the [Turkish] Barbarians vainly trying to invade [Italy] with mercenary troops bought for their savage wars. And above [the map of Italy] hang a snake-bearing inscription which says: "Who placed me, who is so great, above such small things?"

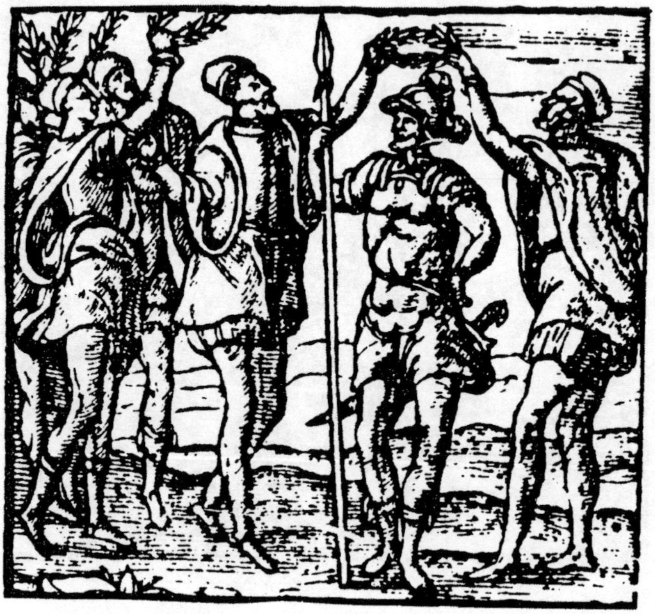

Emblema CXXXIV
OPTIMUS CIVIS

Dum iustis patriam Thrasibulus vindicat armis,
Dumque simultates ponere quemque iubet,
Concors ordo omnis, magni instar muneris, illi
Palladiae sertum frondis habere dedit.
Cinge comam, Thrasibule, geras hunc solus honorem:
In magna nemo est aemulus urbe tibi.

Emblem 134
THE OPTIMUM CITIZEN

When just Thrasibulus returns vindicated by his arms to the homeland [Athens], then ordering one and another to lay aside their rivalries, all the people agree to award him, as the maximum prize, the olive-wreath of Pallas. Place it upon your locks, oh Thrasibulus, and you alone may wear this honor, for there is nobody in the great city to equal you.

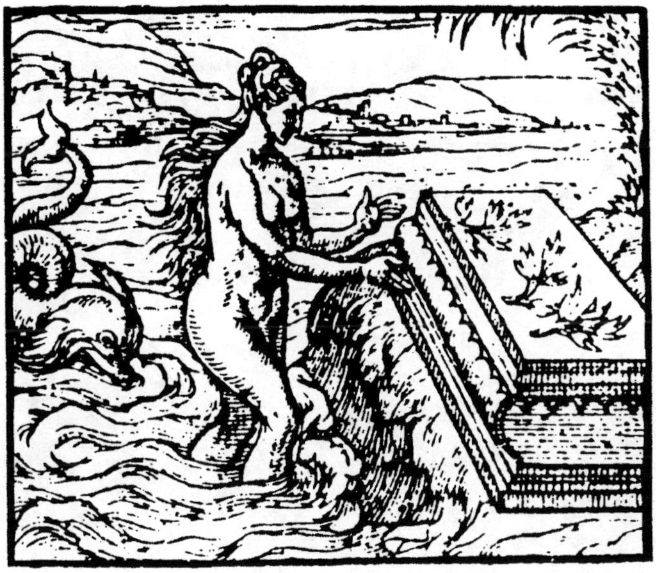

Emblema CXXXV

STRENUORUM IMMORTALE NOMEN

Aecidae tumulum Rhaetaeo in littore cernis,
Quem plerumque pedes visitat alba Thetis.
Obtegitur semper viridi lapis hic amarantho;
Quod numquam herois sit moriturus honos.
Hic Graium murus, magni nex Hectoris. Haud plus
Debet Maeonidae, quam sibi Maeonides.

Emblem 135

THE NAME OF THE STRENUOUS ONE IS IMMORTAL

The tomb of Achilles, placed upon the Rhaetean coast, is often visited by white-footed Thetis. Since the glory of a hero must never die, the lid is always covered with green amaranth. Here lies the bulwark of the Greeks, the slayer of the great Hector. No more does he owe to the Meonian [Homer, for immortalizing his name] than Homer owes to him [Achilles].

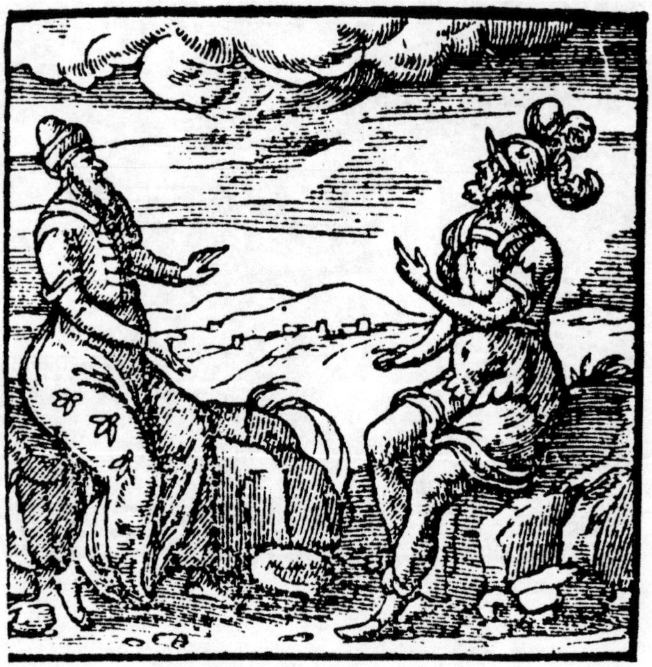

Emblema CXXXVI
NOBILES ET GENEROSI

Aurea Cecropias nectebat fibula vestes,
Cui coniuncta tenax dente cicada fuit:
Calceus, Arcadico suberat cui lunula ritu
Gestatur patribus mullea Romulidis.
Indigenas quod se adsererent, haec signa tulerunt
Antiqua illustres nobilitate viri.

Emblem 136
THE NOBLE AND EMINENT

The Cecropians [Athenians] wore a golden fibula; shaped like a cicada, it pinned their clothes together with its tenacious tooth. It was the custom among the Arcadians to place a little moon upon the upper part of their shoes, and Roman patricians wore it on their footwear. To show that they are native-born, and as ancient signs of nobility, illustrious men bore these signs.

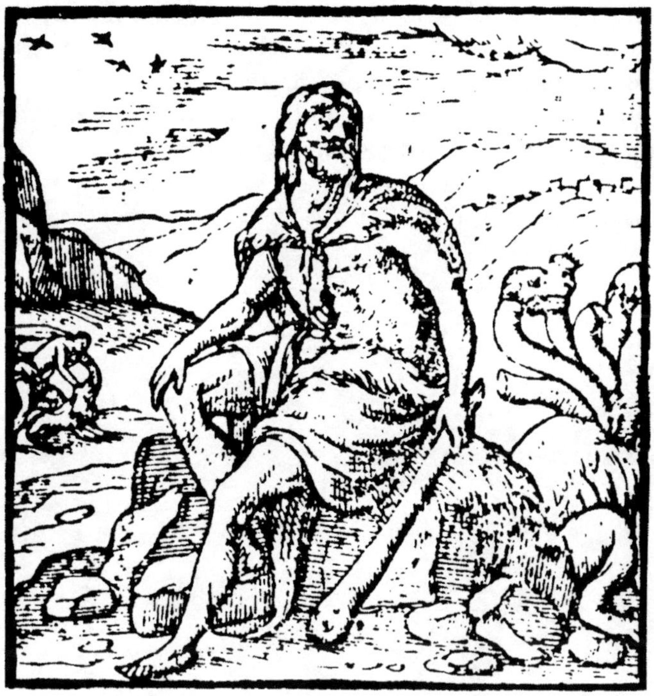

Emblema CXXXVII

DUODECIM CERTAMINA HERCULIS

Roboris invicti superat facundia laudes:
Dicta sophistarum, laqueosque resolvit inanes:
Non furor aut rabies virtute potentior ulla est:
Continuum obscursum sapienti opulentia cedit:
Spernit avaritiam, nec rapto faenore gaudet;
Vincit femineos spoliatque insignibus astus:
Expurgat sordes, et cultum mentibus addit:
Illicitos odit coitus, abigitque nocentes:
Barbaries feritasque dat impia denique poenam:
Unius virtus collectos dissipat hostes:
Invehit in patriam externis bona plurima ab oris:
Docta per ora virum volat, et non interit unquam.

Emblem 137

THE TWELVE LABORS OF HERCULES

Eloquence surpasses praise for invincible strength. It [Hercules and/or eloquence] unties the vain snares and inane sayings of the sophists, and neither fury nor anger are more powerful than virtue. Wealth comes to the wise man due to his unremitting zeal. Virtue spurns avarice and takes no pleasure in robbery or usury. Virtue conquers feminine deceit and pillages their regalia. It cleans filth and augments the cultivation of the mind. It loathes unlawful coitus and drives away evil doers. Barbarism and impious savagery finally pay the penalty. The virtue of a single person disperses the collective enemies. He [Hercules] brings to the homeland great wealth from distant regions. His name flies from the mouths of the learned and it [his fame] shall never die.

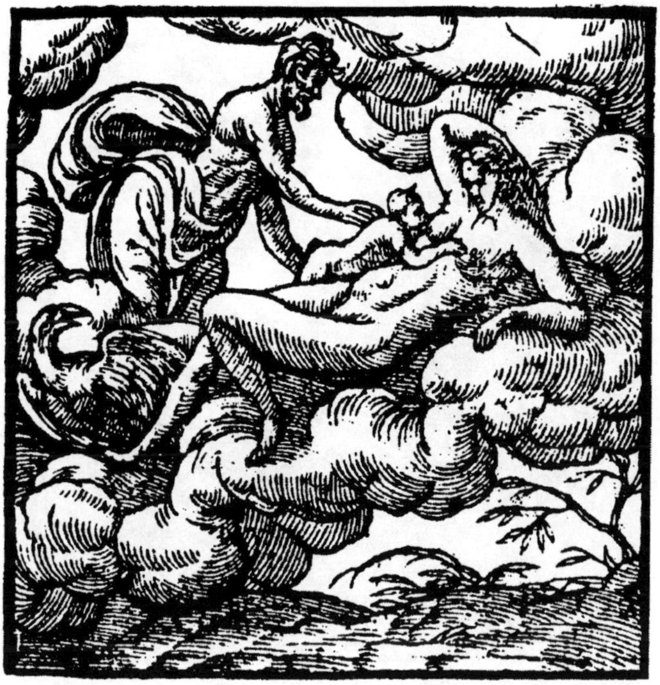

Emblema CXXXVIII

IN NOTHOS

Herculeos spurii semper celebretis honores:
Nam vestri Princeps ordinis ille fuit.
Nec prius esse Deus potuit, quam sugeret infans
Lac, sibi quod fraudis nescia Iuno dabat.

Emblem 138

AGAINST BASTARDS

Oh bastards, forever celebrate the honor of Hercules for he was the first of your spurious race. He couldn't become a god until he sucked the milk which Juno, unaware of her deception [by Jupiter and Alcmena], gave to him as a child.

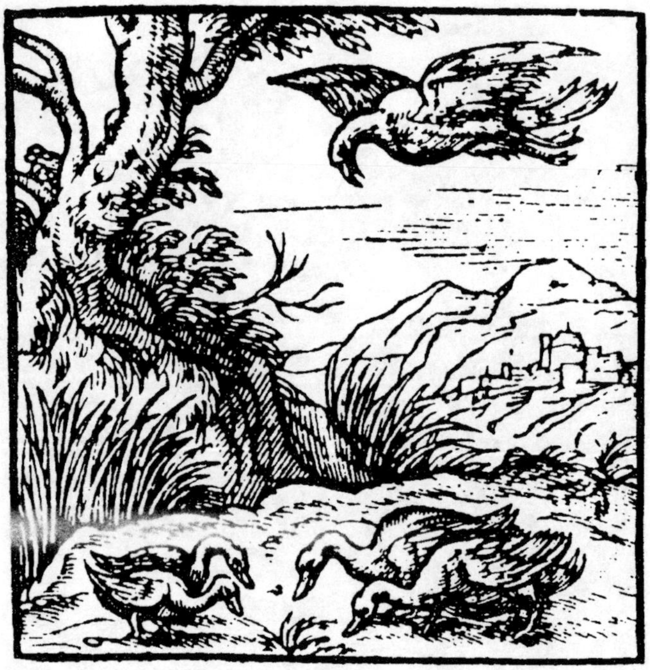

Emblema CXXXIX

IMPARILITAS

Ut sublime volans tenuem secat aera falco;
Ut pascuntur humi graculus, anser, anas:
Sic summum scandit super aethera Pindarus ingens;
Sic scit humi tantum serpere Bacchylides.

Emblem 139

INEQUALITY

Flying high, the falcon cuts through the thin air; meanwhile, the jackdaw, goose and duck feed upon the ground. In the same way, mighty Pindar ascends beyond the highest heaven, and Bacchylides [a clumsy poet] only knows how to slither upon the ground.

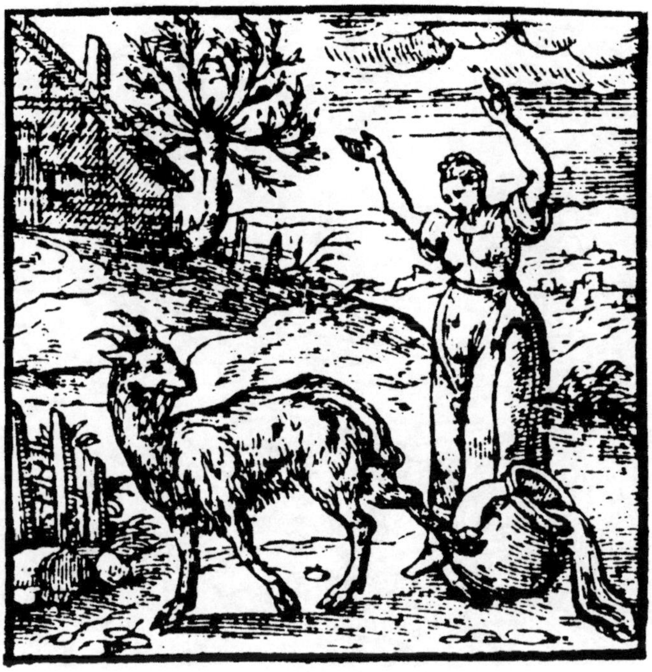

Emblema CXL

IN DESCISCENTES

Quod fine egregios turpi maculaveris orsus,
In noxamque tuum verteris officium;
Fecisti quod capra, sui mulctralia lactis
Cum ferit, et proprias calce profundit opes.

Emblem 140

AGAINST DISSENTERS

Because you besmirched some excellent beginnings with a final clumsy act, hence so you have overturned your proper duties, making them harmful. You have acted like the goat does when it kicks over the milk-pail with its hoof and spills its own riches.

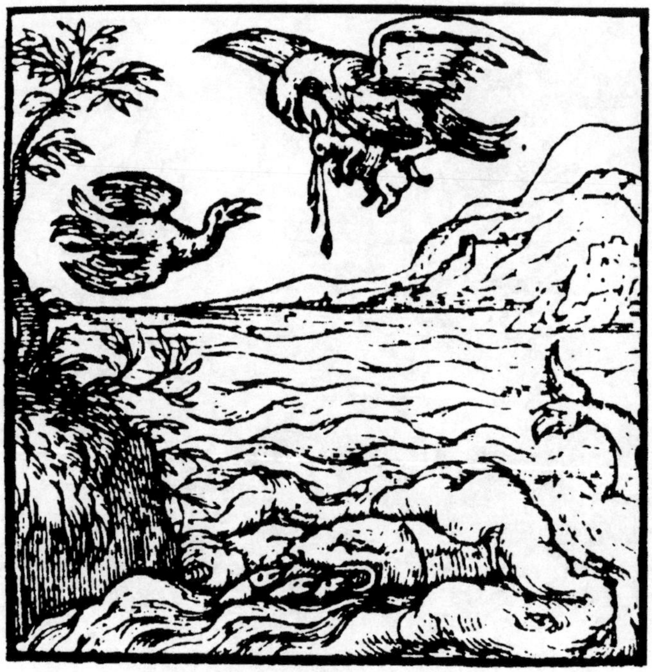

Emblema CXLI

AEMULATIO IMPAR

Altivolam milvus comitatur degener harpem,
Et praedae partem saepe cadentis habet.
Mullum persequitur, qui spretas sargus ab illo
Praeteritasque avidus devorat ore dapes.
Sic mecum Oenocrates agit: at deserta studentum
Utitur hoc lippo curia tamquam oculo.

Emblem 141

UNEQUAL RIVALRY

The degenerate kite accompanies the high-flying harpy-eagle, and often gets part of the falling scraps. The bream pursues the red mullet and avidly devours the meals rejected and left behind by it. The same is done to me [Alciati] by Oenocrates [the wine tippler]: in the lecture-halls abandoned by the students that bleary, half-blinded man is used as an eye.

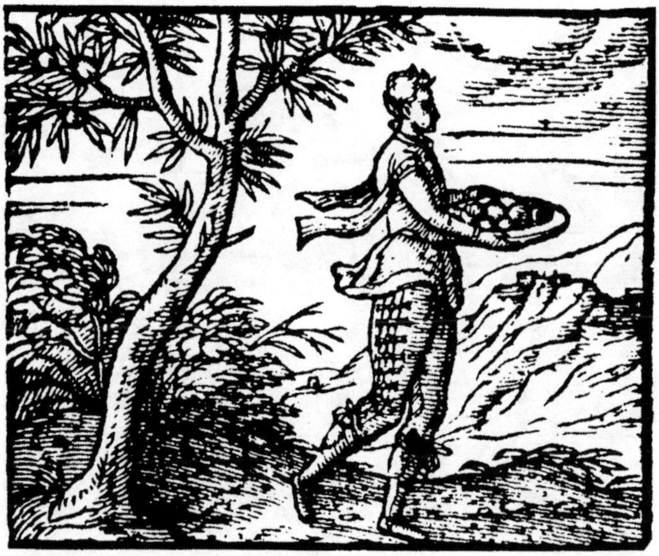

Emblema CXLII

ALBUTII AD D. ALCIATUM SUADENTIS, UT DE TUMULTIBUS ITALICIS SE SUBDUCAT, ET IN GALLIA PROFITEATUR

Quae dedit hos fructus arbor, caelo advena nostro,
Venit ab Eoo Persidis axe prius.
Translatu facta est melior, quae noxia quondam
In patria, hic nobis dulcia poma gerit.
Fert folium linguae, fert poma simillima cordi:
Alciate hinc vitam degere disce tuam.
Tu procul a patria in pretio es maiore futurus;
Multum corde sapis, nec minus ore vales.

Emblem 142

ALBUTIUS CONVINCING ALCIATI TO LEAVE BEHIND THE CHAOS IN ITALY AND TO TEACH IN FRANCE

A foreigner beneath our sky, the first tree which gave these fruits [peaches] came from eastern Persia. Previously poisonous in its homeland, the move improved it, and here it provides for us sweet fruit. Its leaves are tongue-shaped and its fruits look like a heart. Oh Alciati, learn from this how to live your life; in a distant land, you will be more valued than in your homeland. You are very wise in your heart, and your tongue is valued no less.

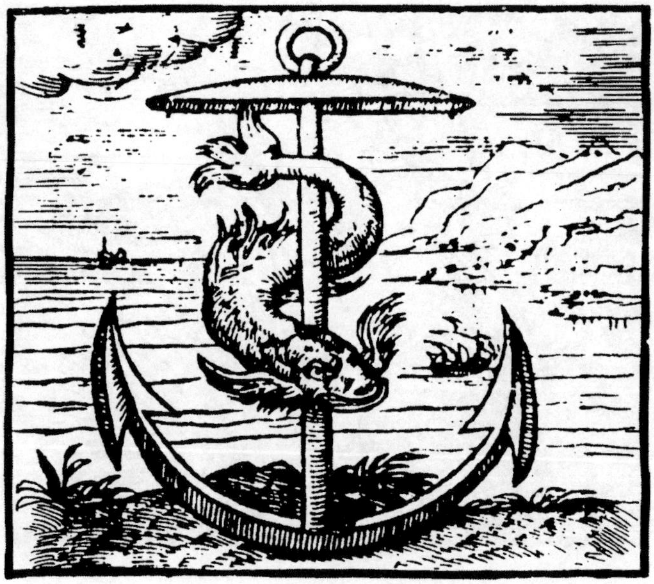

Emblema CXLIII

PRINCEPS SUBDITORUM INCOLUMITATEM PROCURANS

Titanii quoties conturbant aequora fratres,
Tum miseros nautos ancora iacta iuvat:
Hanc pius erga homines Delphin complectitur, imis
Tutius ut possit figier illa vadis.
Quam decet haec memores gestare insignia Reges.
Ancora quod nautis, se populo esse suo!

Emblem 143

THE PRINCE WHO ATTENDS TO THE SECURITY OF HIS SUBJECTS

As long as the Titans brothers [the winds] perturb the waters, an anchor is to be thrown out as an aid to the wretched sailors. The dolphin, devoted to men, wraps himself around the it so that it will be anchored more securely within the depths. It is proper that kings should remember to wear this device. What the anchor is for the sailors, kings should be to their own people!

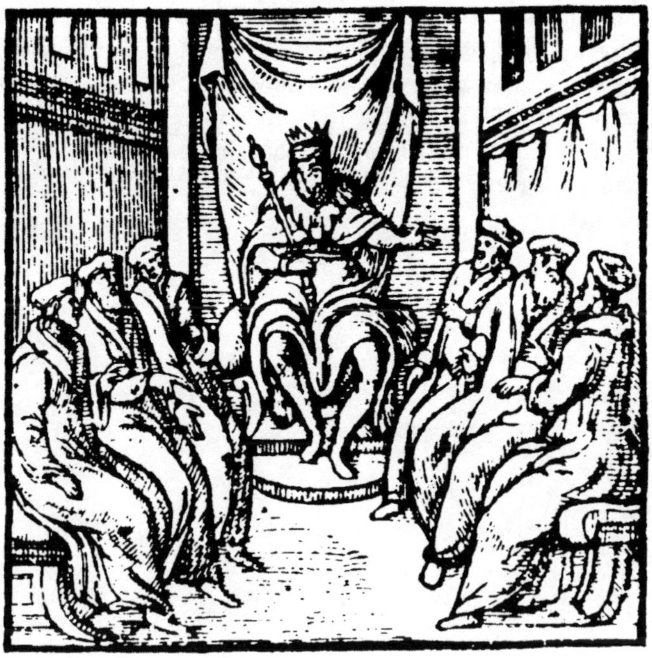

Emblema CXLIV

IN SENATUM BONI PRINCIPIS

Dialogismus

Effigies manibus truncae ante altaria divum
Hic resident, quarum lumine capta prior.
Signa potestatis summae, sanctique Senatus
Thebanis fuerant ista reperta viris.
Cur resident? Quia mente graves decet esse quieta
Iuridicos, animo nec variare levi.
Cur sine sunt manibus? Capiant ne xenia, nec se
Pollicitis flecti muneribusve sinant.
Caecus at est Princeps; quod solis auribus, absque
Affectu, constans iussa Senatus agit.

Emblem 144

ABOUT THE SENATE OF THE GOOD PRINCE

(a dialogue)

Here, in front of the altars of the gods, are installed some statues without hands, and the foremost of these has no eyes. These were devised by the Thebans as the symbols of the the highest power and of Holy Senate. "Why are they seated?" "Because it is fitting that serious judges should have their minds tranquil and that their souls should not be fickle." "Why are they depicted without hands?" "This is so that they can neither accept gifts nor allow that their judgments be swayed by promises or bribes. The Prince is, moreover, blind; with only his ears, and without passion, he steadfastly executes the orders of the Senate."

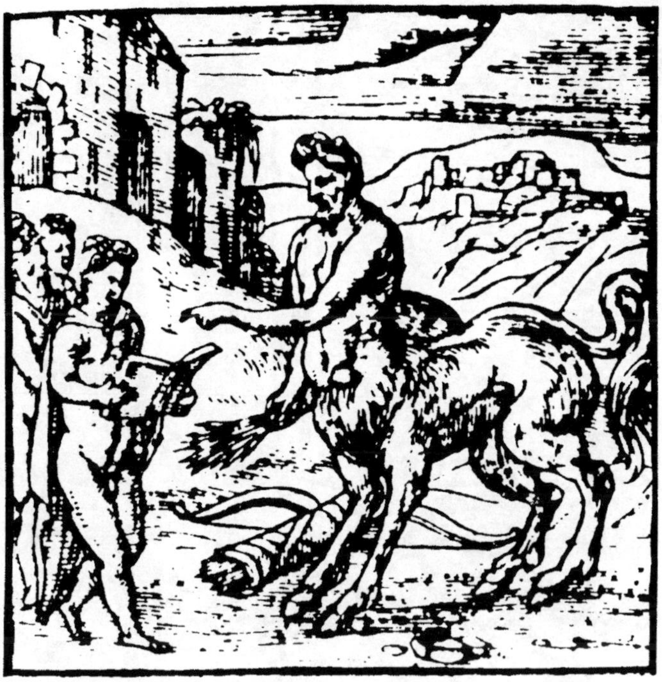

Emblema CXLV

CONSILIARII PRINCIPUM

Heroum genitos, et magnum fertur Achillem
In stabulis Chiron erudisse suis.
Semiferum doctorem, et semivirum Centaurum,
Assideat quisquis Regibus, esse debet.
Est fera, dum violat socios, dum proterit hostes:
Estque homo, dum simulat se populo esse pium.

Emblem 145

THE COUNSELORS OF PRINCES

It is said that Chiron educated in his stable the sons of the heroes and great Achilles. Whoever advises kings ought to be a professor who is half-animal, and a centaur who is half-human. The king becomes a beast when he ravages his allies and when he annihilates his enemies; he becomes a man when he represents himself to his people as being devoted to them.

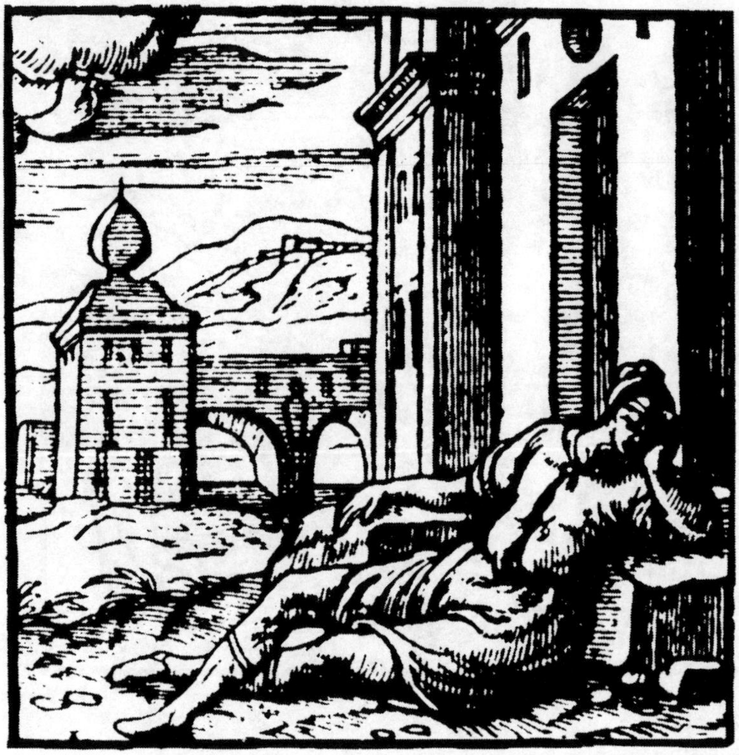

Emblema CXLVI

OPULENTIA TYRANNI, PAUPERTAS SUBIECTORUM

Humani quod splen est corporis, in populi re
Hoc Caesar fiscum dixerat esse suum.
Splene aucto reliqui tabescunt corporis attus,
Fisco aucto arguitur civica pauperies.

Emblem 146

THE TYRANT'S WEALTH IS THE POVERTY OF HIS SUBJECTS

Caesar said that his privy-purse is to the people what the spleen is for the human body: when the spleen swells, the rest of the body begins to waste away. Swollen taxes augur civic impoverishment.

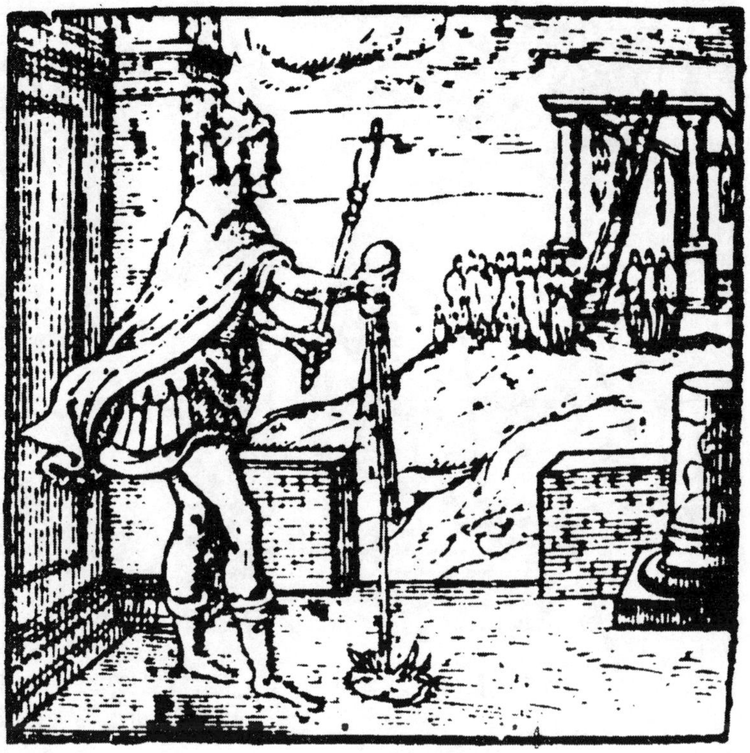

Emblema CXLVII

QUOD NON CAPIT CHRISTUS, RAPIT FISCUS

Exprimit humentes, quas iam madefecerat ante,
Spongiolas cupidi Principis arcta manus.
Provehit ad summum fures, quos deinde coercet.
Vertat ut in fiscum quae male parea suum.

Emblem 147

WHAT CHRIST DOESN'T TAKE, THE TAX MAN STEALS

With a clenched hand, the greedy Prince squeezes wet sponges which he has recently soaked. He elevates thieves to the highest rank, and then he locks them up. Hence, their ill-gotten gains again pour into his treasury.

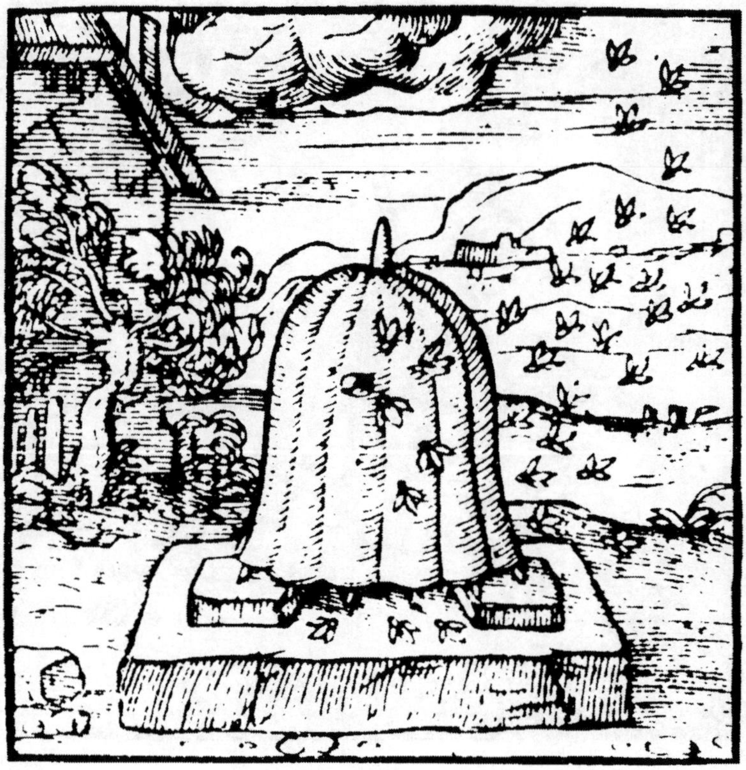

Emblema CXLVIII

PRINCIPIS CLEMENTIA

Vesparum quod nulla unquam Rex spicula figet,
Quodque aliis duplo corpore maior erit;
Arguet imperium clemens moderataque regna;
Sanctaque iudicibus credita iura bonis.

Emblem 148

THE CLEMENCY OF THE PRINCE

The king [sic: "queen"] of the wasps never uses his sting and his body is twice the size of the rest. This argues for a merciful rule and moderated kingship, also that sacred laws should be entrusted to good judges.

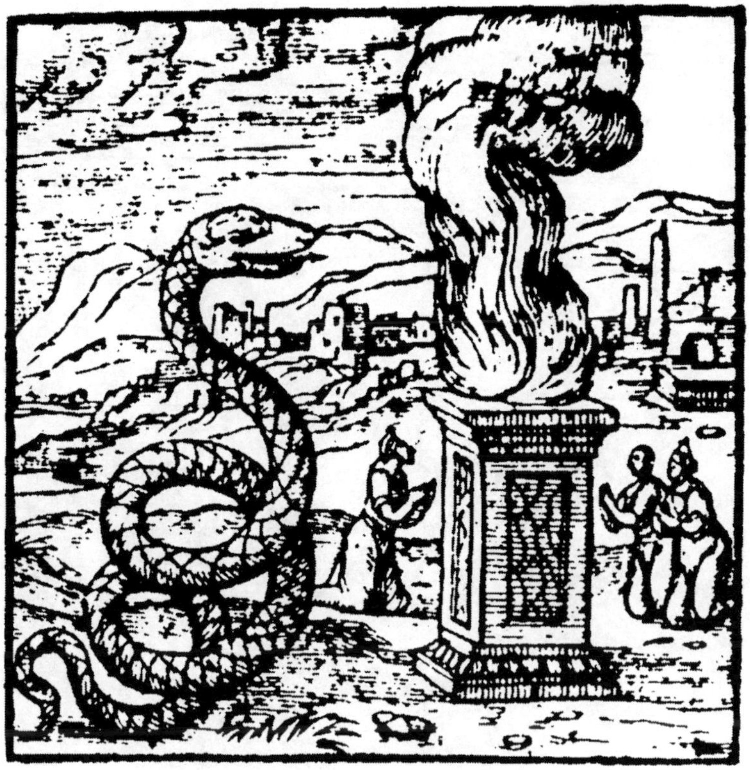

Emblema CXLIX

SALUS PUBLICA

Phoebigena erectis Epidaurius insidet aris,
Mitis, et immani conditur angue Deus.
Accurrunt aegri, veniatque salutifer orant.
Annuit, atque ratas efficit ille preces.

Emblem 149

PUBLIC HEALTH

The son of Phoebe [Asclepius] sits upon altars erected in Epidaurus; although benign, this god disguised himself in the form of an immense serpent. The sick flock to him and pray to him to come to them as a healer. He makes a sign of assent and fulfills the prayers made to him.

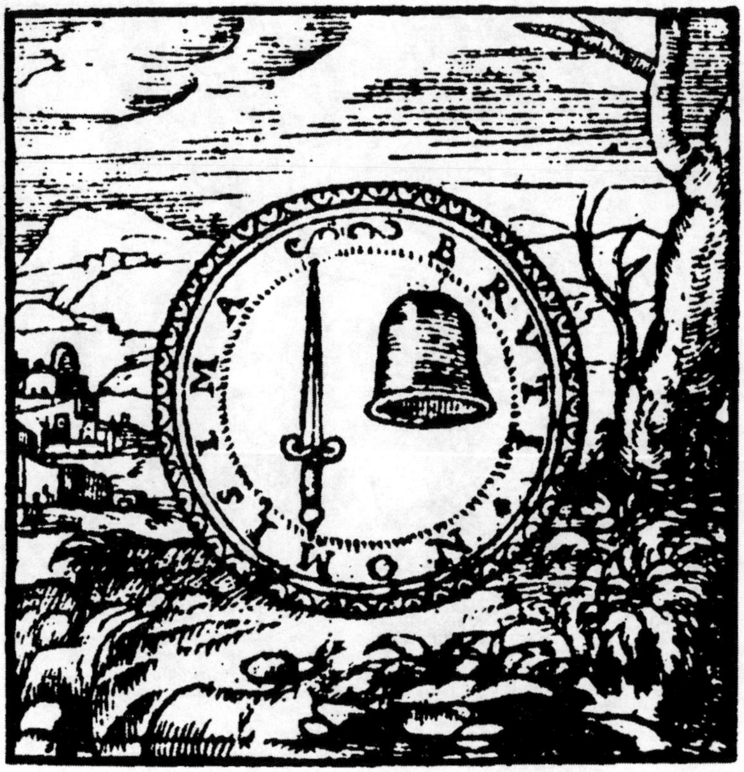

Emblema CL

RESPUBLICA LIBERATA

Caesaris exitio ceu libertate recepta,
Haec ducibus cusa moneta fuit.
Ensiculi in primis, queis pilleus insuper astat,
Qualem missa manu servitia accipiunt.

Emblem 150

THE REPUBLIC LIBERATED

After the death of Caesar, and as though liberty had been restored, the conspirators [led by Brutus] had this coin minted. In the foreground there are daggers, above which a [Phrygian] cap is shown, just like the one which freed slaves receive.

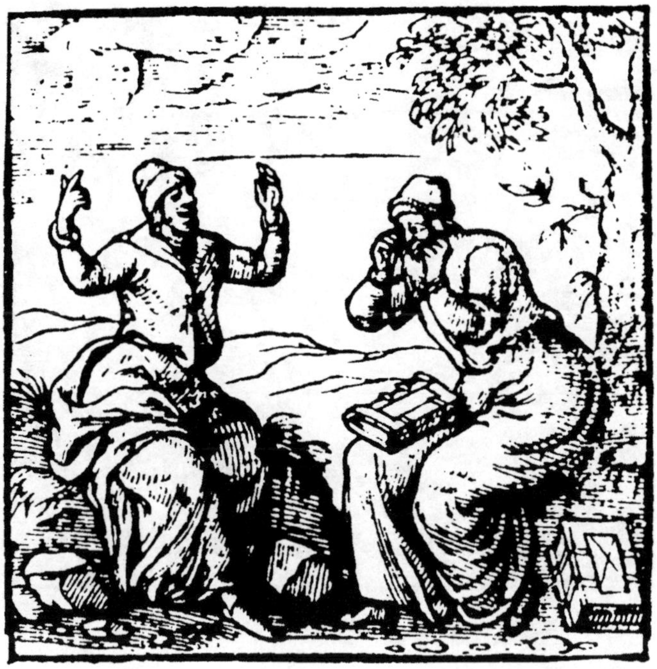

Emblema CLI

IN VITAM HUMANAM

Plus solito humanae nunc defle incommoda vitae,
Heraclite: scatet pluribus illa malis.
Tu rursus, si quando alias, extolle cachinnum,
Democrite: illa magis ludicra facta fuit.
Interea haec cernens meditor, qua denique tecum
Fine fleam, aut tecum quomodo splene iocer.

Emblem 151

ABOUT HUMAN LIFE

You are weeping more than usual because of the misfortunes of human life, oh Heraclitus; evil abounds more and more. To the contrary, more than ever you, oh Democritus, redouble your peals of laughter; life has gotten even more ludicrous. Meanwhile, contemplating life, I wonder whether I will end up weeping with one of you, or if I'll break into laughter with the other.

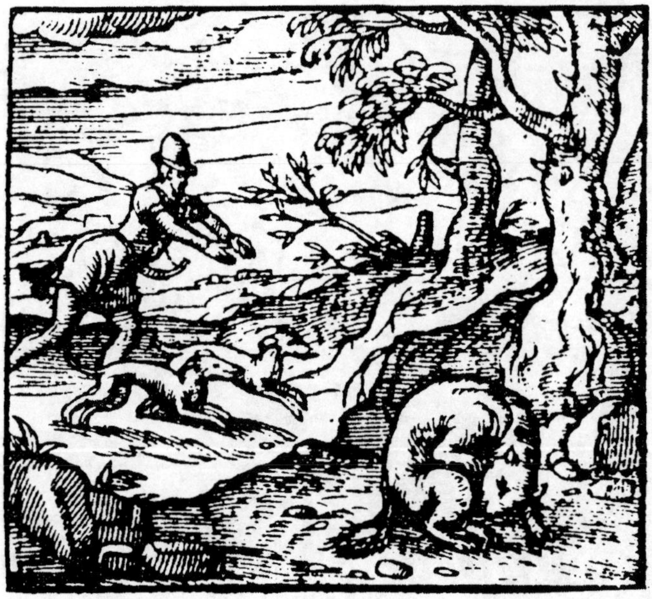

Emblema CLII

AERE QUANDOQUE SALUTEM REDIMENDAM

Et pedibus segnis, tumida et propendulus alvo,
Hac tamen insidias effugit arte fiber.
Mordicus ipse sibi medicata virilia vellit,
Atque abicit, sese gnarus ob illa peti.
Huius ab exemplo disces non parcere rebus,
Et, vitam ut redimas, hostibus aera date.

Emblem 152

SOMETIMES SAFETY IS RANSOMED WITH COINS

Although slow of foot and with a swollen and hanging belly, the beaver escapes from traps by employing this trick. Knowing what those who are pursuing him really prize, chewing himself, he rips off himself his medicinal testicles and casts them aside. Learn from this example not to be sparing of your possessions; give to your enemies the coins they demand for the ransom of your life.

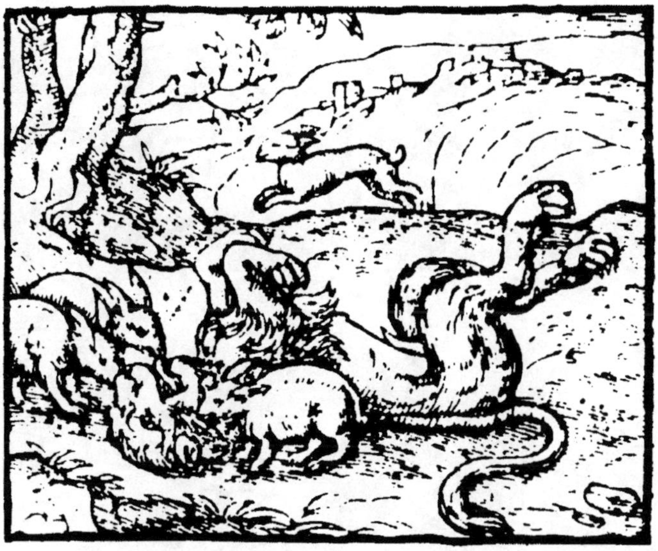

Emblema CLIII

CUM LARVIS NON LUCTANDUM

Aeacidae moriens percussu cuspidis Hector,
Qui toties hosteis vicerat ante suos:
Comprimere haud potuit vocem insultantibus illis,
Dum curru et pedibus nectere vincla parant.
Distrahite ut libitum est: sic cassi luce leonis
Convellunt barbam vel timidi lepores.

Emblem 153

DON'T FIGHT WITH GHOSTS

While expiring after being wounded by the spear wielded by the son of Aeacides [Achilles], Hector, who had so many times been victorious over his enemies, could not restrain himself from speaking to those who were insulting him while they prepared to tie the reins around his feet to drag him behind the chariot. "Tear me apart [he exclaimed] since this is your want; thus do even cowardly hares pull out the whiskers of the dead lion."

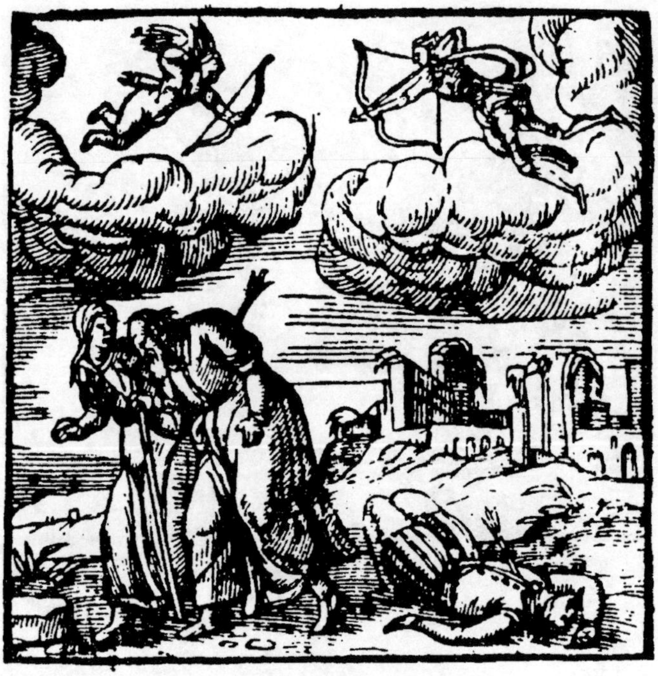

Emblema CLIV

DE MORTE ET AMORE

Errabat socio Mors iuncta Cupidine: secum
Mors pharetras, parvus tela gerabat Amor.
Divertere simul, simul una et nocte cubarunt:
Caecus Amor, Mors hoc tempore caeca fuit.
Alter enim alterius male provida spicula sumpsit;
Mors aurata, tenet ossea tela puer.
Debuit inde senex qui nunc Acheronticus esse.
Ecce amat, et capiti florea serta parat.
Ast ego mutato quia Amor me perculit arcu,
Deficio, iniiciunt et mihi fata manum.
Parce, puer, Mors signa tenens victricia, parce:
Fac ego amem, subeat fac Acheronta senex.

Emblem 154

ABOUT DEATH AND LOVE

Wandering about, Death was joined by his companion Cupid: Death carried his quiver, and little Amor had his arrows. They took lodging and bedded together one night; at that time, not only was Amor blind but also Death, and each one carelessly grabbed the evil stings belonging to the other: Death had seized the golden arrows and the child those made of bone. Behold how an old man, who should have already crossed the Acheron [into Hades], has fallen in love, and how he has adorned his [bald] head with garlands of flowers. However, because Amor struck me down with [Death's] borrowed bow, I am growing weak; the fates are laying their hands upon me. Spare me, oh child; and you, oh Death, carrying your victorious signs, spare me. Let me love, make the old man cross over the Acheron.

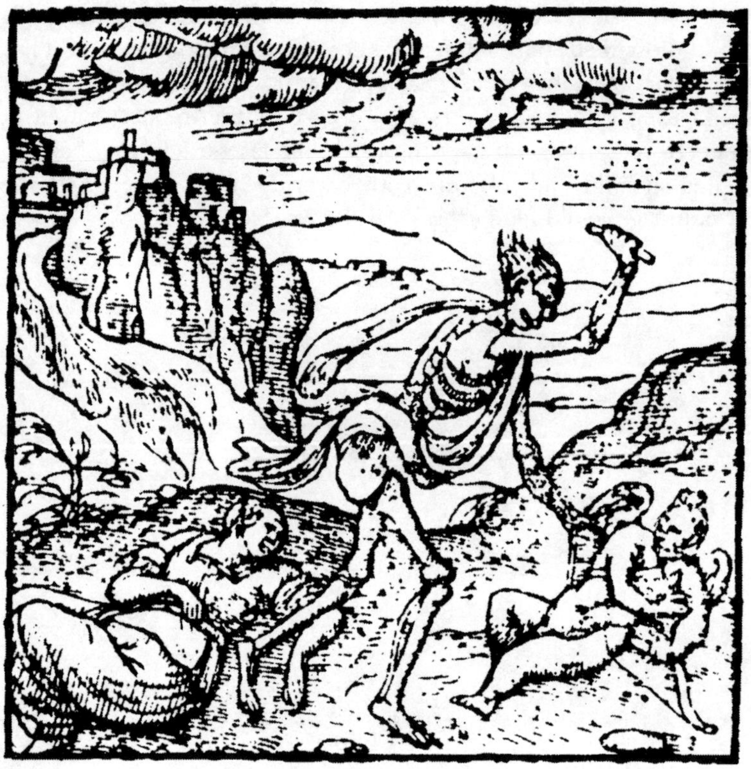

Emblema CLV

IN FORMOSAM FATO PRAEREPTAM

Cur puerum, Mors, ausa dolis es capere Amorem,
Tela tua ut iaceret, dum propria esse putat?

Emblem 155

BEAUTY PREMATURELY STRUCK DOWN BY FATE

Why, oh Death, have you dared to make use of the child Amor? Through your deceptions, he shot off your [lethal] arrows, with him [Cupid] thinking that they were his.

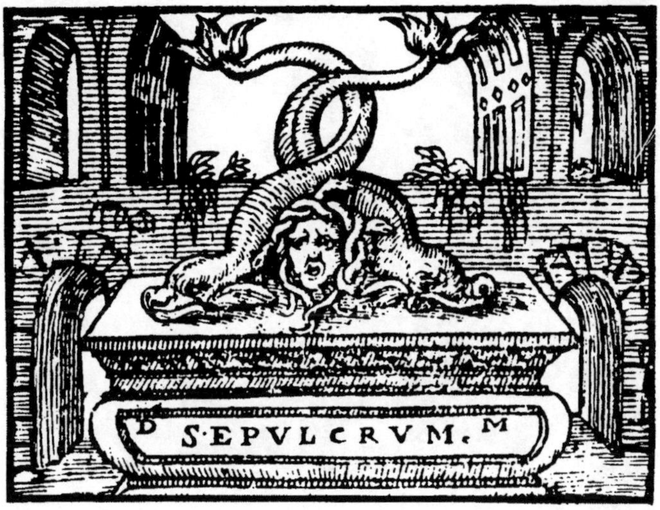

Emblema CLVI

IN MORTEM PRAEPROPERAM

Qui teneras forma allexit, torsitque puellas,
Pulchrior et tota nobilis urbe puer,
Occidit ante diem, nulli mage flendus, Aresti,
Quam tibi, cui casto iunctus amore fuit.
Ergo illi tumulum, tanti monumenta doloris,
Astruis, et querulis vocibus astra feris.
Me sine abis, dilecte: neque amplius ibimus una?
Nec mecum in studiis otia grata teres?
Sed te terra teget; sed fati, Gorgonis ora,
Delphinesque tui signa dolenda dabunt.

Emblem 156

ABOUT A PREMATURE DEATH

The most beautiful and noble boy in all the city, who seduced with his beauty the girls and made them suffer, died before his time. Nobody shall weep more for you, oh Arestus, than you, to whom he was joined by a chaste love. Therefore, you are building a tomb for him as testimony to such great pain and you reach to the stars with your laments: "Why are you going without me, oh lover? Shall we never again be together? Will you never again spend with me pleasing moments of leisure in study? Indeed, the earth shall cover you over, but the Gorgon-head and the dolphins will serve as dolorous signs of your fate."

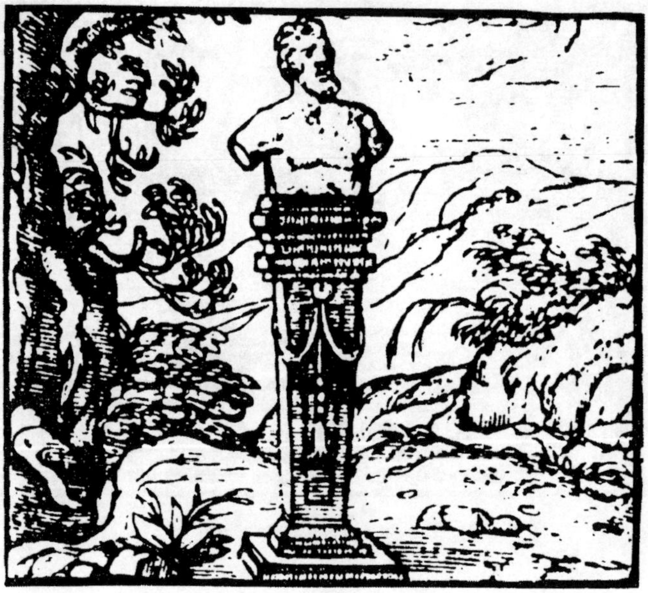

Emblema CLVII

TERMINUS

Quadratum infoditur firmissima tessera saxum,
Stat cirrata super pectore imago tenus,
Et sese nullis profitetur cedere. Talis
Terminus est, homines qui scopus unus agit.
Est immota dies, praefixaque tempora fatis,
Deque ferunt primis ultima iudicium.

Emblem 157

TERMINUS

The base of a squared shaft is firmly buried, and on top of it is a curly-haired image [of a man] cut off at the breast; this declares that he will yields to nobody. This is Terminus [the limit], the one goal that leads men on. It is the fixed day, and the time which has been set by the fates, and in the last events they [the fates] render their judgment over the first day.

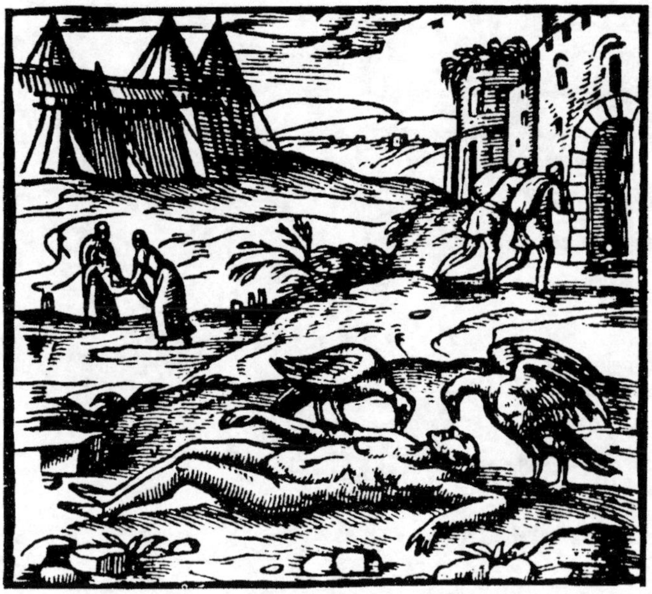

Emblema CLVIII

OPULENTI HEREDITAS

Patroclum falsis rapiunt hinc Troes in armis;
Hinc socii, atque omnis turba Pelasga vetat.
Obtinet exuvias Hector, Graeciaque cadaver.
Haec fabella agitur, cum vir opimus obit.
Maxima rixa oritur; tandem sed transigit heres,
Et corvis aliquid, vulturiisque sinit.

Emblem 158

THE RICH MAN'S INHERITANCE

Here the Trojans are [shown] stripping Patroclus of his borrowed weapons, and there the allies and all the Pelasgian [Greek] troops are moving to prevent it. Hector gets the weapons and Greece retrieves the corpse. This anecdote applies when a rich man dies. This stirs up a great quarrel, but finally the heir concludes the affair. He leaves something to the crows, and grants something else to the vultures.

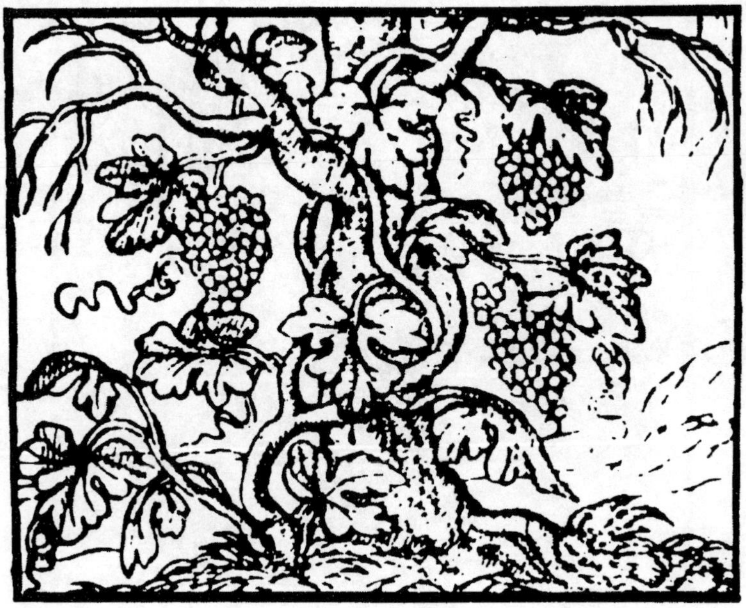

Emblema CLIX

AMICITIA ETIAM POST MORTEM DURANS

Arentem senio, nudam quoque frondibus ulmum,
Complexa est viridi vitis opaca coma:
Agnoscitque vices naturae, et grata parenti
Officii reddit mutua iura suo.
Exemploque monet, tales nos quaerere amicos,
Quos neque disiungat foedere summa dies.

Emblem 159

FRIENDSHIP WHICH ENDURES AFTER DEATH

Dried out by age, a leafless elm has been embraced by a grapevine with thick, green foliage. Acknowledging the vicissitudes of nature, and grateful to its parent, the vine conforms to its oath of mutual obligation. By its own example, we are also advised to seek for ourselves such friends as will not, upon the arrival of that last day [death], disown that pact [of friendship].

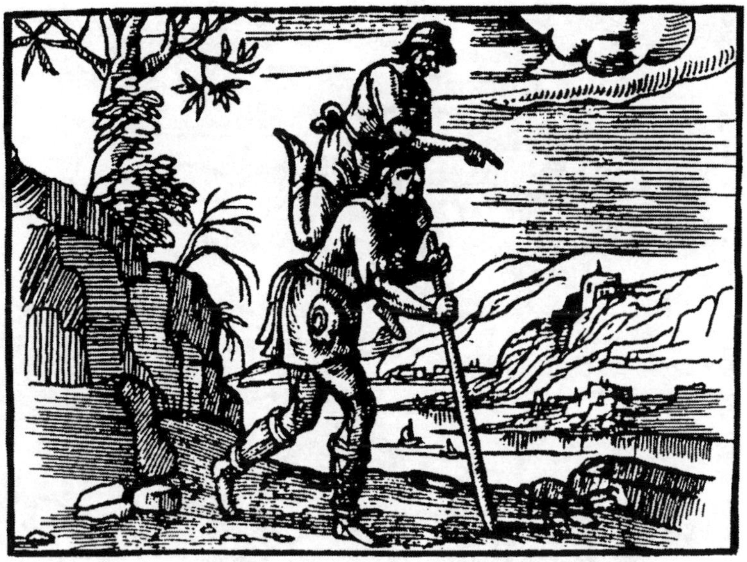

Emblema CLX

MUTUUM AUXILIUM

Loripedem sublatum humeris fert lumine captus:
Et socii haec oculls munera retribuit.
Quo caret alteruter, concors sic praestat uterque:
Mutuat hic oculos, mutuat ille pedes.

Emblem 160

MUTUAL AID

The blind man carries a lame man on his back, and he receives in exchange from his partner the gift of his eyes. Hence, in mutual concord one lends to the other that which he lacks: one exchanges the eyes, and the other exchanges his feet.

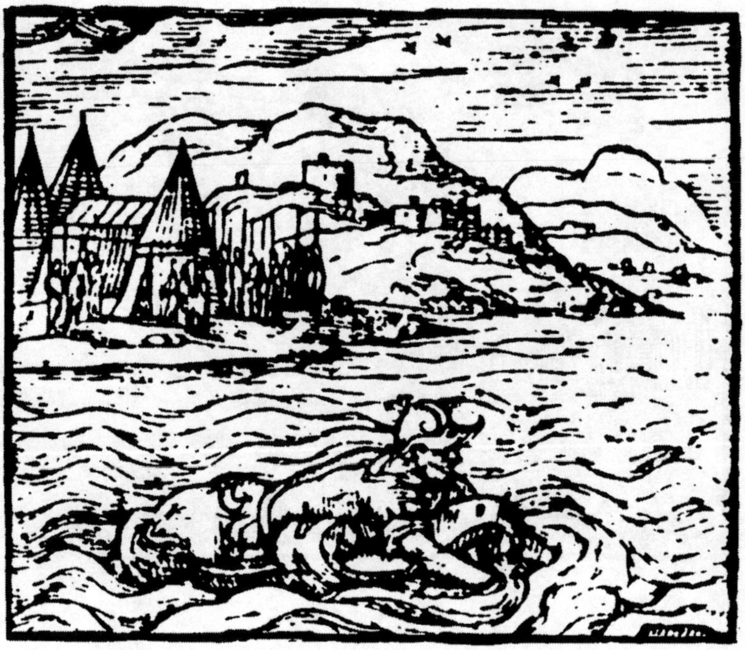

Emblema CLXI

AUXILIUM NUMQUAM DEFICIENS

Bina pericla unis effugi sedulus armis,
Cum premererque solo, cum premererque salo.
Incolumem ex acie clypeus me praestitit: idem
Navifragum apprensus littora adusque tulit.

Emblem 161

HELP IS NEVER WANTING

When I was as much in danger on the land as in the ocean, diligent, I avoided two dangers with a single weapon. My shield kept me safe in battle, and again clasping it, it carried me to the shore when I was shipwrecked.

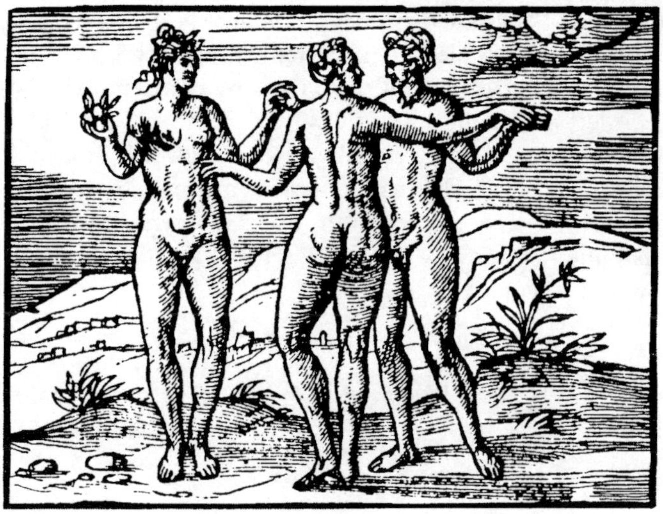

Emblema CLXII

GRATIAE

Tres Charites Venere assistunt, dominamque sequuntur:
Hincque voluptates, atque alimenta parant:
Laetitiam Euphrosyne, speciosum Aglaia nitorem;
Suadela est Pythus, blandus et ore lepos.
Cur nudae? Mentis quoniam candore venustas
Constant, et eximia simplicitate placet.
An quia nil referunt ingrati, atque ascula inanis
Est Charitum? Qui dat munera, nudus eget.
Addita cur nuper pedibus talaria? Bis dat
Qui cito dat: minimi gratia tarda pretii est.
Implicitis ulnis cur vertitur altera? Gratus
Faenerat: huic remanent una abeunte duae.
Iuppiter iis genitor. Caeli de semine divas
Omnibus acceptas edidit Eurynome.

Emblem 162

THE THREE GRACES

(a dialogue)

Taking her as their mistress, the Three Graces [Charities] attend Venus, and they provide her with pleasure and nourishment. They are Euphrosyne, who is happiness, Aglaia, precious splendor, and Pythus [Thalia], who is persuasive with sweet and ingenious speech. "Why are they nude?" "Because beauty corresponds to the candor of the mind, and it takes pleasure in extreme simplicity." "Why do ingrates give nothing, hence the treasure chest of the Graces remains empty?" "Whoever gives away presents is left naked and needy." "Why were winged sandals recently added to them?" "Who gives twice, gives rapidly: a delayed favor is of little worth." "Why do they turn one to face each other with interlocked arms?" "A thankful person lends with interest: for this one, even though the other is absent, the other two remain." Their father is Jupiter, who with his divine semen engendered in Eurynome these goddesses, who are welcomed by all.

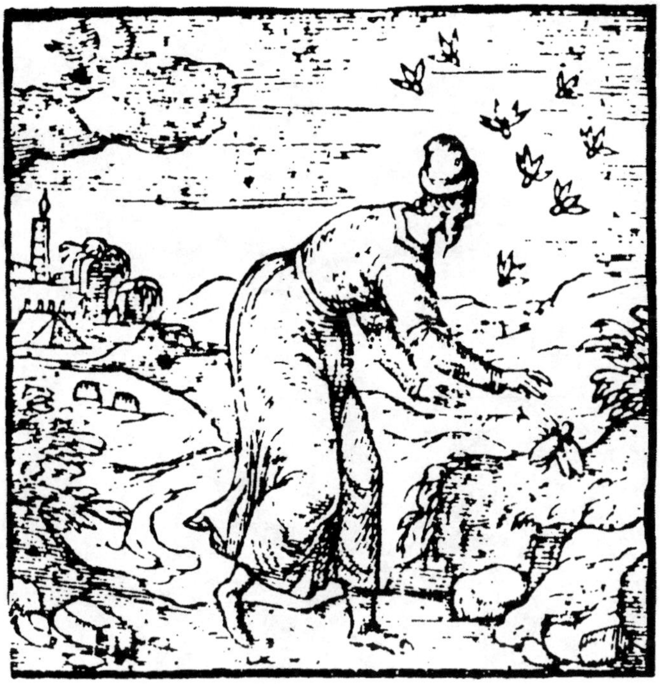

Emblema CLXIII

IN DETRACTORES

Audent flagriferi matulae, stupidique magistri
Bilem in me impuri pectoris evomere.
Quid faciam? Reddamne vices? Sed nonne cicadam
Ala una obstreperam corripuisse ferar?
Quid prodest moscas operosis pellere flabris?
Negligere est satius, perdere quod nequeas.

Emblem 163

AGAINST DETRACTORS

These whip-bearing simpletons and stupid teachers dare to vomit upon me the bile from their impure breasts. What can I do? Shall I throw their vices back to them? But wouldn't that only be like tying down the wing of a buzzing cicada? What use is it to brush away flies with labored blows of the whisk? It's better to ignore what you can't destroy.

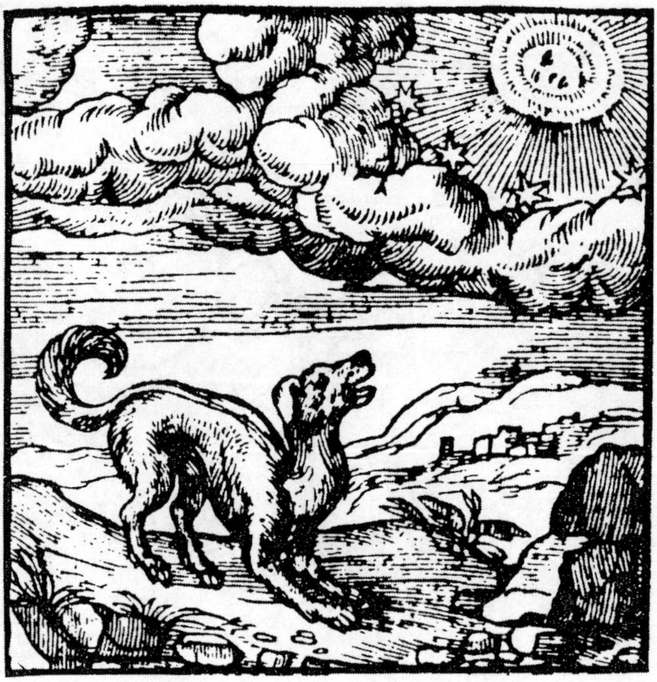

Emblema CLXIV

INANIS IMPETUS

Lunarem noctu, ut speculum, canis inspicit orbem:
Seque videns, alium credit inesse canem,
Et latrat: sed frustra agitur vox irrita ventis,
Et peragit cursus surda Diana suos.

Emblem 164

AN INANE UNDERTAKING

As though it were a mirror, the dog stares at night at the orb of the moon and, seeing himself in it, he thinks it is another dog there and barks. He vainly throws to the winds his useless voice; deaf, Diana [the moon] continues on her course.

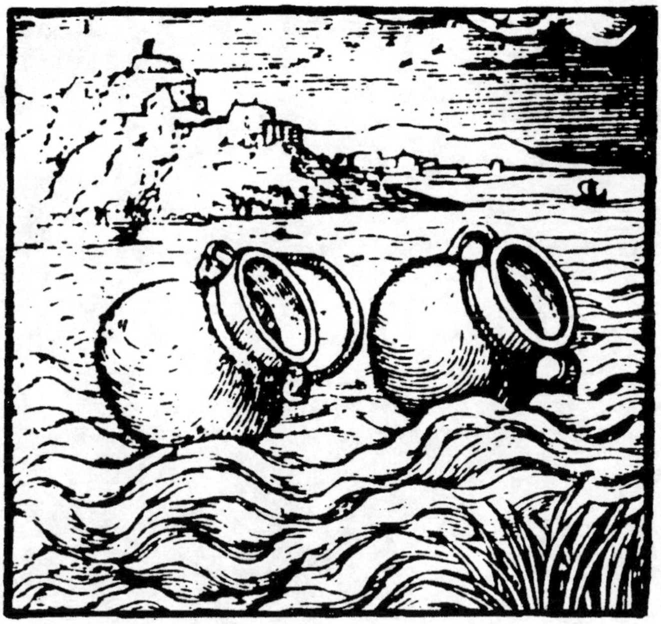

Emblema CLXV

ALIQUID MALI PROPTER VICINUM MALUM

Raptabat torrens ollas, quarum una metallo,
Altera erat figuli terrea facta manu.
Hanc igitur rogat illa, velit sibi proxima ferri,
Iuncta ut praecipites utraque sistat aquas.
Cui lutea, Haud nobis tua sunt commercia curae,
Ne mihi proximitas haec mala multa ferat.
Nam seu te nobis, seu nos tibi conferat unde;
Ipsa ego te fragilis sospite sola terar.

Emblem 165

AN EVIL NEIGHBOR BRINGS ANYBODY HARM

A flood carried away two jugs; one was made of metal, and the other was made by the potter from clay. The metal jug pleaded to the clay pot to draw closer so that, together, they might better brave the rapid waters. Regarding this request, the pot made of clay said: "Your business is not mine, and your proximity will certainly only bring to me much misfortune. Whether the waves drag you to me, or me to you, being fragile, I will be smashed, and you will proceed unharmed."

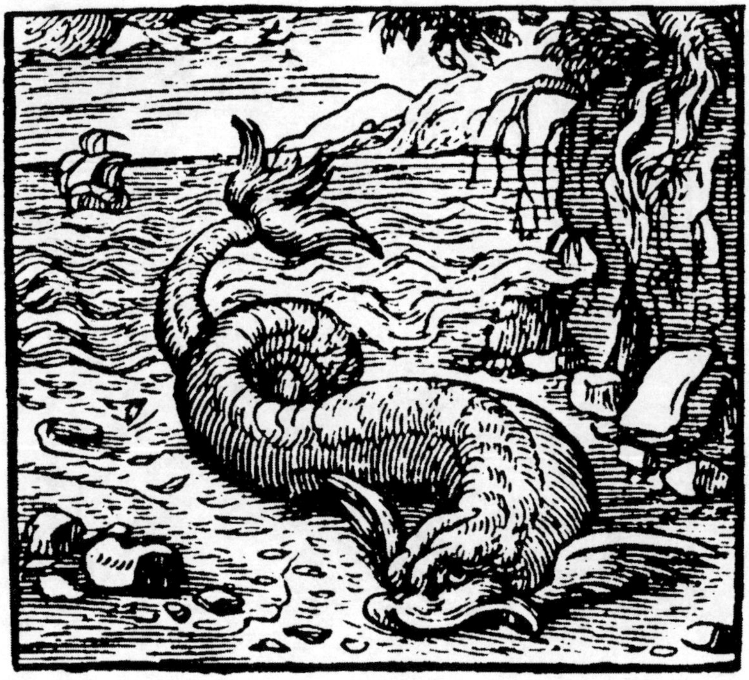

Emblema CLXVI

IN EUM QUI TRUCULENTIA SUORUM PERIERIT

Delphinem invitum me in littora compulit aestus,
Exemplum infido quanta pericla mari;
Nam si nec propriis Neptunus parcit alumnis,
Quis tutos homines navibus esse putet?

Emblem 166

HE WHO PERISHES THROUGH THE CRUELTY OF HIS OWN KIND

Against my will the tide has cast me, the dolphin, upon the beach, so serving as an example of the many dangers presented by the treacherous sea. Hence, if Neptune doesn't look after his pupils, how can anybody think that men are going to be safe upon their ships?

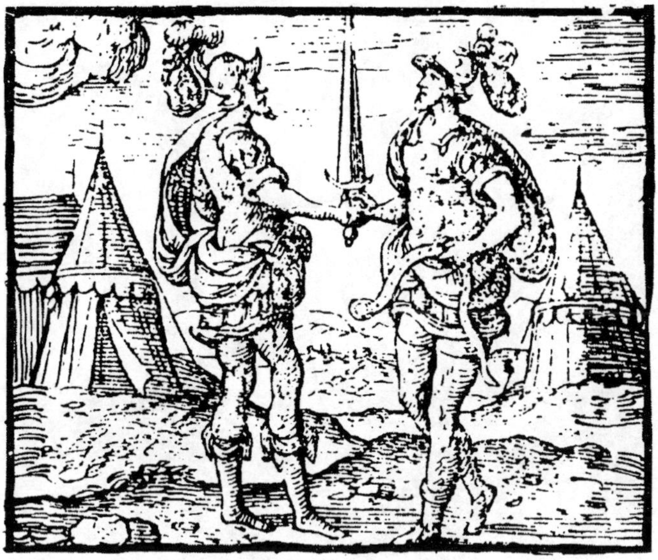

Emblema CLXVII

IN DONA HOSTIUM

Bellorum cepisse ferunt monumenta vicissim
Scutiferum Aiacem, Hectoraque Iliacum
Baltea Priamides, rigidum Telamonius ensem,
Instrumenta suae cepit uterque necis.
Ensis enim Aiacem confecit; at Hectora functum
Traxere Haemoniis cingula nexa rotis.
Sic titulo obsequii, quae mittunt hostibus hostes
Munera, venturi praescia fata ferunt.

Emblem 167

ABOUT GIFTS FROM ENEMIES

Shield-bearing Ajax and Hector the Trojan mutually exchanged the spoils of war; the sword-belt, given by Telamon to Priam, went to Hector, and Ajax got the unbending sword. In accepting these, each one acquired the instrument of his own death. The sword did away with Ajax; tied with the sword-belt to the wheels of [the chariot driven by] the Thessalian [Achilles], Hector was dragged to his death. Hence, the title explains that gifts sent by enemies to enemies under the pretext of courtesy bear the harbingers of [their] fate.

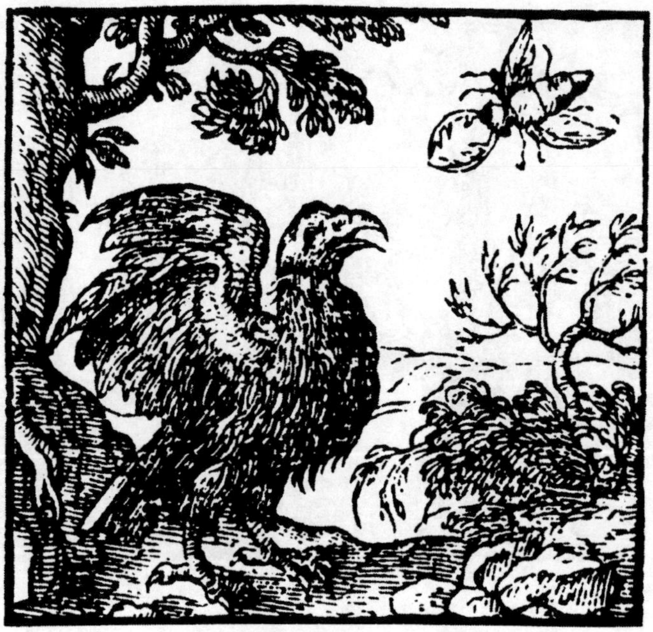

Emblema CLXVIII

A MINIMIS QUOQUE TIMENDUM

Bella gerit Scarabeus, et hostem provocat ultro,
Robore et inferior, consilio superat.
Nam plumis Aquilae clam se neque cognitus abdit,
Hostilem ut nidum summa per astra petat.
Quaque confodiens, prohibet spem crescere prolis:
Hocque modo illatum dedecus ultus abit.

Emblem 168

FEAR ALSO INSIGNIFICANT THINGS

Beyond provoking its enemy, the black beetle makes war upon it. Although it is inferior in strength [to an eagle], it surpasses it through strategy. It hides itself in the eagle's feathers; undiscovered, it seeks out the enemy nest lodged in the starry heights. There, it makes holes in the eggs, so preventing hope for the growth of any offspring. Having avenged the shame inflicted upon it itself in this way, the beetle flies away.

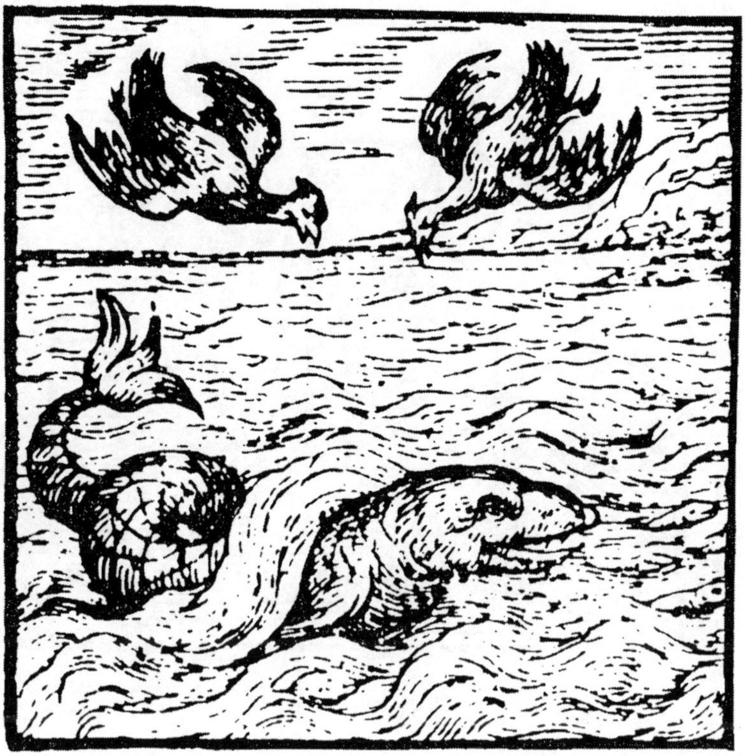

Emblema CLXIX

OBNOXIA INFIRMITAS

Pisciculos Aurata rapit medio aequore sardas,
Ni fugiant pavidae, summa marisque petant.
Ast ibi sunt mergis fulicisque voracibus esca.
Eheu, intuta manens undique debilitas!

Emblem 169

WEAKNESS IS SUBMISSIVE

Even if they do not flee terrified to the surface, the gilt-bream catches the sardines in the middle of the ocean. But even there, on the surface, they become food for voracious diver-birds and coots. Oh my: debility remains defenseless everywhere!

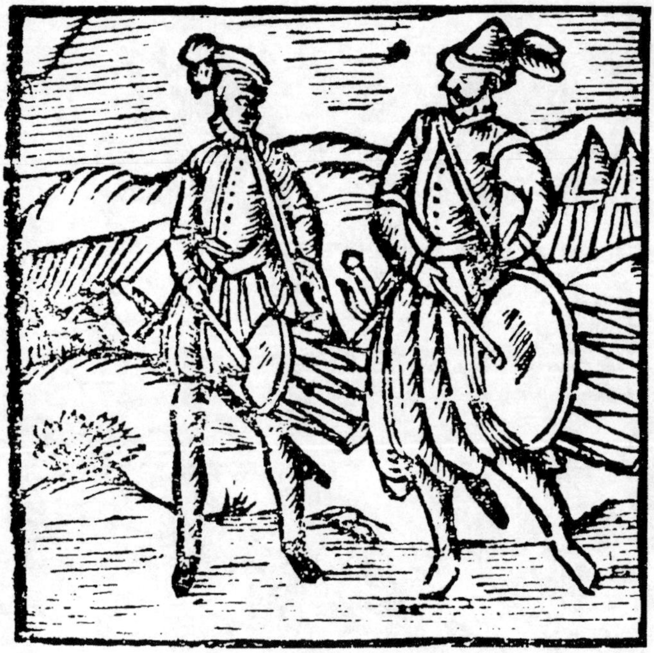

Emblema CLXX

VEL POST MORTEM FORMIDOLOSI

Cetera mutescent, coriumque silebit ovillum,
Si contecta lupi tympana pelle sonent.
Hanc membrana ovium sic exhorrescit, ut hostem
Exanimis quamvis non ferat exanimem.
Sic cute detracta Ziscas, in tympana versus,
Boemos potuit vincere Pontifices.

Emblem 170

TERRIFYING EVEN AFTER DEATH

If the drums covered with wolf-hide sound, the others fall mute and, horrified, the sheepskin keeps its silence. Although the sheep is dead, it cannot endure its dead enemy. In the same way, the skin stripped off of Ziska [the Hussite], then made into a drum, was able to defeat the Bohemian Pontiffs.

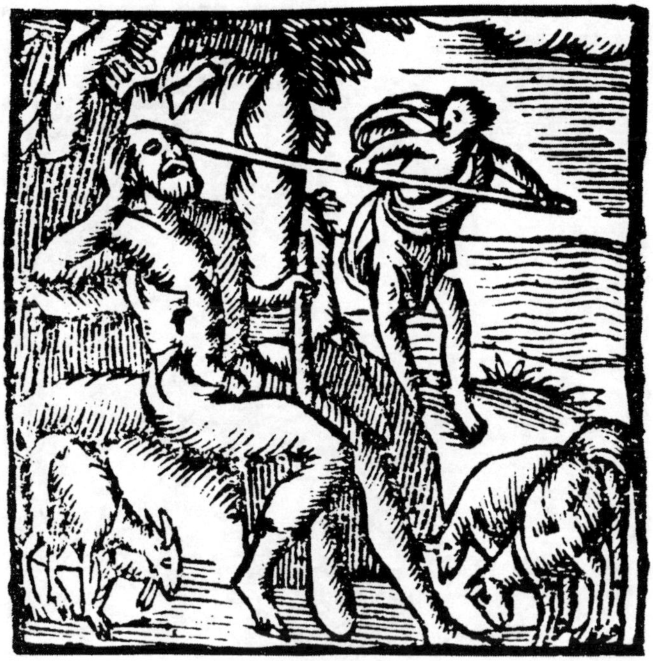

Emblema CLXXI

IUSTA VINDICTA

Dum residet Cyclops sinuosi in faucibus antri,
Haec secum teneras concinit inter aves:
Pascite vos herbas, sociis ego pascar Achivis,
Postremumque Utin viscera nostra ferent.
Audiit haec Ithacus, Cyclopaque lumine cassum
Reddidit; en poenas ut suus auctor habet.

Emblem 171

JUST VINDICATION

While the Cyclops reposes among the young sheep at the entrance to his sinuous lair, he sang these words to himself: "Feed upon the grass for I am going to feed upon the Achaean companians and my guts shall have No-One [Ulysses] for desert." The Ithacan heard him, blinded him, and paid him back. This shows how the author of punishments gets them in his turn.

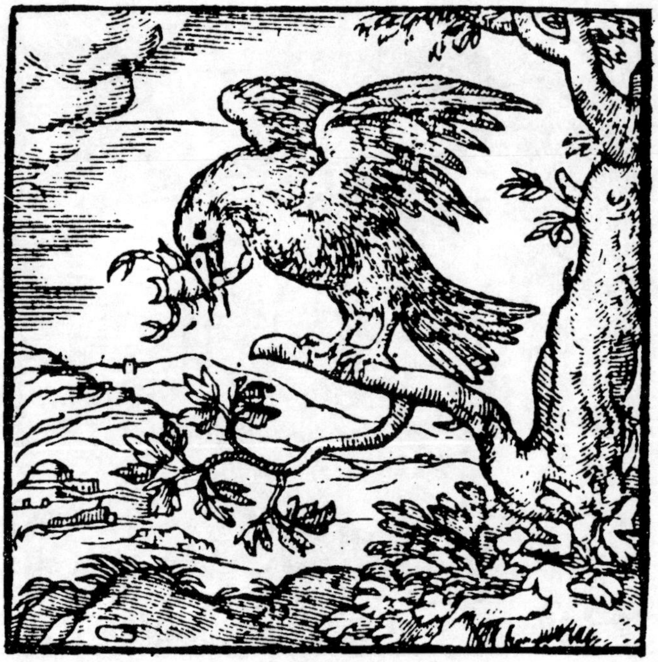

Emblema CLXXII

IUSTA ULTIO

Raptabat volucres captum pede corvus in auras
Scorpion, audaci praemia parta gulae.
Ast ille infuso sensim per membra veneno,
Raptorem in Stygias compulit ultor aquas.
O risu res digna! Aliis qui fata parabat,
Ipse perit, propriis succubuitque dolis.

Emblem 172

JUST REVENGE

A speedy crow took captive in its clawed foot a scorpion; this was a proper prize to its audacious gluttony. The scorpion slowly infused its venom throughout the bird's members and, as an avenger, it pushed its abductor into the Stygian waters. Oh, what a thing worthy of laughter! Whoever prepares death for others, perishes himself, succumbing to his own perfidy.

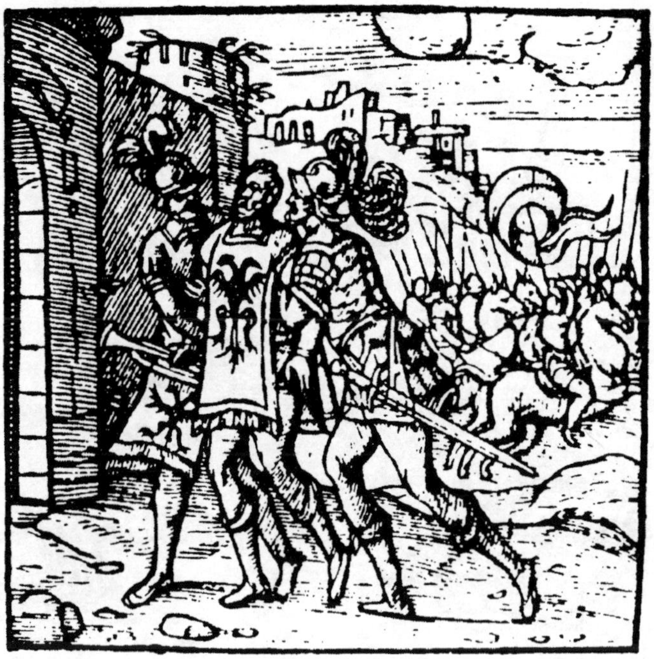

Emblema CLXXIII

PAREM DELINQUENTIS ET SUASORIS CULPAM ESSE

Praeconem lituo perflantem classica, victrix
Captivum in tetro carcere turba tenet.
Queis ille excusat, quod nec sit strenuus armis,
Ullius aut saevo laeserit ense latus.
Huic illi: Quin ipse magis timidissime peccas,
Qui clangore alios aeris in arma cies.

Emblem 173

THE GUILT OF THE DELINQUENT IS SHARED BY HIS INSTIGATOR

The victorious army has imprisoned in a foul jail a bugler who sounded the call of arms. In his defense, he claimed that he took no active part in the battle, nor had he wounded anybody with a brutal sword. They respond: "All the greater then are your sins because, besides being a coward, you called others to arms with the clamor of your trumpet."

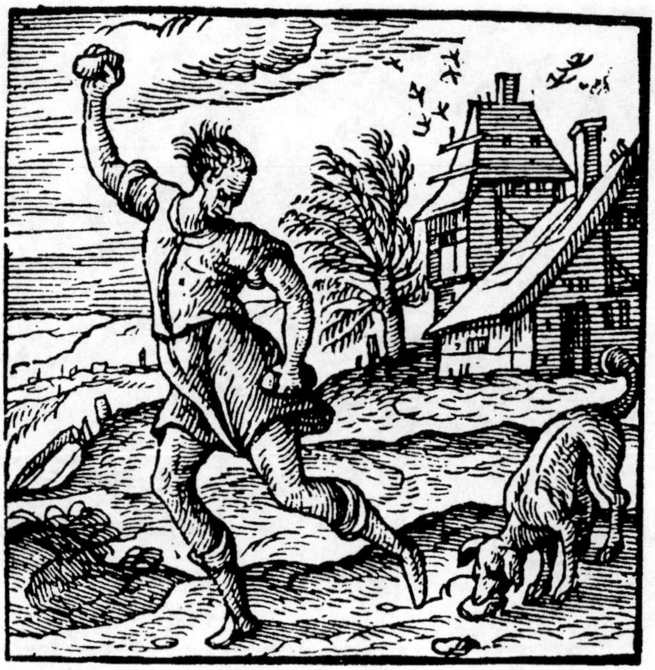

Emblema CLXXIV

ALIUS PECCAT, ALIUS PLECTITUR

Arripit ut lapidem catulus, morsuque fatigat,
Nec percussori mutua damna facit:
Sic plerique sinunt veros elabier hosteis,
Et quos nulla gravat noxia, dente petunt.

Emblem 174

ONE SINS, AND THE OTHER IS PUNISHED

Just as the puppy seizes a stone and tires himself chewing upon it, so he doesn't return the insult to the attacker who threw it at him. In the same way, many let their true enemies escape, only sinking their teeth into those whom no offense weighs down.

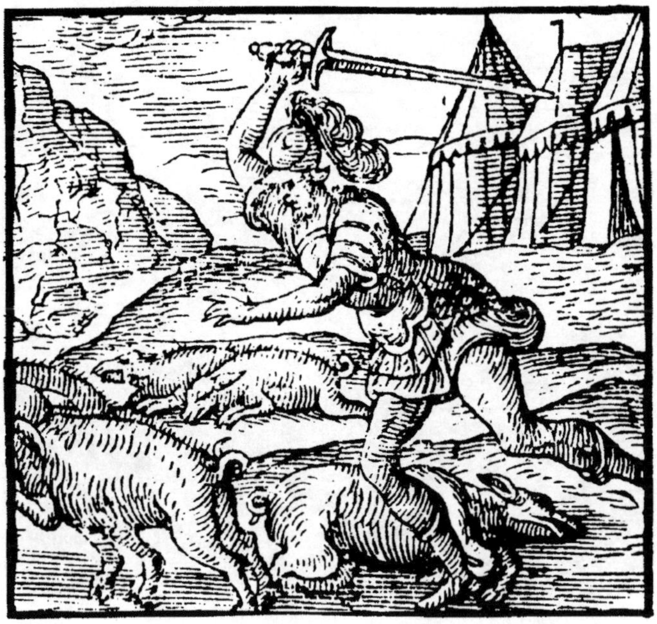

Emblema CLXXV

INSANI GLADIUS

Setigeri medius stabat gregis ensifer Aiax,
Caede suum credens caedere Tantalidas.
Hostia sic tamquam sus succidanea poenas
Pro Laertiade, pro caveaque dabat.
Nescit obesse suis furor hostibus: errat ab ictu,
Consiliique impos in sua damna ruit.

Emblem 175

THE SWORD OF THE INSANE

Standing amidst a bristly herd, Ajax was killing the pigs with his sword because he took them to be the sons of Tantalus [Agamemnon and Menelaus]. The pigs became substitute victims in place of the son of Laertes [Ulysses] and, as it were, they paid the penalty decreed for him. Madness makes one ignorant of how to destroy one's [proper] enemies; its blow misses the target. Deprived of his judgment, Ajax hastened to his own damnation.

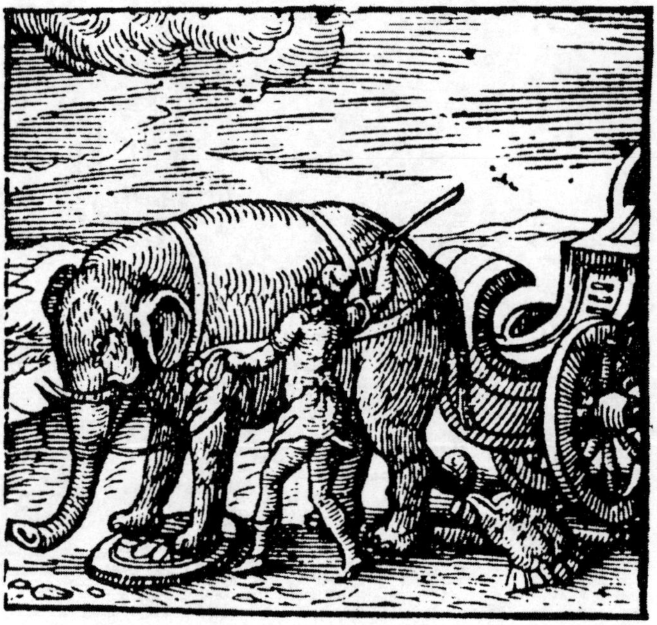

Emblema CLXXVI

PAX

Turrigeris humeris, dentis quoque barrus eburni,
Qui superare ferox Martia bella solet,
Supposuit nunc colla iugo. Stimulisque subactus,
Caesareos currus ad pia templa vehit.
Vel fera cognoscit concordes undique gentes,
Proiectisque armis munia pacis obit.

Emblem 176

PEACE

With towers upon its back, the elephant has ivory tusks; ferocious, it is accustomed to overcome in battle. It has now submitted its neck to the yoke. Disciplined by the goad, it draws the chariots of emperors to the holy temples. Even a beast knows how to recognize men operating in concord where ever it finds them and, throwing down its weapons, its undertakes the obligations of peace.

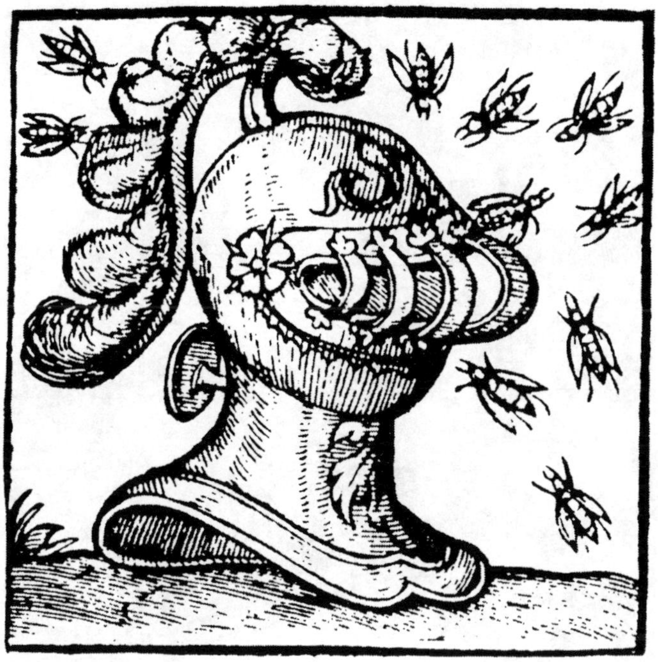

Emblema CLXXVII

EX BELLO PAX

En galea, intrepidus quam miles gesserat, et quae
Saepius hostili sparsa cruore fuit:
Parta pace apibus tenuis concessit in usum
Alveoli, atque favos, grataque mella gerit.
Arma procul iaceant: fas sit tunc sumere bellum,
Quando aliter pacis non potes arte frui.

Emblem 177

PEACE AFTER WAR

Here is a helmet worn by an intrepid soldier, and it was often splattered with the blood of enemies. When peace came, the little bees were permitted to use it as a hive, then with honeycombs producing delicious honey. Lay your arms aside: only embark upon war when you can no longer enjoy the arts of peace in any other way.

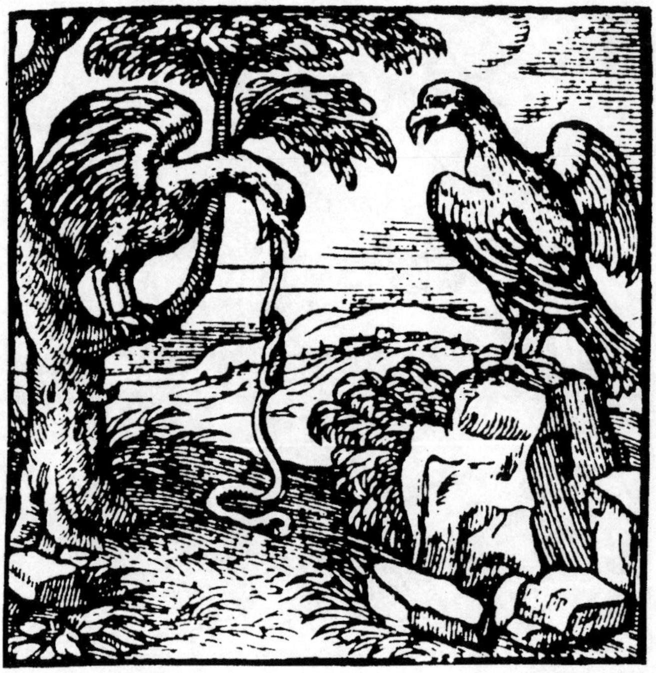

Emblema CXXVIII

EX PACE UBERTAS

Grandibus ex spicis tenues contexe corollas,
Quas circum alterno palmite vitis eat.
His comptae Alcyones tranquilli in marmoris unda
Nidificant, pullus involucresque fovent.
Laetus erit Cereri, Baccho quoque fertilis annus,
Aequorei si rex alitis instat erit.

Emblem 178

ABUNDANCE AFTER PEACE

Weaving delicate garlands from the larger sheaves, alternating grape leaves in a circle, kingfishers make their nests upon the tranquil surface of the waves; and there they care for their flightless chicks. The year will be fruitful in Ceres and Bacchus [wheat and wine] if the king acts as a counterpart to these sea birds.

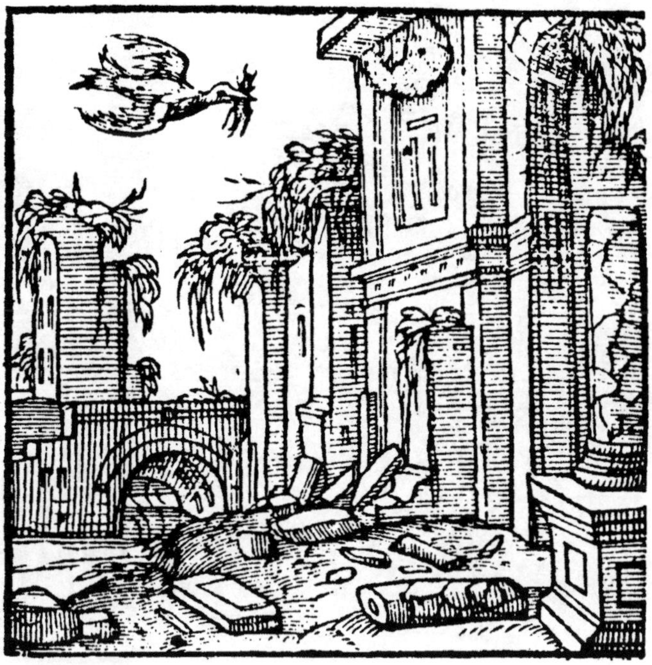

Emblema CLXXIX

DOCTOS DOCTIS OBLOQUI NEFAS ESSE

Quid rapis, heu, Progne vocalem saeva cicadam,
Pignoribusque tuis fercula dira paras?
Stridula stridentem, vernam verna, hospita laedis
Hospitam, et aligeram penniger ales avem?
Ergo abice hanc praedam: nam musica pectora summum est
Alterum ab alterius dente perire nefas.

Emblem 179

ONE SCHOLAR SHOULD NOT MALIGN ANOTHER

Why, oh brutal Procne [turned into a swallow], do you steal the singing cicada and make it into a loathsome meal for your own chicks? You who chatters, would you do damage to another who chatters? You, who sings in spring, would you do it to another who does the same;? Would you, the guest, act so to another guest? Would you, a bird with wings, do so to another winged being? Release, then, this prey. The worst crime is to have one musical soul perish from the tooth of the other.

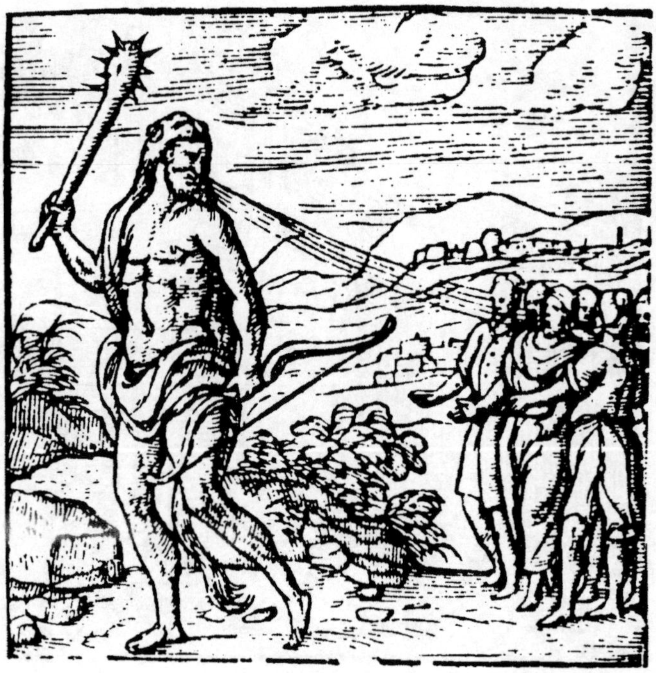

Emblema CLXXX

ELOQUENTIA FORTITUDINE PRAESTANTIOR

Arcum laeva tenet, rigidam fert dextera clavam,
Contegit et Nemees corpora nuda leo.
Herculis haec igitur facies? Non convenit illud
Quod vetus, et senio tempora cana gerit.
Quid quod lingua illi levibus traiecta catenis,
Queis fissa facileis allicit aure viros?
Anne quod Alciden lingua, non robore Galli
Praestantem populis iura dedisse ferunt?
Cedunt arma togae, et quamvis durissima corda
Eloquio pollens ad sua vota trahit.

Emblem 180

ELOQUENCE EXCELS FORCE

(a dialogue)

With a bow in his left hand, he carries in his right the hard club and covers his naked body with the [skinned] Nemean lion. "So, is this the image of Hercules? But one thing does not pertain, that he is [shown] old and with graying temples. Why, with his tongue pierced with fine chains, does he so easily pull behind him men who have those chains affixed to their ears?" "Is it not stated by the Gauls that the extraordinary Alcides [Hercules] gave laws to the peoples by the power of his tongue — and not by his weapons? Arms must yield before togas [senatorial robes], and he whose real strength lies in eloquence attracts towards himself the votes of even those whose hearts may be hardened."

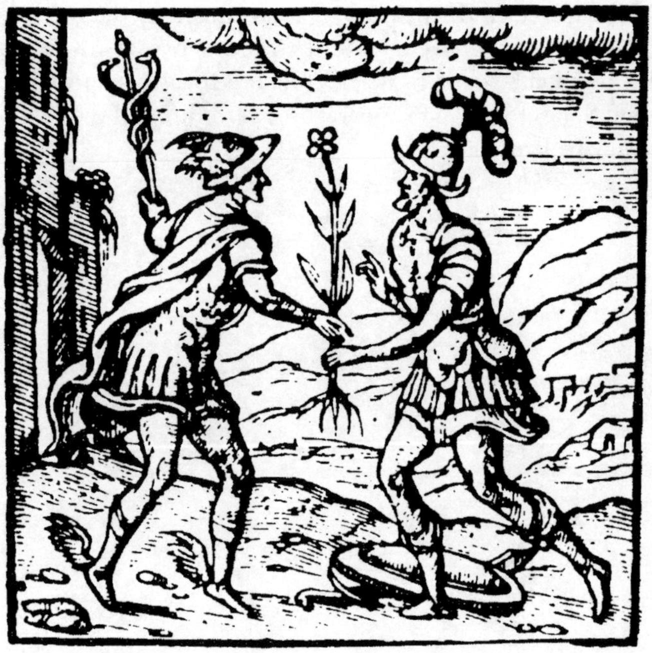

Emblema CLXXXI

FACUNDIA DIFFICILIS

Antidotum Aeae medicata in pocula Circes
Mercurium hoc Ithaco fama dedisse fuit.
Moly vocant: id vix radice evellitur atra,
Purpureus sed flos, lactis et instar habet.
Eloquii candor facundiaque allicit omnes:
Sed multi res est tanta laboris opus.

Emblem 181

ELOQUENCE IS DIFFICULT

It is well known how Mercury gave the Ithacan [Ulysses] an antidote for the drugged brews of Circe. It is called the moly plant, and its black root is pulled up with some difficulty. It is purple, but the flowers produce a kind of milk. Although the brilliance and fecundity of eloquence attracts everybody, it is an opus [or work of art] arising from much work and many efforts.

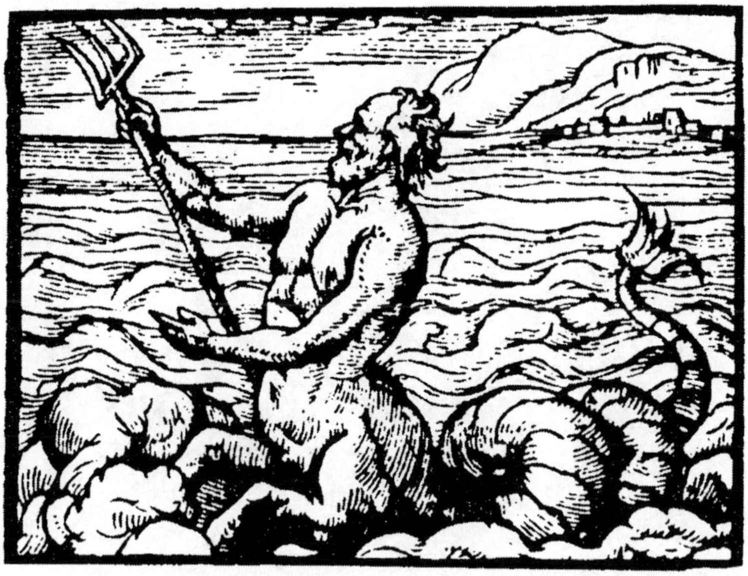

Emblema CLXXXII

ANTIQUISSIMA QUAEQUE COMMENTITIA

Pallenaee senex, cui forma est histrica, Proteu,
Qui modo membra viti fers, modo membra feri:
Dic age, quae species ratio te vertit in omnes,
Nulla sit ut vario certa figura tibi?
Signa vetustatis, primaevi et praefero secli,
De quo quisque suo somniat arbitrio.

Emblem 182

WHATEVER IS MOST ANCIENT IS IMAGINARY

(a dialogue)

"Old man from Pallenia, oh Proteus, you have as many shapes as an actor has roles. Why are your members sometimes that of a man, and sometimes that of an animal? Come on, tell me, what can be the reason for you to change into all manner of shapes, and yet you have no fixed figure of your own?" "I reveal the signs belonging to the most remote ages, ancient and prehistoric, and each man imagines them according to his whimsy."

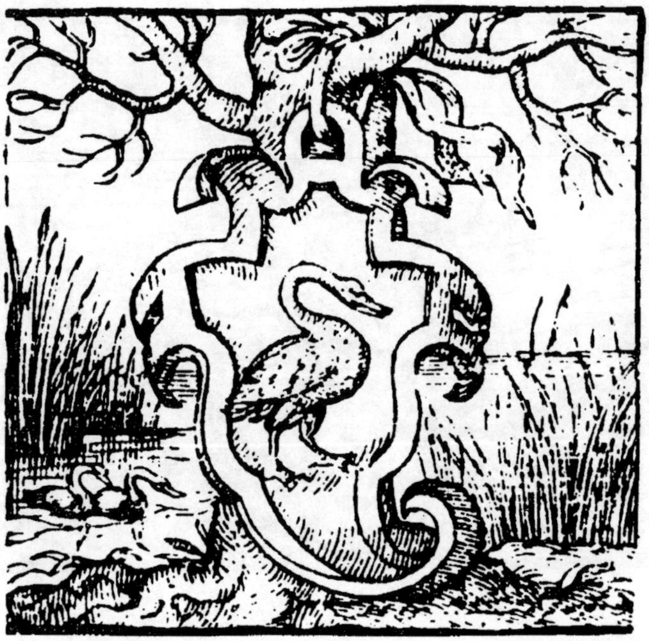

Emblema CLXXXIII

INSIGNIA POETARUM

Gentiles clypeos sunt qui in Iovis alite gestant,
Sunt quibus aut serpens, aut leo, signa ferunt:
Dira sed haec vatum fugiant animalia ceras,
Doctaque sustineat stemmata pulcher Olor.
Hic Phoebo sacer, et nostrae regionis alumnus:
Rex olim, veteres servat adhuc titulos.

Emblem 183

THE BADGE OF THE POETS

There are those who display on their family shields either the bird of Jupiter [an eagle], or a serpent, or a lion. But let all those savage animals flee from the waxen writing-tablets of the vatic poets; let the beautiful Swan support their learned pedigrees. This bird is sacred to Phoebus [Apollo], and it is a student in our region [Italy]: formerly a king, it still retains its old titles.

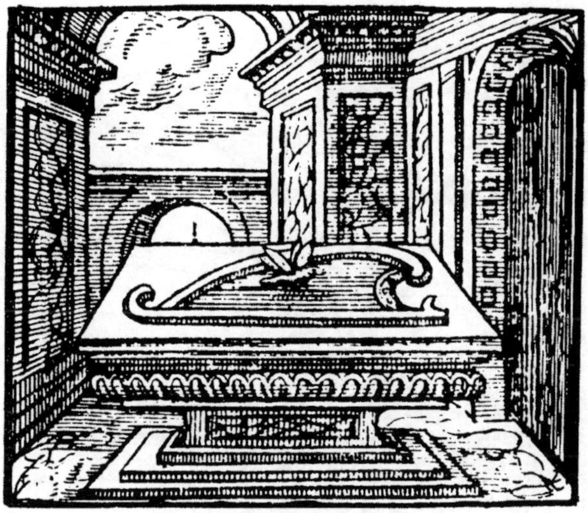

Emblema CLXXXIV

MUSICAM DIIS CURAE ESSE

Locrensis posuit tibi, Delphice Phoebe, cicadam
Eunomus hanc, palmae signa decora suae.
Certabat plectro Sparthyn commissus in hostem,
Et percussa sonum pollice fila dabant.
Trita fides rauco coepit cum stridere bombo,
Legitimum harmonias et vitiare melos:
Tum citharae argutans suavis sese intulit ales,
Quae fractam impleret voce cicada fidem:
Quaeque allecta, soni ad legem descendit ab altis
Saltibus, ut nobis garrula ferret opem.
Ergo tuae ut firmus stet honos, o sancte, cicadae,
Pro cithara hic fidicen aeneus ipsa sedet.

Emblem 184

MUSIC IS THE CONCERN OF THE GODS

Eunomus the Locrian dedicated to you, oh Delphic Apollo, this cicada as a worthy sign of his own triumph. Challenged by a Spartan, he competed against his lyre and, plucked with his thumb, the strings were resounding. Then one of them, worn out, began to emit a sour sound and the buzzing corrupted the rightful harmony of the music. Then a delightful, chirping cicada hopped upon the cithara to compensate with its voice for the broken string. Seduced by the sound, the cicada had descended from the woody heights so that its chirping voice might help us with its art work. Hence, so that the honor due to your cicada may become eternal, oh holy one, the bronze image of the lutist perches here above the cithara.

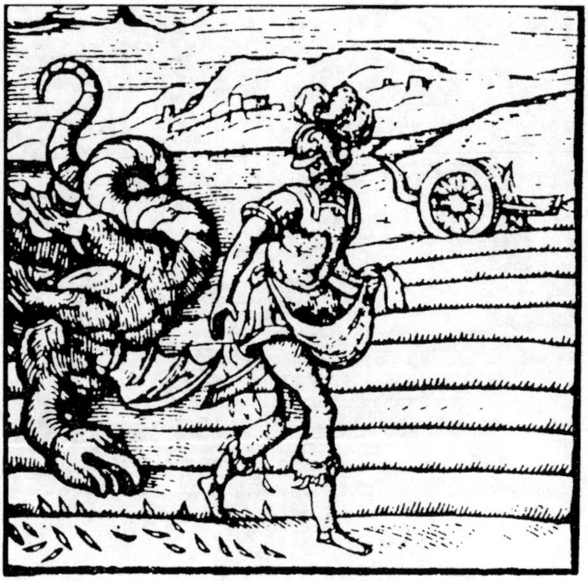

Emblema CLXXXV

LITTERA OCCIDIT, SPIRITUS VIVIFICAT

Vipereos Cadmus dentes ut credidit arvis,
Sevit et Aonio semina dira solo:
Terrigenum clypeata cohors exorta virorum est,
Hostili inter se qui cecidere manu.
Evasere, quibus monitu Tritonidos armis
Abiectis data pax, dextraque iuncta fuit.
Primus Agenorides elementa, notasque magistris
Tradidit, iis suavem iunxit et harmoniam.
Quorum discipulos contraria plurima vexans,
Non nisi Palladia qui dirimuntur ope.

Emblem 185

THE LETTER KILLS AND THE SPIRIT VIVIFIES

As it is believed, Cadmus sowed the dragon's teeth, dire seeds, in the fields of Aonius [Boethia]. A shield-bearing cohort sprang up from the earth [the Spartae], and they began to kill one another with a hostile hand. The only ones who saved themselves were those who threw down their weapons following the counsel of Tritonia [Athena]; peace was made and they shook hands. Agenor [the father of Cadmus] was the first to transmit the letters of the alphabet to the teachers; he united these with sweet harmony. His disciples later saw themselves vexed by many polemics; these were only reconciled with the help of Pallas [Athena].

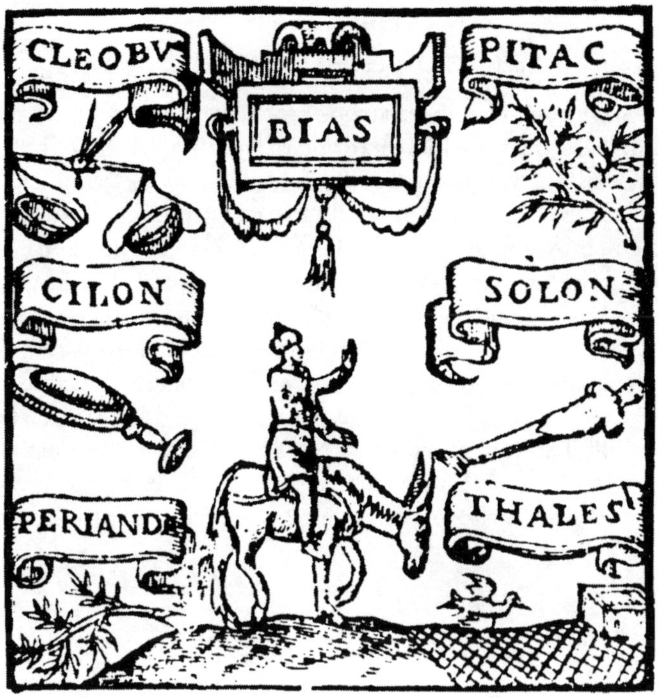

Emblema CLXXXVI

DICTA SEPTEM SAPIENTUM

Haec habeas, septem Sapientum effingere dicta,
Atque ea picturis qui celebrare velis.
Optimus in rebus modus est, Cleobulus ut inquit:
Hoc trutinae examen, sive libella docet.
Noscere se Chilon Spartanus quemque iubebat:
Hoc speculum in manibus, vitraque sumpta dabunt.
Quod Periander ait, frena adde, Corinthius, irae:
Puleium admotum naribus efficiet.
Pittacus at, ne quid, dixit, nimis, haec eadem aiunt,
Contracto qui git ore liquefaciunt.
Respexisse Solon finem iubet. Ultimus agris
Terminus haud magno cesserot ipse Iovi.
Heu, quam vera Bias; est copia magna malorum:
Musimoni insideat effice Sardus eques.
Ne praes esto, Thales dixit; sic illita visco
In laqueos sociam parra, meropsque trahit.

Emblem 186

SAYINGS OF THE SEVEN WISE MEN

Here you have portrayed the sayings of the seven wise men; in case you wish to celebrate them, these are made known to you in paintings. As Cleobulus stated: "Due measurement is best in everything," and this is shown by the accuracy of the balance or by a pair of scales. Chilon the Spartan ordered everyone to "Know thyself"; this will be represented by a mirror or a looking-glass held in the hands. What Periander from Corinth stated was "Curb your anger": the sprig of mint held to the nose helps. Pittacus advised "Nothing in excess," and the same thing is said by those who, with their lips twisted, are chewing coriander. Solon demanded that the end of things be foreseen: the final boundary stone [*terminus*] in a field will not ever yield before mighty Jupiter. Oh my, how great is the truth expressed by Bias: "There is a great abundance of evil!" This is pictured with a Sardinian riding upon a sheep-goat hybrid. Stated Thales, "Don't become a bondsman": hence, the barn-owl or bee-eater bird smeared with bird-lime is shown attracting its companions into the net.

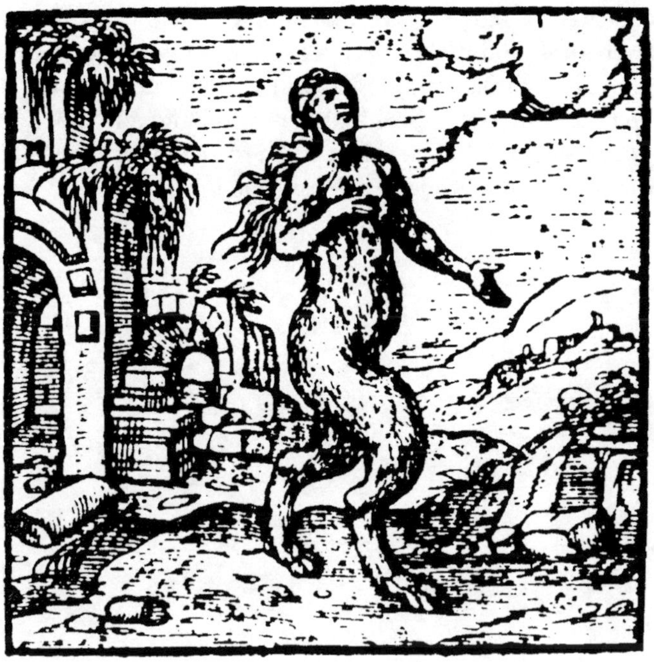

Emblema CLXXXVII

SUBMOVENDAM IGNORANTIAM

Quod monstrum id? Sphinx est. Cur candida virginis ora,
Et volucrum pennas, crura leonis haber?
Hanc faciem assumpsit rerum ignorantia: tanti
Scilicet est triplex causa et origo mali.
Sunt quos ingenium leve, sunt quos blanda voluptas,
Sunt et quos faciunt corda superba rudes.
At quibus est notum, quid Delphica littera poscit,
Praecipitis monstri guttura dira secant.
Namque vir ipse bipesque tripesque et quadrupes idem est,
Primaque prudentis laurea, nosse virum.

Emblem 187

IGNORANCE MUST BE BANISHED

(a dialogue)

"What monster is this?" "It is the Sphinx." "Why does it have the shining face of a virgin and the thick plumage of a bird and the feet of a lion?" "Ignorance assumed this appearance because the cause and origin of so many evils is threefold. There are those for whom a weak mind makes them ignorant; others are made so by their compliant sexual appetites, and others as due to their haughty hearts. But those who know what is inscribed in the Delphic text will slit the cruel throat of the dangerous monster. Since man is himself a biped, also a tripod and a tetrapod [or three- and four-footed, according to the lethal riddle posed to Oedipus by the Sphinx], the preeminent crown given to the prudent is to know man."

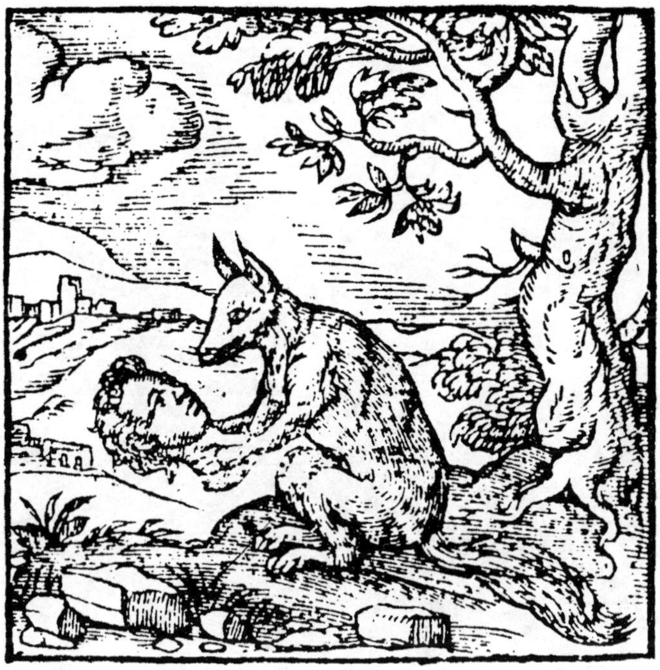

Emblema CLXXXVIII

MENTEM, NON FORMAM, PLUS POLLERE

Ingressa vulpes in Choragi pergulam,
Fabre expolitum invenit humanum caput,
Sic eleganter fabricatum, ut spiritus
Solum deesset, caeteris vivisceret.
Id illa cum sumpsisset in manus, ait,
O quale caput est! Sed cerebrum non habet.

Emblem 188

THE MIND, NOT BEAUTY, IS THE MORE WORTHY

A fox ventured inside the workshop of a stage-manager and found there a beautifully rendered human head, and it was so elegantly carved that it only lacked breath to make it alive in all other aspects. Taking it in its hands, the fox said: "Oh, what a beautiful head—but it has no brain!"

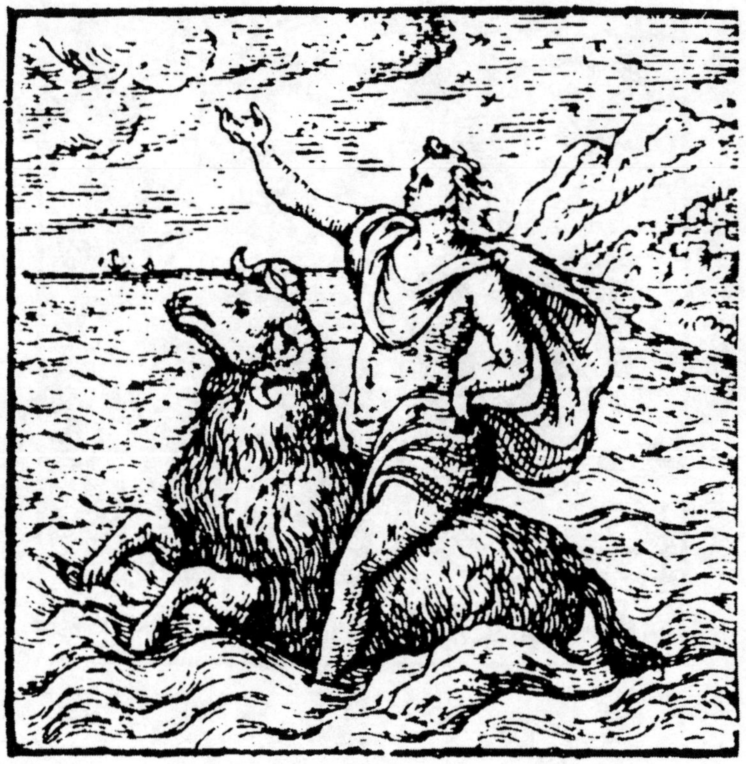

Emblema CLXXXIX

DIVES INDOCTUS

Tranat aquas residens pretioso in vellere Phryxus,
Et flavam impavidus per mare scandit ovem.
Ecquid id est? Vir sensu hebeti, sed divite gaza,
Coniugis, aut servi quem regit arbitrium.

Emblem 189

AN UNLEARNED RICH MAN

Phryxus crosses the waters enthroned upon the precious fleece, fearlessly riding through the ocean bestride the golden sheep. And who is like that? If very rich in treasure, but still lacking in wits, a man may be ruled by the arbitrary caprices of his wife — or even his slave.

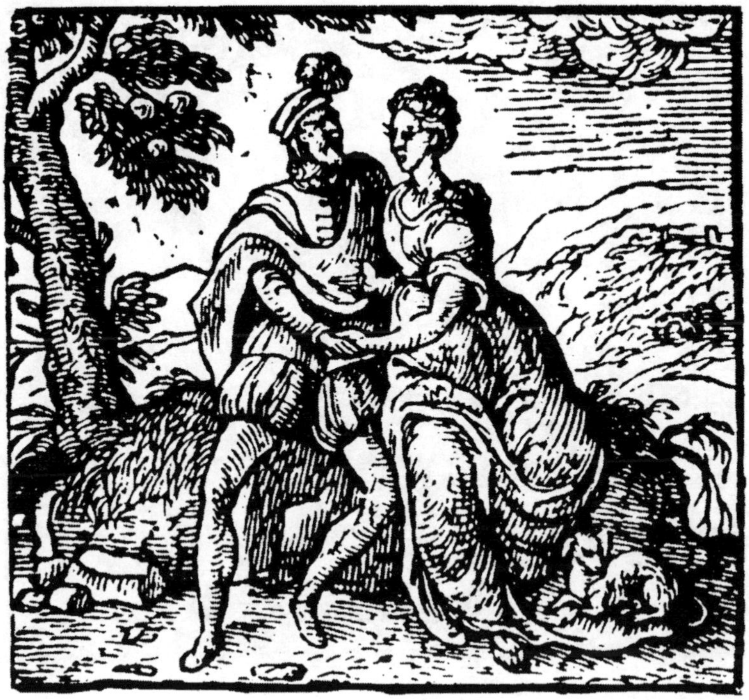

Emblema CXC

IN FIDEM UXORIAM

Ecce puella, viro quae dextra iungitut: ecce
Ut sedet, ut catulus lusitat ante pedes!
Haec fidei est species: Veneris quam si educat ardor,
Malorum in laeva non male ramus erit:
Poma etenim Veneris sunt. Sic Schoeneida vicit
Hippomenes, petit sic Galatea virum.

Emblem 190

ABOUT THE FIDELITY OF A WIFE

Behold a girl joined with her right hand to her husband: behold how she is seated, and see how a puppy is playing at her feet! This is the image of fidelity: if the fire of Venus nourishes her, it is proper that there be put to the left a branch of apples, for these are fruits of Venus. Thereby, the daughter of Schoeneus [Atalanta] defeated Hippomenes, and thus Galatea sought a husband [Acis].

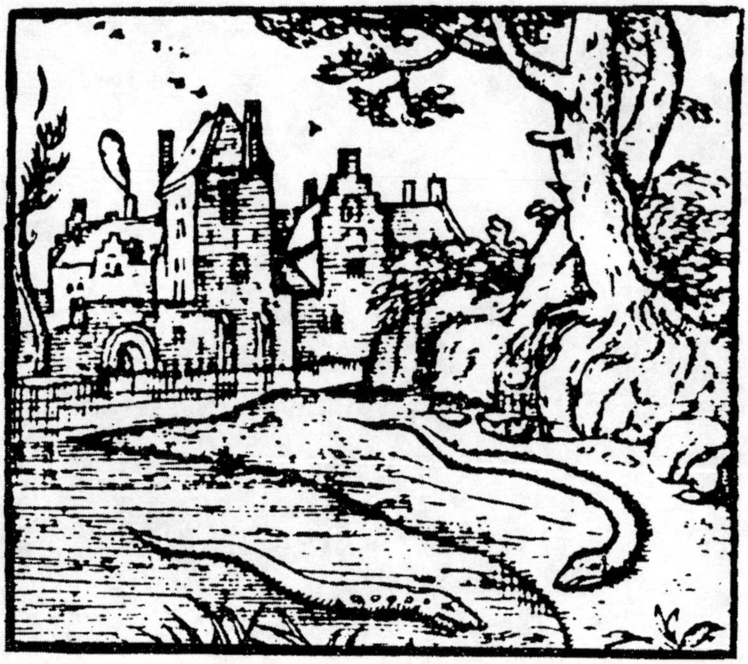

Emblema CXCI

REVERENTIAM IN MATRIMONIO REQUIRI

Cum furit in Venerem, pelagi se littore sistit
Vipera, et ab stomacho dira venena vomit:
Muraenamque ciens ingentia sibila tollit,
At simul amplexus appetit illa viri.
Maxima debetur thalamo reverentia: coniux
Alternum debet coniubi et obsequium.

Emblem 191

MARRIAGE REQUIRES RESPECT

When it becomes infuriated by love [or Venus], the viper places itself on the beach and vomits from its stomach the dire venom. It then emits loud hisses to summon the eel, and she simultaneously longs for the embraces of the male. The maximum reverence is due to the marriage-bed: one spouse owes to the other spouse reciprocal allegiance.

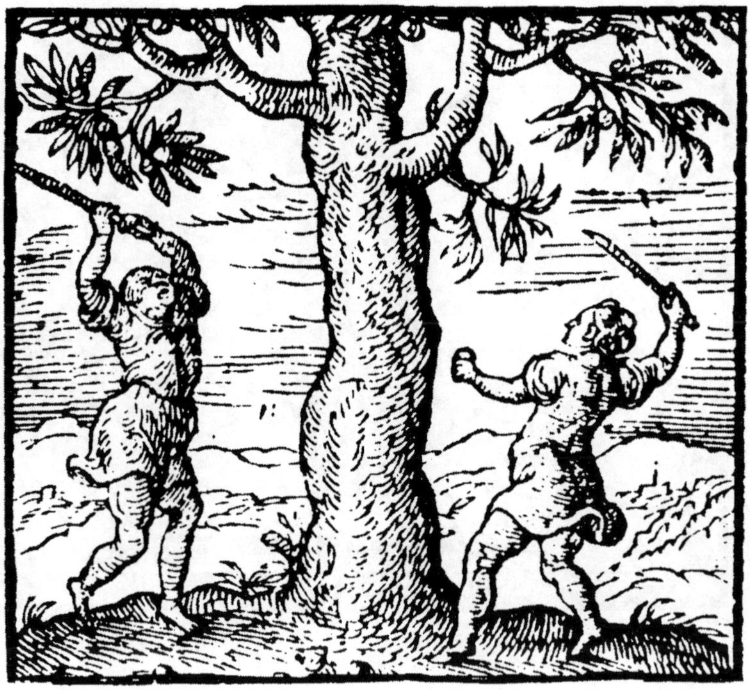

Emblema CXCII

IN FECUNDITATEM SIBI DAMNOSAM

Ludibrium pueris lapides iacientibus, hoc me
In trivio posuit rustica cura nucem:
Quae laceris ramis, perstrictoque ardua libro,
Certatim fundis per latus omne petor.
Quid sterili posset contingere turpius? Eheu,
Infelix, fructus in mea damna fero!

Emblem 192

FECUNDITY HARMING ITSELF

Here you see me used as a plaything by boys pitching rocks at me, a walnut tree, installed in a crossroads by the rustic concern for nuts. Towering aloft with tattered branches and bruised bark, I am unerringly attacked from all sides with slings. How could something so shameful happen to a sterile tree? Oh, woe is me: I bear the fruits of my own damnation!

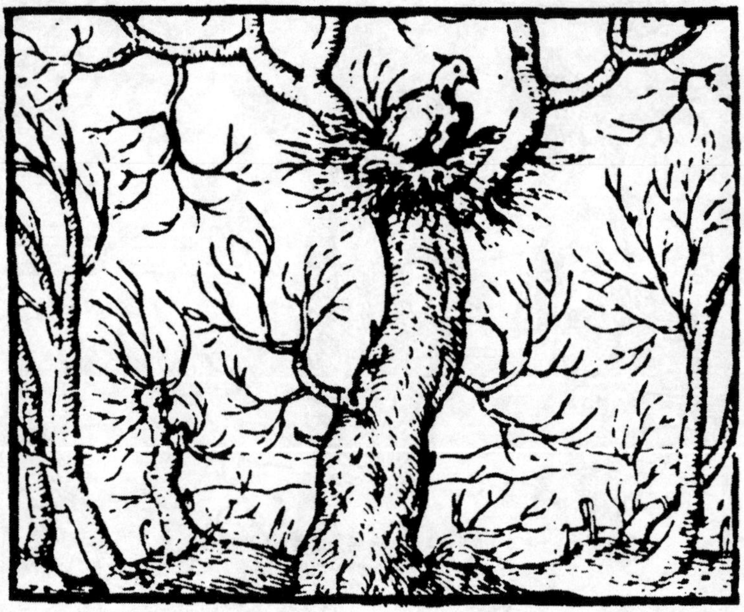

Emblema CXCIII

AMOR FILIORUM

Ante diem vernam boreali cana palumbes
Frigore nidificat, praecoqua et ova fovet:
Mollius et pulli ut iaceant. Sibi vellicat alas,
Queis nuda hiberno deficit ipsa gelu.
Ecquid Colchi pudet, vel te, Progne improba? Mortem
Cum volucris propriae prolis amore subit?

Emblem 193

LOVE FOR CHILDREN

Anticipating spring in winter's cold, the white ring-dove makes its nest and attends to the prematurely hatched eggs. So that her chicks may lie more softly, she plucks her wings; in this manner, stripped, she dies from the wintery frost. Doesn't this shame you, oh you from Colchis [Medea], or you, oh cruel Procne [another famous filiocide], that a bird would confront death for the love of her children?

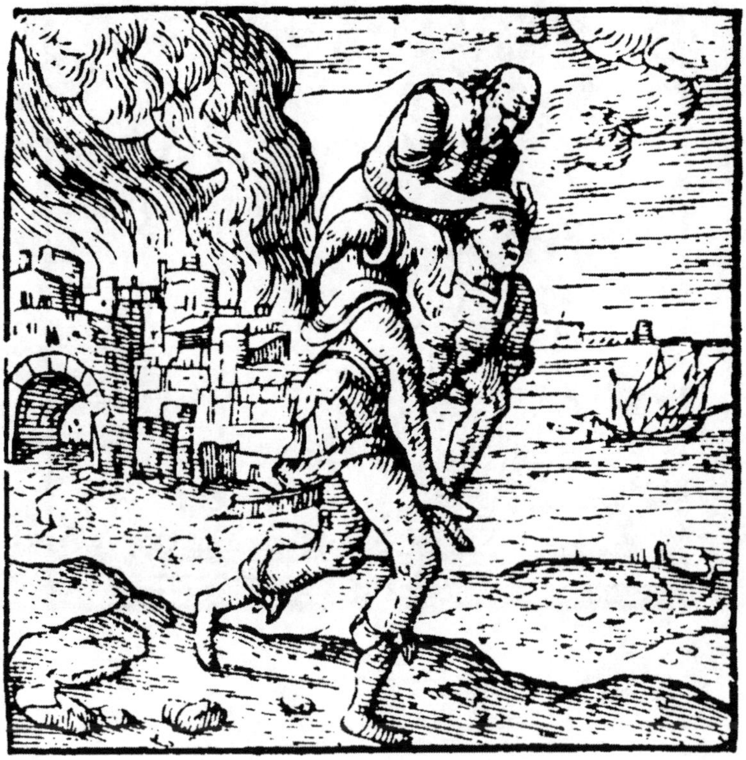

Emblema CXCIV

PIETAS FILIORUM IN PARENTES

Per medios hosteis patriae cum ferret ab igne
Aeneas humeris dulce parentis onus:
Parcite, dicebat: vobis sene adorea rapto
Nulla erit, erepto sed patre summa mihi.

Emblem 194

THE SONS' DEVOTION FOR THEIR PARENTS

In the midst of the enemy, while carrying upon his back the sweet burden of his father [Anchises] to save him from his homeland [Troy] put to the torch, Aeneas kept on saying: "Spare us; for you, for having taken prisoner an old man, there will be no reward for valor, but mine shall be the greatest glory for having rescued my father."

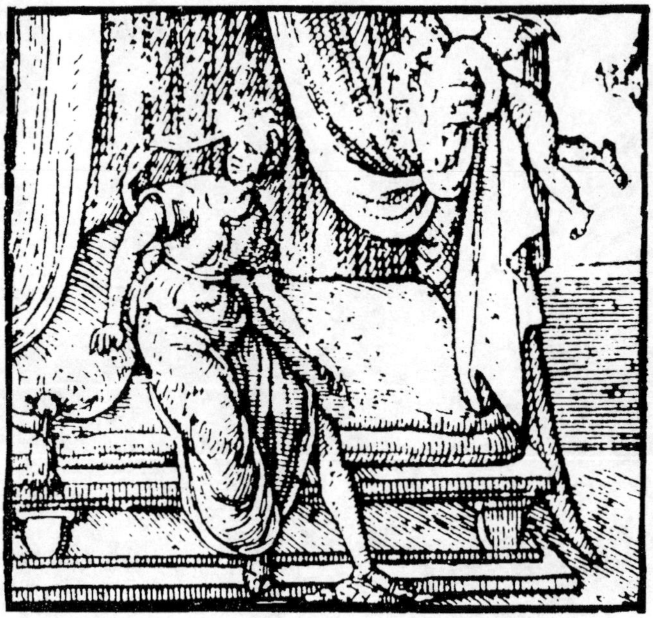

Emblema CXCV

MULIERIS FAMAM, NON FORMAM VULGATAM ESSE OPORTERE

Alma Venus, quaenam haec facies? Quid denotat illa
Testudo, molli quam pede, Diva, premis?
Me sic effinxit Phidias, sexumque referri
Femineum nostra iussit ab effigie:
Quodque manere domi, et tacitas decet esse puellas,
Supposuit pedibus talia signa meis.

Emblem 195

BETTER THAT A WOMAN'S REPUTATION BE PUBLICIZED THAN HER BEAUTY

(a dialogue)

"Whose face is this, oh nourishing Venus? What, oh Goddess, is the meaning of the turtle which you press upon with your soft foot?" "This is how Phidias [the sculptor] portrayed me, and with our image he ordered that the female sex be symbolized. He put such an sign beneath my feet to indicate that it is befitting for girls to stay at home and to keep silent."

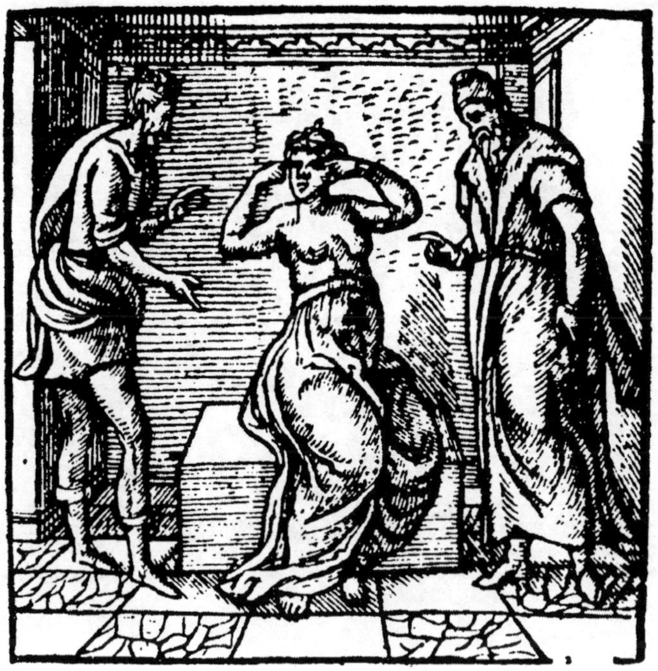

Emblema CXCVI

IN PUDORIS STATUAM

Penelope desponsa sequi cupiebat Ulyssem,
Ni secus Icarius mallet habere pater.
Ille Ithacam, hic offert Spartem. Manet anxia virgo.
Hinc pater, inde viri mutuus urget amor.
Ergo sedens velat vultus, obnubit ocellos:
Ista verecundi signa pudoris erant.
Queis sibi praelatum Icarius cognovit Ulyssem,
Hocque Pudori aram schemate constituit.

Emblem 196

ABOUT A STATUE OF MODESTY

Betrothed to Ulysses, Penelope was eager to accompany him, but Icarius, her father, was inclined to keep her with him. Ulysses offered her Ithaca, and Icarius offered Sparta. The virgin remained anxious. On the one hand, her father was pressuring her and, on the other, she was urged on by the love she shared with the man [Ulysses]. Therefore, she sits with her face veiled and covers her eyes: these were the bashful signs of modesty. By these manifestations Icarius learned that Ulysses was preferred over him, and the father had an altar with this design built to honor Modesty.

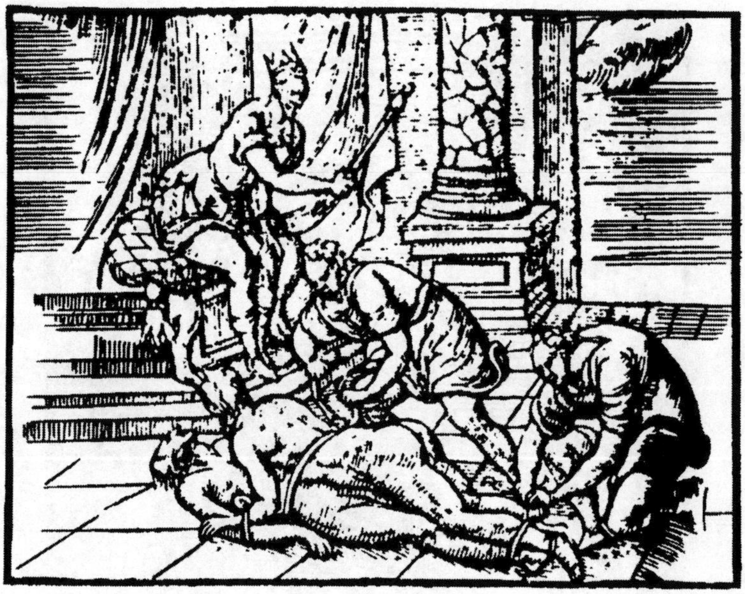

Emblema CXCVII

NUPTA CONTAGIOSO

Dii meliora piis, Mezenti, cur age sic me
Compellas? Emptus quod tibi dote gener;
Gallica quem scabies, dira et mentagra perurit:
Hoc est quidnam aliud, dic mihi saeve pater,
Corpora corporibus quam iungere mortua vivis,
Efferaque Etrusci facta novare ducis?

Emblem 197

MARRIED TO AN INFECTED MAN

(a dialogue)

"May the gods grant a better fate to the pious, oh Mezentius." "Why do you call me to account with that name [of an ancient tyrant]?" "Because of the son-in-law which you bought with a dowry, the one who is [as you knew] consumed by the French pox [syphilis] and covered with horrible eruptions. Tell me, oh savage father, what is this if not uniting dead bodies to the living and bringing them out for burial? Are you not renewing the deeds of the Etruscan leader [Mezentius]?"

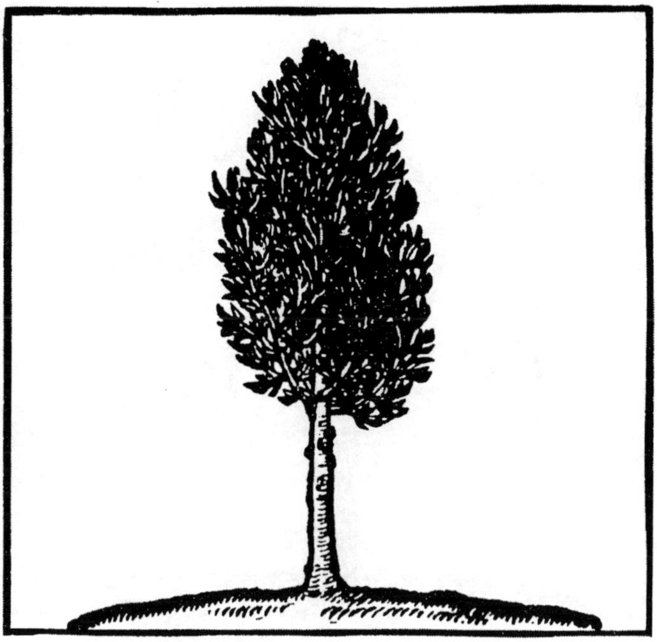

Emblema CXCVIII

CUPRESSUS

Indicat effigies metae, nomenque Cupressi
Tractandos parili conditione suos.
Aliud
Funesta est arbor, procerum monumenta Cupressus,
Quale apium plebis, comere fronde solet.
Aliud
Pulchra come est, pulchro digestaeque ordine frondes;
Sed fructus nullus haec coma pulchra gerit.

Emblem 198

THE CYPRESS

Its conical shape and its name, Cypress, indicates that one's own kind must be treated on equal terms. Otherwise: The cypress is a funereal tree belonging to the monuments honoring nobles, and in the same way that parsley regularly covers plebeian graves with its leafage. Otherwise: Its crown is beautiful, and its leaves are arranged in a beautiful order, but this beautiful crown yields no fruit.

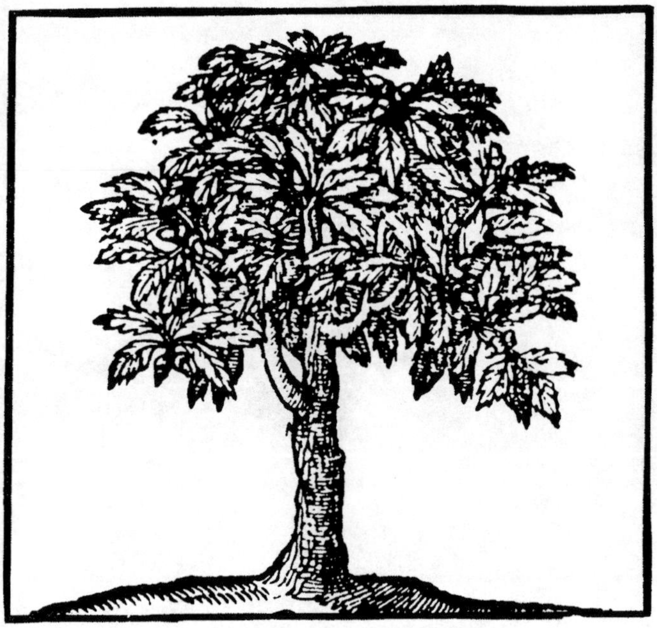

Emblema CXCIX

QUERCUS

Grata Iovi est quercus, qui nos servatque fovetque:
Servanti civem querna corona datur.
Aliud
Glande aluit veteres, sola nunc proficit umbra:
Sic quoque sic arbos officiosa Iovis.

Emblem 199

THE LIVE OAK

The live oak is pleasing to Jupiter, who preserves us and cherishes us: a crown of oak leaves is given to him who watches over a fellow citizen. Otherwise: Its acorns used to feed the ancients, but now we only profit from its shade; one way or the other, however, the tree of Jupiter lends its services.

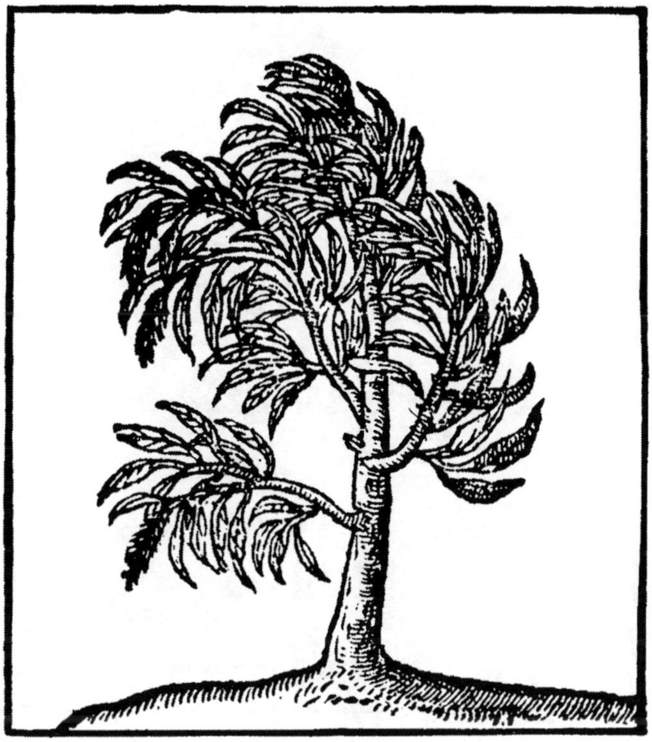

Emblema CC

SALIX

Quod frugisperdam salicem vocitarit Homerus,
Clitoriis homines moribus adsimilat.

Emblem 200

THE WILLOW

The willow, which Homer called a "fruit-loser," can be likened to those men with Clitorian customs [that is, homosexuals].

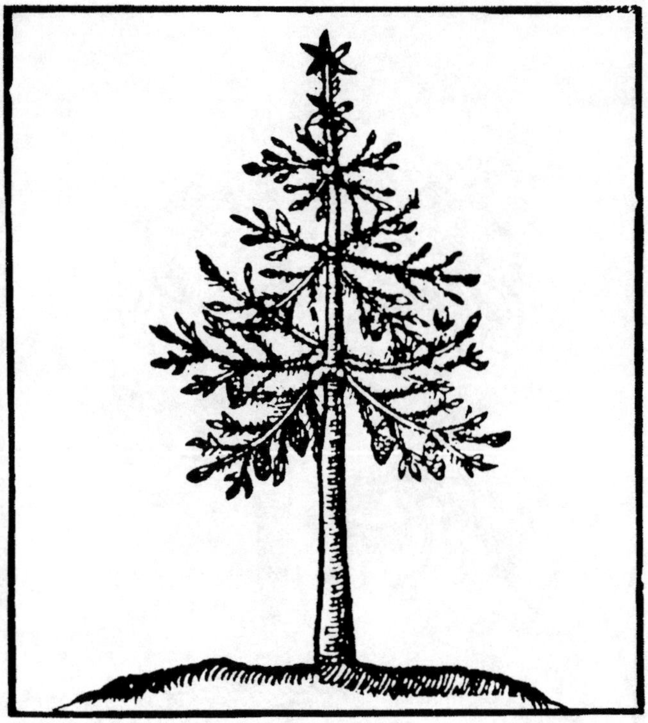

Emblema CCI

ABIES

Apta fretis Abies in montibus editur altis:
Est et in adversis maxima commoditas.

Emblem 201

THE FIR

Suited for [making ships sailing] the high seas, the fir grows upon high mountains: in adverse circumstances, great advantage may be taken from it.

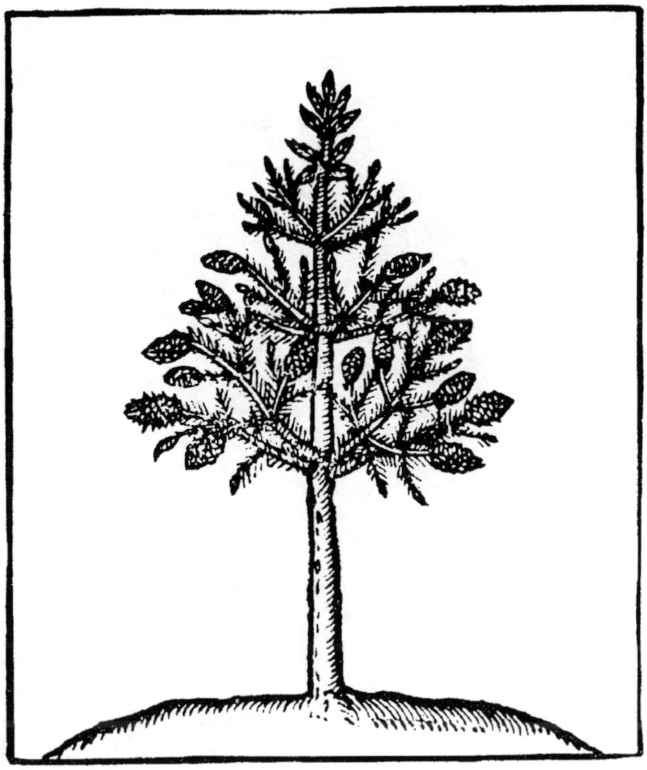

Emblema CCII

PICEA

At picea emittat nullos quod stirpe stolones,
Illius est index, qui sine prole perit.

Emblem 202

THE PINE

Since the pine produces no offshoots from its roots, it is a symbol for the one who dies without offspring.

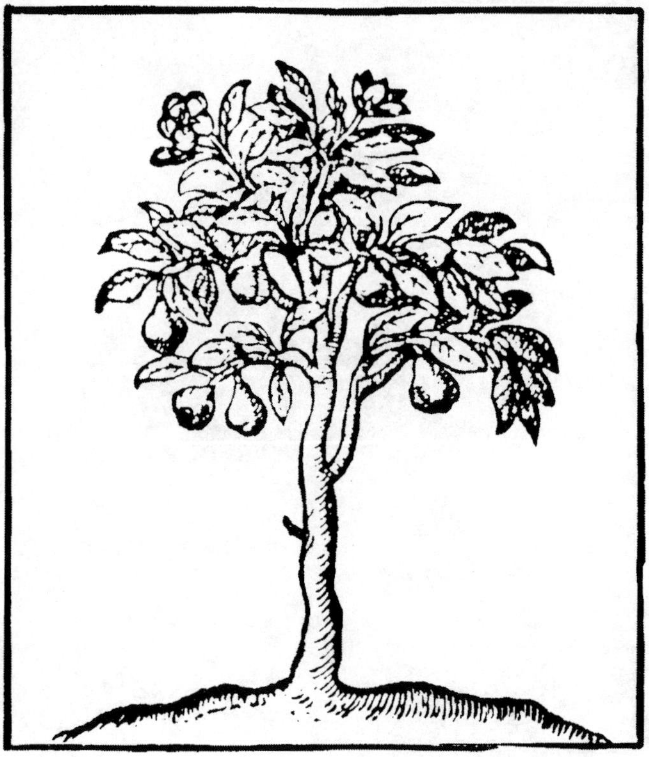

Emblema CCIII

COTONEA

Poma novis tribui debere Cydonia nuptis
Dicitur antiquus constituisse Solon:
Grata ori et stomacho cum sint, ut et halitus illis
Sit suavis, blandus manet et ore lepos.

Emblem 203

THE QUINCE

It is said that Solon decreed the ancient Cretan obligation of giving quinces to newly-weds. They are pleasing to the mouth and stomach, and they also sweeten the breath, leaving the mouth seductively charming and winsome.

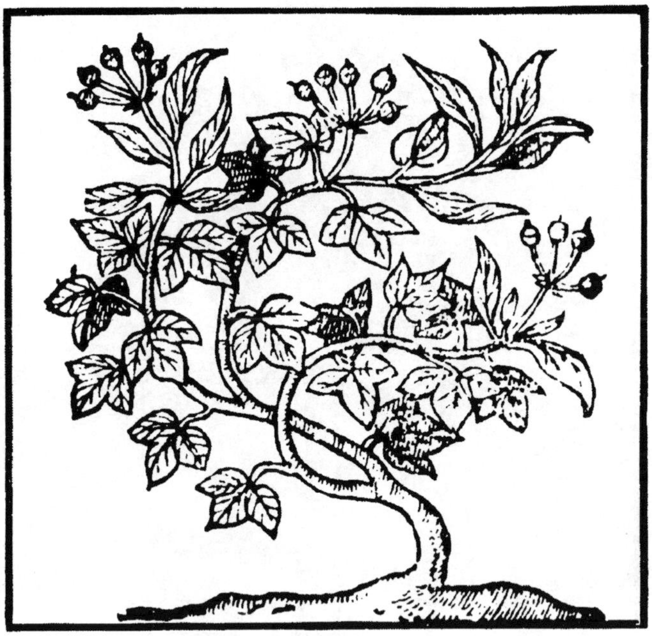

Emblema CCIV
HEDERA

Haudquaquam arescens hederae est arbuscula, Cisso
Quae puero Bacchum dona dedisse ferunt:
Errabunda, procax, auratis fulva corymbis,
Exterius viridis, caetera pallor habet.
Hinc aptis vates cingunt sua tempora sertis:
Pallescunt studiis, laus diuturna viret.

Emblem 204
IVY

It is said that Bacchus gave as a present to the child Cissus the ivy bushes which never wither. Ivy is errant and wanders brashly, and it is made tawny with its golden clusters; green on top, the back of its leaves are pale. This is why the brows of poets are bound with ivy garlands: they become pale due to their studies, but their glory flourishes for a long time.

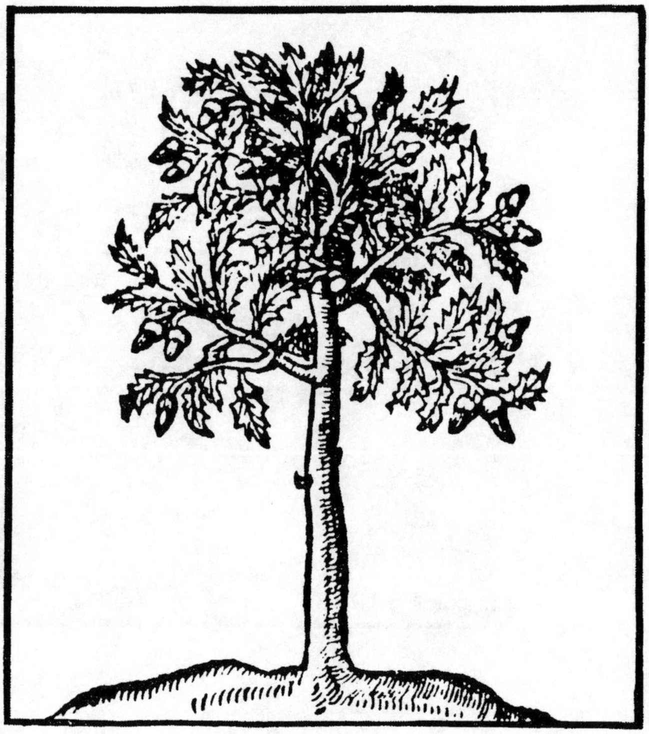

Emblema CCV

ILEX

Duritie nimia quod sese rumperit llex,
Symbola civilis seditionis habet.

Emblem 205

THE HOLM-OAK

Since its excessive hardness causes it to burst apart, the holm-oak becomes the symbol of civil insurrection.

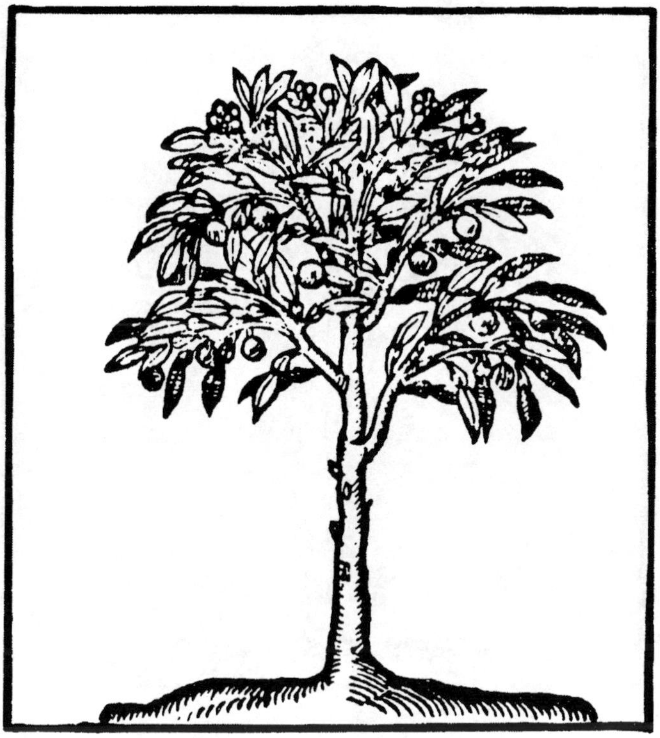

Emblema CCVI

MALUS MEDICA

Aurea sunt Veneris poma haec: iucuntus amaror
Indicat, est Graecis sic *glukupikros* amor.

Emblem 206

THE ORANGE

These are the golden apples of Venus: a pleasing bitterness indicates the orange, so love is also called by the Greeks "bitter-sweet."

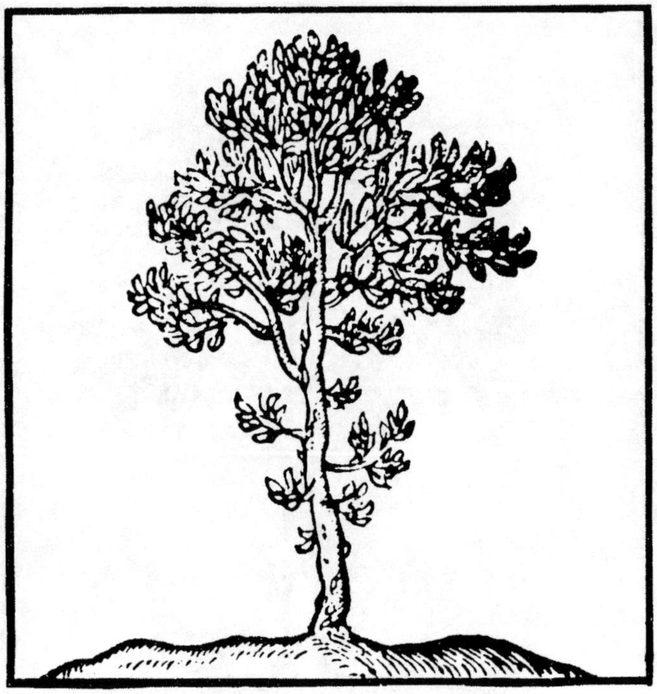

Emblema CCVII

BUXUS

Perpetuo viridis, crispoque cacumine buxus,
Unde est disparibus fistula facta modis,
Deliciis apta est teneris et amantibus arbor:
Pallor inest illi, pallet et omnis amans.

Emblem 207

THE BOX-WOOD

The box-wood is perpetually green and it has a curly crown. Flutes are made from it in different modes. It is a tree suited to pleasures and and it is appropriate for the affectionate and lovers: pallor distinguishes it, and every lover grows pale.

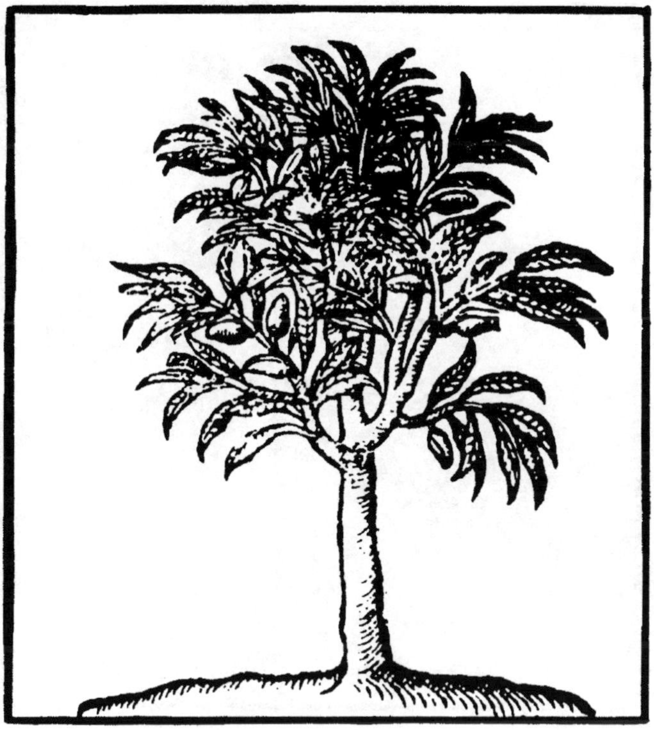

Emblema CCVIII

AMYGDALUS

Cur properan follis praemittis, amygdale, flores?
Odi pupillos praecocis ingenii.

Emblem 208

THE ALMOND

(a dialogue)

"Why do you hasten to display your flowers, oh almond-tree, before you grow your leaves?" "I hate the students with precocious talents."

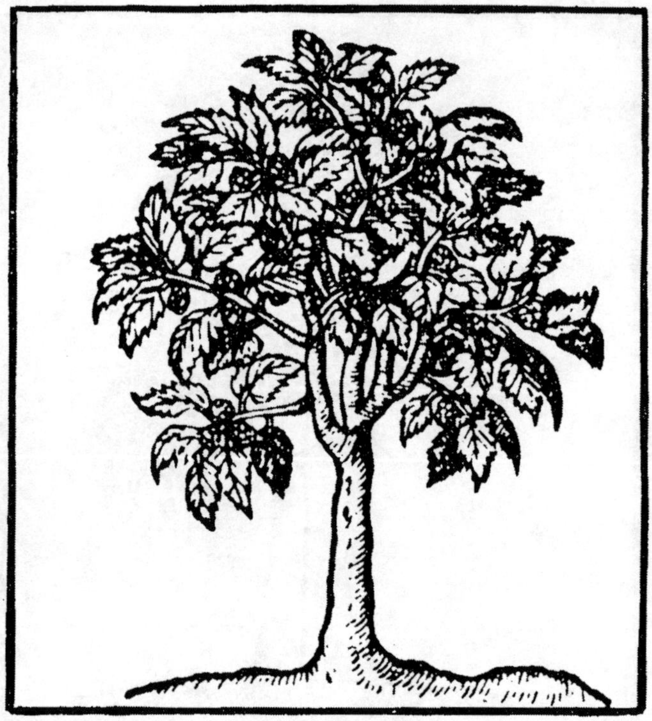

Emblema CCIX

MORUS

Serior at morus nisi frigore lapso
Germinat: et sapiens nomina falsa gerit.

Emblem 209

THE MULBERRY

On the other hand [and with reference to the almond], more sensibly, the mulberry only germinates after the frosts quit: and, being wise, it is falsely named [*morus*, meaning "crazy, extravagant"].

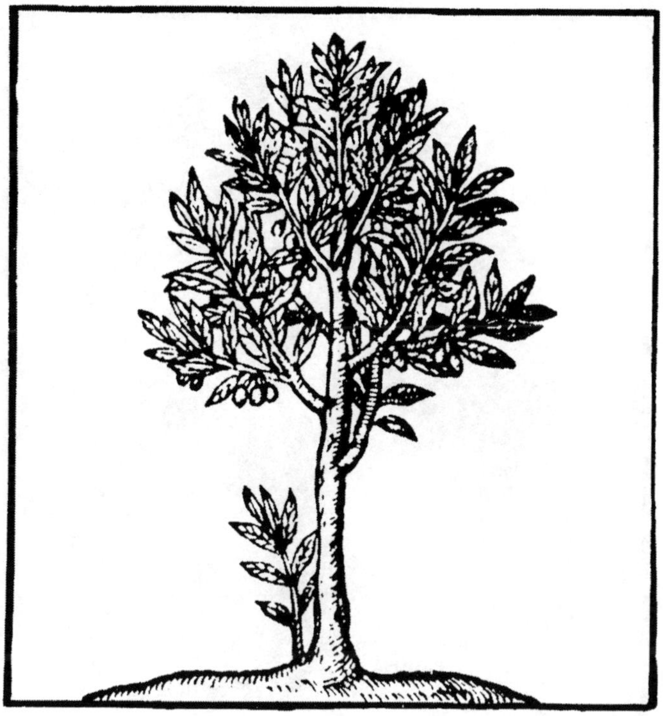

Emblema CCX

LAURUS

Praescia venturi Laurus, fert signa salutis:
Subdita pulvillo somnia vera facit.
Aliud
Debetur Carlo superatis Poenis:
Victrices ornent talia serta comas.

Emblem 210

THE LAUREL

Reading the future, the Laurel brings signs of salvation. Placed under a pillow, it induces truthful dreams. Otherwise: a laurel wreath is due to Charles [V] for having conquered the Carthaginians [sic: the Turks at Tunis]: let such garlands adorn the heads of victors.

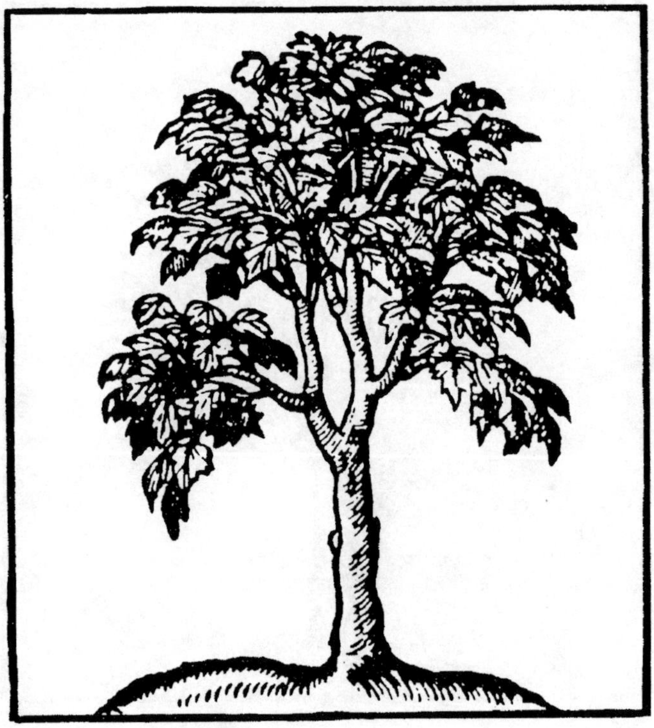

Emblema CCXI

POPULUS ALBA

Herculeos crines bicolor quod populus ornet,
Temporis alternat noxque diesque vices.

Emblem 211

THE WHITE POPLAR

Because the two-colored poplar adorns the mane of Hercules, day and night alternate in the succession of time.

Appendix: The "Suppressed" Emblem

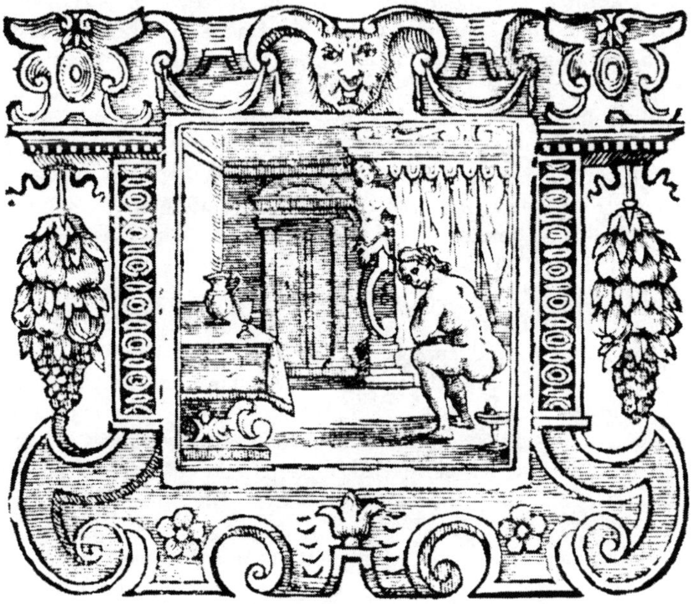

Emblema LXXX

ADVERSUS NATURAM PECCANTES.

Turpe quidem dictu, sed et est res improba factu,
Excipiat siquis choenice ventris onus.
Mensuram, legisque modum hoc excedere sanctae est,
Quale sit incesto pollui adulterio.

Emblem 80
AGAINST THOSE SINNING AGAINST NATURE

It is quite shocking to relate, but even more is it a foul deed whenever anyone chooses to dump the burden of his bowels into a food bowl. This act stands for all offenses exceeding the canonic measure of sacred law, just as when one is willingly defiled by sexual pollution, incest and adultery.

According to the erudite commentary of Johann Thuilius, as published in 1621:

> To date, no one has produced a picture for this emblem and, as for the verses themselves [*epigramma*], previous commentators have just "lightly brushed these aside" (as the saying goes). Nevertheless, and employing quite unrestrained words, I shall by no means shy away from tackling this rather obscene matter [*rem turpiculam*], especially as this trifle [*zizania*] really demands a most thorough pruning. For this reason, the future artist is instructed, in advance, as follows [*propter sic pictori praejuvi*]: let there be pictured a bed closed on all sides by curtains and, beside it, let there be displayed a naked man who unloads his gut into a golden dish [*homo nudus ventrem in pateram auream exoneret*]. ... In regards to what actually goes on within that curtained bed, let that remain my concern, and let it be known also only by our artist, for here one is anxious to spare chaste eyes and, thereby, chaste minds [*castis oculis, & ... mentibus*]. For this reason, to be sure, the emblem had been relegated to the end [*calcem reiectum fuit*] by Minos [Claude Mignault, an earlier commentator] since it was judged by him to be unsuited for tender ears and thus unseemly for extended interpretation [*explicatione prolixor*]. To the contrary, and just as Virgil put it, I am not ashamed to gather up pearls from a dung-heap [*ex stercore margaritas legere*]. Therefore, let's get to the [interpretive] matter at hand.
>
> I notice an allusion here to one of the *Symbola* of Pythagoras, the one which Plutarch interprets as follows in his treatise *De educatione puerorum*: "Food ought not be consigned to a chamber-pot [*cibos in scaphio non ponendos*]." Certainly this signifies [according to Plutarch] that: "It is improper to allow lofty thoughts to be conveyed to an empty mind; speech, after all, is food for the intellect [*intelligentiae cibus est*], but this food may be rendered unclean by human vileness [*quem impurum reddit hominum nequitia*]." ... On the other hand, it appears that this emblem [by Alciati] was drawn from the fifth book of Artemidorus' *De insomniis*, where he had this to say: "Somebody had a dream to the effect that he had loosened his bowels into a food-bowl [*choenicem alvum exonerare*]. In addition to this foulness, and since he had incestuous relations with his sister, he was damned [*cum sorore cubitasset, damnatus est*]." Indeed, since a choenix represents "a measure," thus its meaning is likened to "a law" [*mensura enim est choenix: at quidem mensura legi similis est*]. In this way, he [Artemidorus' pre–Freudian dreamer] had confessed to doing a deed which broke the law because he committed an act considered inadmissible by the laws of all the Greek city-states.
>
> I [Thuilius] am therefore certainly ready to wager that when Alciati conceived of this emblem he must have been recalling a certain distich by Martial, the one discussing Bassa: "You, oh Bassa, are not even ashamed to unload the wretched load of your guts upon gold; you drink from crystal — and you do some costly shitting!" [*Ventris onus misero, nec te pudet, excipis auro, Bassa. Bibis vitro — carius ergo cacas!*]. Moreover [I believe] that this epigram [by Alciati] had been intended to be compared to a certain criminal act, the perversity of male buggery [*masculae Veneris flagitium*], and so, even separately from the Motto, the emblem [as a whole] bears

> comparison with Bassa, he who is "*carius cacat* [a costly crapper]." Indeed, what else [other than buggery] could be more in the nature of a reversal of the natural sequence [*hysteron proteron*]? Is there [likewise] any more foully ugly abuse [*turpior abusus*] than the dumping of one's excrements upon [expensive] gold whilst drinking from [inexpensive] glass and crockery? In this sense, such a loathsome exchange of containers [*tam execrando vasorum permutatio*] is surely *contra naturam*, that is "against nature" according to the definition of this perversion [*flagitium*] as is accepted by most jurists. So much for my opinion concerning this emblem, for which I have provided this picture and, as for the rest, I may now leave that to the reader's judgment [*de reliquo, lectoris isto iudicium*].

(J. Thuilius, *Andreae Alciati Emblematua cum commentariis. ... Opera et vigiliis Ioannis Thuilii ... Patavij apud Petrum Paulum Tozzium....* Padua: Tozzi, 1621, pp. 353–56.)

Select Bibliography

For annotated editions of Alciati's emblem-book, see the following works listed below: Daly and Callahan (eds.); Daza Pinciano (trans.); López; Mignault; Sánchez Brocense; Sebastián (ed., 1985); Thuilius. See also Aesop; the various bestiaries (Hassig [ed.], Sebastián [ed., 1986], White [ed.]); Brant; Cartari; Colonna; Conti; Covarrubias; Erasmus; Giovio; Gracián; *Greek Anthology*; Horapollo; Loyola; Menestrier; Picinelli; Sequeyros (trans.); Tesauro; Valeriano; Whitney.

Abbondanza, R. "The Methodology of Andrea Alciati." In E. Cochrane (ed.), *The Late Renaissance in Italy*. London: Macmillan, 1970, pp. 77–90.

Aesop. *Fables of Aesop*, ed. S. A. Handford. Harmondsworth: Penguin, 1964.

Alciati, A. *Emblematum liber*. Augsburg: Steyner, 1531 (editio princeps; available in microfiche from Inter-Documentation Company, Leiden, the Netherlands).

Allen, D. C. "Ben Jonson and the Hieroglyphics." *Philological Quarterly* XVIII, 1939, pp. 290–300.

Bagley, A. L., et al. (eds.). *The Telling Image: Explorations in the Emblem*. New York: AMS, 1995.

Balavoine, C. "Les Emblèmes d'Alciat: sens et contresens." *L'Emblème à la Renaissance*. Paris: Sedes, 1982, pp. 49–60.

Bauer, L. F. "Seventeenth-Century Naturalism and the Emblematic Interpretation of Paintings," *Emblematica* III, 1988, pp. 209–22.

Becker, J. "'De duystere sin van de geschilderde figueren': Zum Doppelsinn in Rätsel, Emblem und Genrestück." In J. Müller Hofstede (ed.), *Wort und Bild in der niederländische Kunst und Literatur des 16. und 17. Jahrhunders*. Erfstads: Olms, 1984, pp. 17–29.

Bertonasco, M. F. *Crashaw and the Baroque*. Tuscaloosa: University of Alabama Press, 1971.

Bialostocki, J. "Rembrandt's 'Terminus.'" *Wallraf-Richartz Jahrbuch* XXVII, 1966, pp. 49–60.

Boas, G. (ed.) *The Hieroglyphics of Horapollo*. Princeton NJ: Princeton University Press, 1983.

Bolzoni, L. *The Gallery of Memory: Literary and Iconographical Models in the Age of the Printing Press*. Toronto: University of Toronto Press, 2001.

Brant, S. *Das Narrenschift*, ed. H. A. Junghans. Stuttgart: Reclam, 1980.

_____. *The Ship of Fools*, trans. E. H. Zeydel. New York: Dover, 1962.

Callahan, V. W. "The Erasmus-Alciati Friendship." *Acta Conventus Neo-Latini Lovaniensis*. Munich: Fink, 1973, pp. 133–41.

_____. "The Mirror of Princes. Erasmian Echoes in Alciati's *Emblematum Liber*." *Acta Conventus Neo-Latini Amstelodamensis*. Munich: Fink, 1979, pp. 183–96.

_____. "Uses of the Planudean Anthology:

Thomas More and Andrea Alciati." *Acta Conventus Neo-Latini Boloniensis.* Munich: Fink, 1985, pp. 399–412.

_____. "Andrea Alciato's 'Palm Tree' Emblem: A Humanist Document." *Emblematica* VI/2, 1992, pp. 219–35.

_____. "Erasmus's Adages: A Pervasive Element in the Emblems of Alciato." *Emblematica* IX,1995, pp. 241–56.

Cartari, V. *Le Imagini de i dei de gli antichi....* Venice: Valgrisi, 1571; facs. rpt. New York: Garland, 1976.

Chew, S. C. "Time and Fortune." *English Literary History* VI, 1939, pp. 83–113.

_____. *The Pilgrimage of Life.* New Haven CT: Yale University Press, 1962.

Clements, R. J. *Picta Poesis: Literary and Humanistic Theory in Renaissance Emblem Books.* Rome: Edizioni di Storia e Letteratura, 1966.

Colonna, F. *Hypnerotomachia Poliphili: The Strife of Love in a Dream.* trans. J. Godwin. London: Thames & Hudson, 1999.

Conti (Comes), N. *Mythologiae, sive explicationum fabularum.* Venice: Trino, 1567; facs. rpt., New York: Garland, 1976.

Covarrubias Orozco, S. *Tesoro de la lengua castellana o española,* ed. M. Camarero. Madrid: Castalia, 1994.

Cummings, R. "Alciato's Emblem 41: 'Unum nihil, duos plurimum posse.'" *Emblematica* X, 1996, pp. 399–413.

_____. "Alciato's *Emblemata* as an Imaginary Museum." *Emblematica* X, 1996, pp. 245–81.

Curtius, E. R. *European Literature and the Latin Middle Ages.* Princeton NJ: Princeton University Press, 1990.

Daly, P. M. "Emblematic Poetry of Occasional Meditation." *German Life and Letters* XXV, 1972, pp. 126–39.

_____. "Goethe and the Emblematic Tradition." *Journal of English and German Philology* LXXIV, 1975, pp. 388–412.

_____. "A Note on Shakespeare's Sonnet 116: A Case of Emblematic Association." *Shakespeare Quarterly* XXVIII, 1977, 515–16.

_____. "The Bibliographic Basic for Emblem Studies." *Emblematica* VIII, 1994, pp. 151–75.

Daly, P. M. *Literature in the Light of the Emblem: Structural Parallels between the Emblem and Literature in the Sixteenth and Seventeenth Centuries.* Toronto: University of Toronto Press, 1998.

_____. (ed.) *Andrea Alciato and the Emblem Tradition: Essays in Honor of Virginia Woods Callahan.* New York: AMS Press, 1989.

Daly, P. M., and Callahan, V. W. (eds.) *Andreas Alciatus: Index Emblematicus (The Latin Emblems; Emblems in Translation).* Toronto: University of Toronto Press, 1985 (2 vols.).

Daza Pinciano, B. (trans.) *Alciato: Emblemas,* ed. M. Soria. Madrid: Editora Nacional, 1975.

Demetz, P. "The Elm and the Vine: Notes Towards the History of a Marriage Topos." *Publications of the Modern Language Association.* LXXIII, 1958, pp. 521–32.

Dimler, G. R. "The *Imago Primi Saeculi*: Jesuit Emblems and the Secular Tradition." *Thought* LVI, 1981, pp. 438–48.

Droulers, E. *Dictionnaire des attributs, allégories, emblèmes et symboles.* Tourhout: Brepols, 1948.

Drysdall, D. "A Lawyer's Language Theory: Alciato's *De verborum significatione.*" *Emblematica* IX, 1995, pp. 269–92.

_____. "Self-Analysis and Self-Awareness for Students: Alciato's Application of an Emblem." *Emblematica* IX, 1995, pp. 393–400.

Erasmus. *The Adages of Erasmus,* trans. M. M. Phillips. Cambridge: Cambridge University Press, 1964.

Fabiny, T. (ed.) *Shakespeare and the Emblem: Studies in Renaissance Iconography and Iconology.* Szeged: Attila József University, 1984.

Fowler, A. D. S. "Emblems of Temperance in *The Faerie Queene,* Book II." *Review of English Studies* XXXVI, 1960, pp. 143–49.

Franits, W. "The Relationship between Emblems and Dutch Paintings of the Seventeenth Century." *Marsyas.* XXII, 1983–5, pp. 25–32.

Freeman, R. "George Herbert and the Emblem Books." *Review of English Studies* XVII, 1941, pp. 150–65.

Gállego, J. *Vision et symboles dans la peinture espagnole du siècle d'or.* Paris: Klincksieck, 1968.

Giehlow, K. *Der Hieroglyphenkunde des Humanismus in der Allegorie der Renaissance.* Vienna: Tempsky, 1915.

Giovio, P. *Dialogo dell'imprese militari et amorose.* Venice: L. Domenichi, 1556 (available in microfiche from Inter-Documentation Company, Leiden, the Netherlands).

Glendinning, N. "Goya and Van Veen: An Emblematic Source for Some of Goya's Late Drawings." *Burlington Magazine* CXIX, 1977, pp. 568–71.

Gombrich, E. H. "Icones symbolicae. The Visual Image in Neo-Platonic Thought." *Journal of the Warburg and Courtauld Institutes* XI, 2948, pp. 163–92.

Gracián, B. *Agudeza y arte de ingenio.* [rpt.] Madrid: Austral, 1957.

The Greek Anthology. trans. Peter Jay. Harmondsworth: Penguin, 1981.

Green, H. *Shakespeare and the Emblem Writers.* London: Truebner, 1870.

_____. *Andrea Alciati and His Books of Emblems: A Biographical and Bibliographical Study.* London: Truebner, 1872; rpt. New York: Burt Franklin, 1976.

Hassig, D. (ed.) *The Mark of the Beast: The Medieval Bestiary in Art, Life, and Literature.* New York: Routledge, 2000.

Heckscher, W. S. "Pearls from a Dungheap: Andrea Alciati's 'Offensive' Emblem, 'Adversus naturam peccantes.'" In *Art the Ape of Nature: Studies in Honor of H.W. Janson.* New York: Abrams, 1981, pp. 291–311.

_____. *A Selective List of Secondary Sources Dealing with Andrea Alciati and His Book of Emblems.* Princeton: Princeton University Press, 1985.

_____. *Art and Literature: Studies in Relationship.* Baden-Baden: Koerner, 1985.

_____. *The Princeton Alciati Companion: A Glossary of Neo-Latin Words used by Andrea Alciati and the Emblem Book Writers of His Time, Including a Bibliography of Secondary Sources.* New York: Garland, 1989.

_____. "Andrea Alciati's Laurel Tree and Its Symbolic Traditions." *Emblematica* VI, 1992, pp. 207–18.

Heckscher, W. S., and Wirth, K-A. "Emblem, Emblembuch." *Reallexikon der deutschen Kunstgeschichte.* Stuttgart: Metzler, 1959, vol. 5, cols. 85–228.

Henebry, W. M. "Writing with Dumb Signs: Memory, Rhetoric, and Alciato's *Emblemata.*" *Emblematica* X, 1996, pp. 211–44.

Henkel, A., and Schöne, A. *Emblemata. Handbuch zur Sinnbildkunst des XVI. und XVII. Jahrhunderts.* Stuttgart: Metzler, 1976.

Hervey, M. F. S. *Holbein's "Ambassadors": The Picture and the Men.* London: National Gallery, 1900.

Hill, E. K. "What Is an Emblem?" *Journal of Aesthetics and Art Criticism* XXIX, 1970, pp. 261–65.

Hocke, G. R. *Manierismus in der Literatur: Sprach-Alchemie und esoterische Kombinationskunst.* Hamburg: Rohwolt, 1959.

Hoen, N. A. *Aspects of Classical Mythology in Renaissance Emblems.* Ann Arbor: UMI Press, 1975.

Höltgen, K. "Eine Emblemfolge in Donnes Holy Sonnet XIV." *Archiv für das Studien der neueren Sprachen* CC, 1963, pp. 347–52.

Homann, H. *Studien zur Emblematik des 16. Jahrhunderts: Sebastian Brant, Andrea Alciati, Johannes Sambucus, Mathias Holtzwart, Nicolaus Taurellus.* Utrecht: Haevitjens, Dekker & Guntert, 1973.

Horapollo *see* Boas.

Iversen, E. *The Myth of Egypt and Its Hieroglyphics in European Tradition.* Princeton NJ: Princeton University Press, 1993.

Johnson, E. D. "Some Examples of Shakespeare's Use of the Emblem Books." *Baconia* XXIX, 1945, pp. 19–65.

Jongh, E. de. *Zinne- en Minnebeelden in de Schilderkunst van de Zeventiende Eeuw.* Amsterdam: Nederlandse Stichting Openbaar Kunstbezit, 1967.

_____. (ed.) *Tot Lering en Vermaak.* Amsterdam: Rijksmuseum, 1976.

Jongh, E., Dittrich, L., and Renger, K. (eds.) *Die Sprache der Bilder: Realität und Bedeutung in der niederländischen Malerei des 17. Jahrhunderts.* Braunschweig: Herzog Anton-Ulrich Museum, 1978.

Kauffmann, H. "Rubens und Isabella Brant in der Geissblattlaube," in *Form und Inhalt: Kunstgeschichtliche Studien.* Stuttgart: Schmitt, 1950, pp. 257–74.

Kiefer, F. "The Conflation of Fortuna and Occasio in Renaissance Thought and Iconography." *Journal of Medieval and Renaisance Studies.* IX/1, 1979, pp. 1–27.

Klein, R. "La Théorie de l'expression figurée dans les traités italiens sur les 'imprese,' 1555–1612," *Bibliothèque d'Humanisme et de la Renaissance* XIX, 1957, pp. 320–41.

Knott, B. "Nothing to Do with Cupid? A Discussion of Alciato's Emblem 112." *Emblematica* IX, 1995, pp. 415–27.

Köhler, J. *Der "Emblematum liber" von Andreas Alciatus (1492–1550): Eine Untersuchung zur Entstehung, Formung antiker Quellen und pädagosischen Wirkung im 16. Jahrhundert.* Hildesheim: Verlag August Lax, 1986.

Konecny, L. *Mezi textem a obrazem: Miscellanea z historie emblematiky.* Prague: Národni knihovna Ceské republiky, 2002.

Ladner, G. B. "Vegetation Symbolism and the Concept of Renaissance," in *De Artibus Opuscula XL: Essays in Honor of Erwin Panofsky.* New York: New York University Press, 1961, pp. 303–22.

Lederer, J. "John Donne and the Emblematic Practice." *Review of English Studies* XXII, 1946, pp. 182–200.

Lee, R. W. *Ut Pictura Poesis: The Humanistic Theory of Painting*. New York: Norton, 1967.
Levitine, G. "Some Emblematic Sources of Goya." *Journal of the Warburg and Courtauld Institutes* XXII, 1959, pp. 106–31.
_____. "The Elephant of Goya." *Art Journal* XX, 1961, pp. 12–19.
_____. "Goya, les emblèmes et la revanche de l'âne emportant des reliques." *Gazette des Beaux-Arts* XCIII, April 1979, pp. 39–48.
Lewis, A. C. *Emblem Books and English Drama. A Preliminary Survey, 1581–1600*. Ann Arbor: University Microfilms, 1951.
López, D. *Declaración Magistral sobre las Emblemas de Andrés Alciato*. Valencia: Vilagrasa, 1655; facs. ed., Menston, Yorkshire: Scolar Press, 1973.
Loyola, I. *The Spiritual Exercises of St. Ignatius*, trans. A. Mottola. Garden City NY: Image, 1964.
Manning, J. "Alciati and Philostratus's *Icones*." *Emblematica* I, 1986, pp. 207–210.
Margolin, J-C. "Alciato, a Champion of Humanism in the Eyes of Eramus." *Emblematica* IX, 1995, pp. 369–89.
Masson, A. *L'Allégorie*. Paris: Presses Universitaires, 1974.
Menestrier, C-F. *L'art des emblèmes*. Lyons: Coral, 1662 (available in microfiche from Inter-Documentation Company, Leiden, the Netherlands).
Miedema, H. "The Term 'Emblema' in Alciati." *Journal of the Warburg and Courtauld Institutes* XXXI, 1968, pp. 234–50.
Mignault, C. *Emblemata cum expliatione, v. c. Andreae Alciati Medidanensis Iurisconsulti. Per Cl. Minoem....* Leyden, 1591 (available in microfiche from Inter-Documentation Company, Leiden, the Netherlands).
Moffitt, J. F. *Caravaggio in Context, Painterly Naturalism and Humanist Texts*. Jefferson, NC: McFarland, 2004.
_____. "Goya y los demonios: *El autorretrato con el doctor Arrieta* y la tradición del '*Ars Moriendi*.'" *Goya: Revista de arte*, no. 163, 1982, pp. 12–23.
_____. "Velázquez, Fools, Calabacillas and Ripa." *Pantheon: Internationale Zeitschrift für Kunst* XL/4, 1982, pp. 304–9.
_____. "Diego Velázquez, Andrea Alciati, and the *Surrender at Breda*." *Artibus et historiae: Rivista internazionale di arti visive* III/5, 1983, pp. 75–90.
_____. "An Emblematic Alchemical Source for Duchamp's *Large Glass* in a Preparatory Drawing of 1912 Called *La mariée mise à nu par les célibataires*." *Cauda Pavonis: The Hermetic Text Society Newsletter* II/2, 1983, pp. 1–4.
_____. "Paul Klee's *Twittering Machine* and the Emblematic 'Birds-in-Bondage-Vile' Theme." *Studies in Iconography* IX, 1983, pp 135–74.
_____. "Orientaciones actuales en la investigación emblemática sobre arte y cultura del Siglo de Oro español." *Cuadernos internacionales de historia psicosocial del arte* II, 1983, pp. 31–43.
_____. "Who is the *Old Man in a Golden Helmet?*" *Art Bulletin* LXVI/3, 1984, pp. 417–27.
_____. "Un grabado emblemático de Goya: '*El disparate desordenado o matrimonial*.'" *Goya: Revista de arte*, nos. 187/8, 1985, pp. 77–80.
_____. "*The Count-Duke of Olivares on Horseback*: An Emblematic Equestrian by Velázquez." *Konsthistorisk Tidskrift* LV, 1986, pp. 149–67.
_____. "Observations on the Origins and Meanings of 'Goya with the Devils' in the 1820 *Self-Portrait with Dr. Eugenio García Arrieta*." *Bulletin of the Minneapolis Art Institute* LXV, 1986, pp. 36–49.
_____. "Las Cruces oroszlánjai: Hogy kerül egy közigazgatási épület elé egy bronz oroszlán pár?" In J. Pál (ed.), *A Reneszánsz szimbolizmus: ikonográfia, emblematika, Shakespeare*. Szeged, Hungary: József Attila University Press, 1987, pp. 245–51.
_____. "Francisco Goya and Sebastián de Covarrubias Orozco (More on Goya's 'Moral Emblems')." *Boletín del seminario de estudios de arte y arqueología de la Universidad de Valladolid* LIII, 1987, pp. 271–300.
_____. "Goya's Emblematic *Portrait of Don Manuel María Osorio de Moscoso y Alvarez de Toledo*." *Konsthistorisk Tidskrift* LVI, 1987, pp. 145–56.
_____. "Velázquez y el significado del retrato ecuestre barroco." *Goya: Revista de arte*, no. 202, 1988, pp. 207–15.
_____. "L'amour et les oiseaux: Emblématique aviaire chez Paul Klee." *Mélusine: Cahiers du Centre de Recherche sur le Surréalisme* X, 1989, pp. 97–108.
_____. "Un dibujo del *Descubrimiento de Ariadne* por Jusepe Ribera." *Archivo español de arte* LXII/no. 246, 1989, pp. 193–94.
_____. "The Fifteen Emblematic 'Genre-Scenes' in the *Nova Poemata* (1624)." *Konsthistorisk Tidskrift* LVIII, 1989, pp. 157–65.
_____. "How 'Modern' is Minimalist Art? The Case of Pol Bury's *Sphere Upon a Cube* (1971)." *Hoogsteder-Naumann Mercury* IX, 1989, pp. 42–46.

_____. "The Prince and the Prime Minister: The Site and the Significance of Velázquez's *Equestrian Lesson of Prince Baltasar Carlos.*" *Studies in Iconography* XII, 1989, pp. 90–120.

_____. "*El Viejo del Casco de Oro:* Un cuadro atribuído a Rembrandt." *Ephialte: Lecturas de historia del arte* I, 1989, pp. 211–29.

_____. "An Emblematization of Philip IV in the Salón de Reinos." *Pantheon: Internationale Jahreszeitschrift für Kunst* XLVIII, 1990, pp. 70–75.

_____. "Francisco Pacheco and Jerome Nadal: New Light on the Flemish Sources of the Spanish 'Picture-within-the-Picture.'" *Art Bulletin* LXXII/4, 1990, pp. 631–38.

_____. "'Hut-and-Tortoise': An 'Ecological' Topos from Vitruvius in George Wither's *Collection of Emblemes.*" *Ars longa: Cuadernos de arte* I, 1990, pp. 35–42.

_____. "A Hidden Sphinx by Agnolo Bronzino, '*ex tabula Cebetis Thebani.*'" *Renaissance Quarterly* XLVI, 1993, pp. 277–307.

_____. "El maravillosa *Libro Mudo* de la Alquimia." *Ars longa: Cuadernos de arte*, no. 4, 1993, pp. 7–13.

_____. "Los '*Emblemas Morales*' de Francisco de Goya y de Sebastián de Covarrubias." *Goya: Revista de arte*, nos. 241–2, 1994, pp. 45–56.

_____. "Una emblematización de Felipe IV y el clave alciatino del Salón de Reinos del Buen Retiro." *Actas del primer simposio internacional de emblemática.* Teruel: Instituo de Estudios Turolenses, 1994, pp. 255–77.

_____. "Rubens's *Duke of Lerma, Equestrian* Amongst 'Imperial Horsemen.'" *Artibus et Historiae: An Art Anthology* XV/ no. 29, 1994, pp. 99–110.

_____. "Marcel Duchamp, la emblemática alquímica, y el *Atalanta Fugiens.*" *Texturas* IV, 1994/95, pp. 57–75.

_____. "Un 'cómic-book' hermético: El maravilloso *Libro Mudo* de la alquimia." *Xiloca*, no. 16, 1995, pp. 171–201.

_____. "Francisco Goya, Cesare Ripa, and Allegorical Senescence." *Mitteilungen der Carl Justi Vereinigung* VII, 1995, pp. 35–40.

_____. "Francisco Goya, Andrea Alciati, and Emblematic Evacuation." *Source: Notes in the History of Art* XV/3, 1996, pp. 20–27.

_____. "The Forgotten Role of a 'Determined Christian Knight' in Titian's Depiction of *Charles V, Equestrian, at Mühlberg,*" *Gazette des Beaux-Arts* CXLIII, Jan. 2001, pp. 37–52.

_____. "'Poisoned Love' Posited in an Emblematic Lizard by Caravaggio." *Gazette des Beaux-Arts* CXLIV, July/August 2002, pp. 1–18.

Moffitt, J. F., and Liedtke, W. "Velázquez, Olivares, and the Baroque Equestrian-Portrait." *The Burlington Magazine* CXII/3, 1981, pp. 529–37.

Morreale, M. "Los *Emblemata* de Alciato en el *Tesoro de la lengua castellana* de Sebastián de Covarrubias." *Nueva revista de filología hispánica* XL, 1992, pp. 343–81.

Nilsson, S. A. "The Ass Sequence in *Los Caprichos.*" *Konsthistorisk Tidskrift* XLVIII, 1978, pp. 27–38.

Nordström, F. *Goya, Saturn and Melancholy.* Stockholm: Almqvist & Wiksell, 1956.

Ong,W. J. "From Allegory to Diagram in the Renaissance Mind: A Study in the Significance of the Allegorical Tableau." *Journal of Aesthetics and Art Criticism* XVII/4, 1959, pp. 423–40.

Panati, C. *Words to Live By: The Origins of Conventional Wisdom and Commonsense Advice.* New York: Penguin, 1999.

Panofsky, E. "Der gefesselte Eros." *Oud Holland* L, 1933, pp. 193–217.

_____. *The Iconography of Correggio's Camera di San Paolo.* London: Warburg Institute, 1961.

Patch, R. P. *The Goddess Fortuna in Medieval Literature.* Oxford and New York: Oxford University Press, 1928.

Picinelli, F. *Mundus symbolicus, in emblematum universitate formatus, explicatus, et tam sacris quam profanis eruditionibus ac sententiis illustratus*, ed. A. Erath. Cologne: Demen, 1694; facs. rpt., New York: Garland, 1976.

Porteman, K. "The Early Reception of Alciato in the Netherlands." *Emblematica* IV, 1989, pp. 243–55.

Praz, M. *Studies in Seventeenth-Century Imagery.* Rome: Edizioni di Storia e Letteratura, 1975.

Reichenberger, K. "Das Schlangensymbol als Sinnbild von Zeit und Ewigkeit: Ein Beitrag zur Emblematik in der Literatur des 16. Jahrhunderts." *Zeitschrift für romanische Philologie* LXXXI, 1956, pp. 346–51.

_____. "Ruhmesverlangen als Ausdruck der schöpferischen Persönlichkeit: Zur Interpetation eines Alciatiemblems." *Bibliothek und Wissenschaft* III, 1966, pp. 219–28.

Ripa, C. *Baroque and Rococo Pictorial Imagery*, ed. E. A. Maser. New York: Dover, 1971.

_____. *Iconologia, ovvero descrittione d'imagini delle virtù, vitii, affetti, passioni humane, corpi celesti, mondo e sue parti.* Padua: Tozzi, 1611; facs. rpt., New York: Garland, 1976.

Rodríguez de la Flor, F. *Emblemas: Lecturas de la imagen simbólica*. Madrid: Alianza, 1995.

Röttgen, H. *Caravaggio: Der irdische Amor, oder Der Sieg der fleischlischen Liebe*. Frankfurt a/M: Fischer, 1996.

Rupp, M. "Apta pictura et concinna imago: Der Flusskrebs bei Sebastian Brant und Albrecht Dürer, Marcello Virgilio de Adriani und Andrea Alciato." *Zeitschrift für Deutsches Altertum und Deutsche Literatur* CXXVII, 1998, pp. 169–81.

Russell, D. S. "Alciati's Emblems in Renaissance France." *Renaissance Quarterly* XXXIV, 1981, pp. 534–54.

_____. "Emblems and Hieroglyphics: Some Observations on the Beginnings and the Nature of Emblematic Forms." *Emblematica* I, 1986, pp. 227–43.

Salerno, L. "Poesia e simboli nel Caravaggio: I dipinti emblematici." *Palatino* X, 1966, pp. 106–12.

Sánchez Brocense, F. *Comment. in And. Alciati Emblemata*.... Lyons: Rovillé, 1573 (available in microfiche from Inter-Documentation Company, Leiden, the Netherlands).

Sánchez Pérez, A. *La Literatura emblemática española (siglos XVI y XVII)*. Madrid: Sociedad General Española de Librería, 1977.

Saunders, A. "Alciati and the Greek Anthology." *Journal of Medieval and Renaissance Studies* XII, 1982, pp. 1–18.

Schenk zu Schweinsberg, E. *Das Bilderrätsel*. Hildesheim: Olms, 1973.

Schöne, W. *Peter Paul Rubens: Die Geissblattlaube: Doppelbildnis des Künstlers mit Isabella Brant*. Stuttgart: Reclam, 1956.

Sebastián, S. *Contrarreforma y barroco: Lecturas iconográficas e iconológicas*. Madrid: Alianza, 1981.

_____. "*Theatro Moral de la Vida Humana*, de Otto Vaenius: Lectura y significado de los emblemas." *Boletín del Museo e Instituto Camón Aznar* XIV, 1983, pp. 7–92.

_____. *Emblemática e historia del arte*. Madrid: Cátedra, 1995.

_____. (ed.) *Alciato: Emblemas*. Madrid: Akal, 1985.

_____. *El Fisiólogo atribuido a San Epifanio, seguido de El Bestiario Toscano*. Madrid: Tuero, 1986.

Selig, K. L. "The Spanish Translations of Alciato's 'Emblemata.'" *Modern Language Notes* LXX, 1955, pp. 354–59.

_____. "Gracián and Alciato's 'Emblemata.'" *Comparative Literature* VIII, 1956, pp. 1–11.

_____. "The Commentary of Juan de Mal Lara to Alciato's 'Emblemata.'" *Hispanic Review* XXIV, 1956, pp. 26–41.

_____. "Philostratus' 'Imagines' and Alciati's 'Emblemata.'" *Modern Language Notes* LXXII, 1957, pp. 247–61.

_____. *Studies on Alciato in Spain*. New York: Garland, 1990.

_____. *Studies on Cervantes*. Kassel: Reichenberger, 1993.

Sequeyros, M. (trans.) *Anteojo de larga vista, o idea de la agudeza, e ingeniosa locución*. Madrid: A. Marín, 1714 (see Tesauro).

Seznec, J. *The Survival of the Pagan Gods: The Mythological Tradition and Its Place in Renaissance Humanism and Art*. New York: Torchbooks, 1961.

Shearman, J. *Mannerism: Style and Civilization*. Harmondsworth: Penguin, 1967.

Silcox, M. V. " 'Gleanings Out of Other Mens Harvestes': Alciato in Whitney's *A Choice of Emblemes*." in Bath, M., et al. (eds.), *The Art of the Emblem: Essays in Honor of Karl Josef Hültgen*. New York: AMS, 1998, pp. 161–200.

Simpson, D. P. *Cassell's New Compact Latin Dictionary*. New York: Laurel, 1979.

Soria, M. S. "Goya's Allegories of Fact and Fiction." *Burlington Magazine* XC, 1948, pp. 196–200.

Steadman, J. M. "Una and the Clergy: The Ass Symbol in *The Faerie Queene*." *Journal of the Warburg and Courtauld Insitutes* XXI, 1958, pp. 134–37.

_____. "*Aeropagitica* and the *Hieroglyphica* of Goropius Becanus." *Notes and Queries* VII, 1961, 181–2.

_____. "Falstaff as Actaeon: A Dramatic Emblem." *Shakespeare Quarterly* XIV, 1963, pp. 230–44.

Sullivan, M. A. "Bruegel's Proverbs: Art and Audience in the Northern Renaissance." *Art Bulletin* LXXIII, 1991, pp. 431–66.

Tacchi Venturi, P. *S. Ignacio de Loyola en el arte de los siglos XVII y XVIII*. Rome: Stock, 1929.

Tesauro, E. *Il Cannocchiale Aristotelico*. Turin: Sinbaldo stampatore, 1670 (available in microfiche from Inter-Documentation Company, Leiden, the Netherlands).

Tervarent, G. *Attributs et Symboles dans l'Art Profane 1450–1600*. Geneva: Droz, 1958.

_____. "Eros and Anteros, or Reciprocal Love in Ancient and Renaissance Art." *Journal of the Warburg and Courtauld Institutes* XXVIII, 1965, pp. 205–8.

Thuilius, J. (ed.) *Andreae Alciati emblematua cum commentariis. ... Opera et vigiliis Ioan-*

nis Thuilii....Patavij apud Petrum Paulum Tozzium..., Padua: Tozzi, 1621 (available in microfiche from Inter-Documentation Company, Leiden, the Netherlands).

Traupman, J. C. *The New College Latin and English Dictionary*. New York: Bantam, 1971.

Tung, M. "A List of Flora and Fauna in Peacham's *Minerva Britanna* and Alciati's *Emblemata* Together with Possible Models in Contemporary Illustrations." *Emblematica* I, 1986, pp. 345–357.

_____. "A Serial List of Aesopic Fables in Alciati's *Emblemata*, Whitney's *A Choice of Emblemes*, and Peacham's *Minerva Britanna*." *Emblematica* I, 1989, pp. 315–29.

Tuve, R. *Allegorical Imagery: Some Mediaeval Books and Their Posterity*. Princeton NJ: Princeton University Press, 1977.

Valeriano, P. *Les Hiéroglyphiques de Ian-Pierre Valerian*, trans. J. de Montylard. Lyons: Frellon, 1615; facs. rpt., New York: Garland, 1976.

Verheyen, E. "Eros et Antéros." *Gazette des Beaux-Arts* LXV, 1965, pp. 321–40.

Volkmann, L. "Hieroglyphik und Emblematik des Giorgio Vasari." In *Werden und Wirken, ein Festgruss K. W. Hiersemann*. Leipzig: Koehler, 1924, pp. 409–19.

_____. *Bilderschriften der Renaissance: Hieroglyphik und Emblematik in ihren Beziehungen und Fortwirkungen*. Rpt., Nieuwkoop: B. de Graaf, 1962.

Warncke, C-P. *Sprechende Bilder — sichtbare Wörte. Das Bildverständnis in der frühen Neuzeit*. Wiesbaden: Wolfenbüttler Forschungen, 1987.

Weiss, R. *The Renaissance Rediscovery of Classical Antiquity*. Oxford: Blackwell, 1969.

White, T. H. (ed.) *The Bestiary: A Book of Beasts*. New York: Capricorn, 1960.

Whitney, G. *A Choice of Emblemes (1586)*, ed. H. Green. New York: Blom, 1967.

Wilkenfield, R. B. "Act and Emblem: The Conclusion of *Samson Agonistes*." *English Literary History* XXXII, 1965, pp. 160–68.

Wind, E. "Aenigma Termini." *Journal of the Warburg and Courtauld Institutes* I, 1937-8, pp. 66–69.

_____. *Pagan Mysteries in the Renaissance: An Explanation of Philsophical and Mystical Sources of Iconography in Renaissance Art*. New York: Norton, 1968.

Wittkower, R. "Chance, Time and Virtue." *Journal of the Warburg and Courtauld Institutes* I, 1937–8, pp. 313–21.

_____. *Allegory and the Migration of Symbols*. London: Thames and Hudson, 1977.

Wolffhardt, E. "Beiträge zur Pflanzensymbolik." *Zeitschrift für Kunstwissenschaft* VIII, 1954, 177–201.

Yates, F. "The Emblematic Conceit in Giordano Bruno's *De Gli Eroici Furori* and in the Elizabethan Sonnet Sequences." *Journal of the Warburg and Courtauld Institutes* VI, 1943, pp. 101–21.

_____. *The Art of Memory*. Chicago: University of Chicago Press, 1966.

Young, A. R. "Facsimiles, Microform Reproductions, and Modern Editions of Emblem Books." *Emblematica* I, 1986, pp. 109–56.

Zafra, R., and Azanza, J. J. (eds.) *Emblemata aurea: La emblemática en el arte y la literatura del Siglo de Oro*. Madrid: Akal, 2000.

Zimmerman, J. E. *Dictionary of Classical Mythology*. New York: Bantam, 1966.

Index